Alice & Zoroku 4

story & art by TETSUYA IMAI

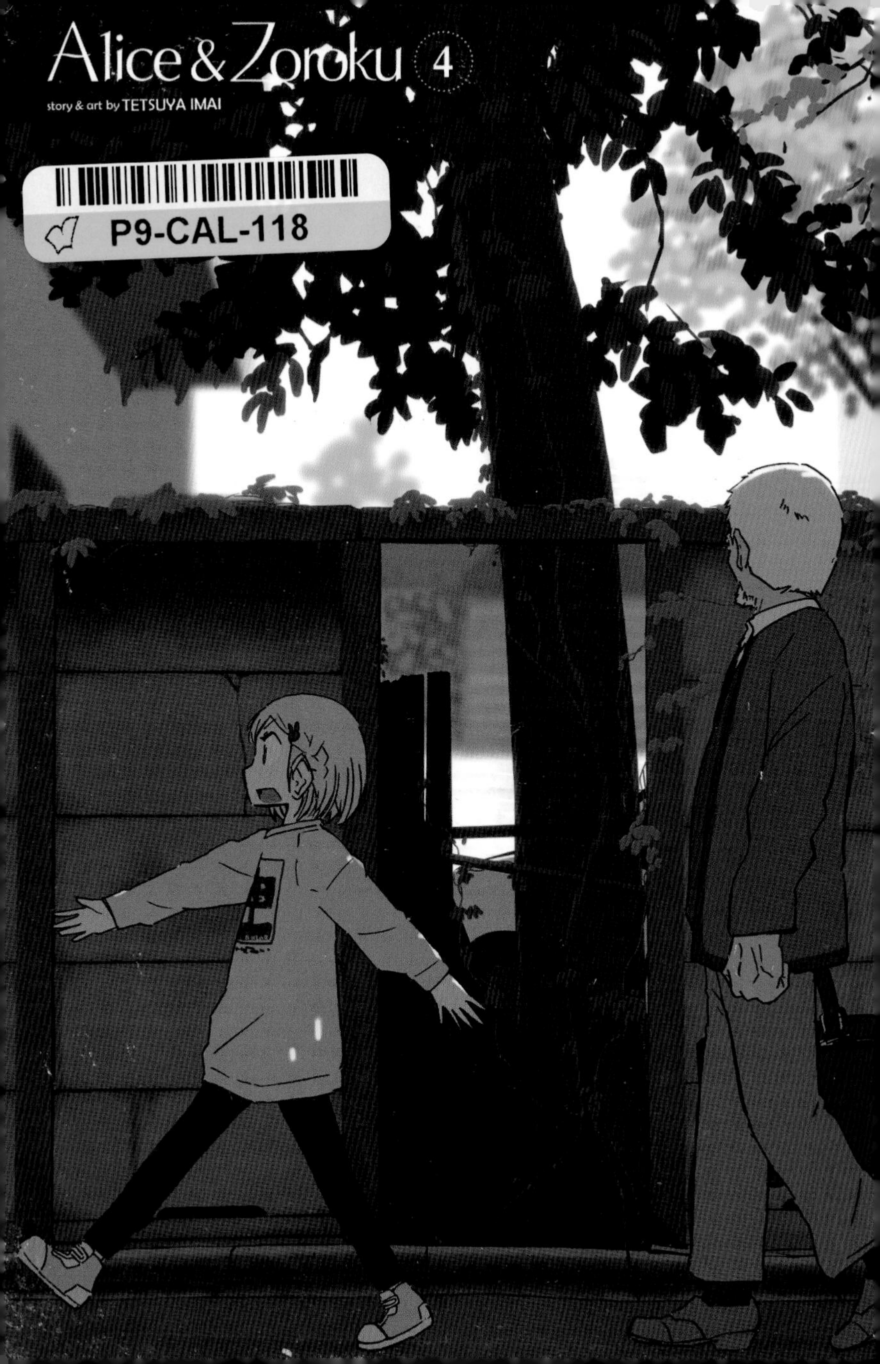

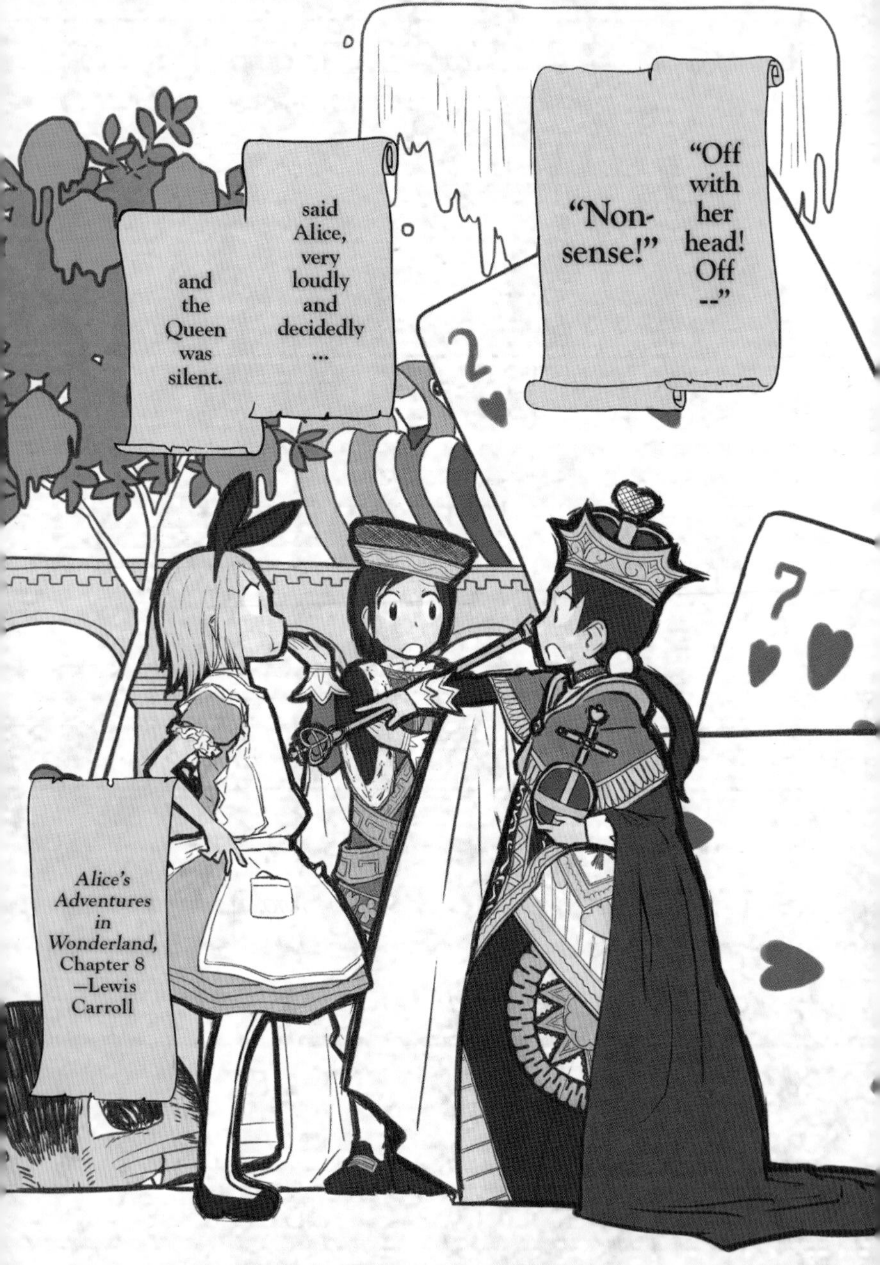
"Off with her head! Off --"
"Non-sense!"
said Alice, very loudly and decidedly ...
and the Queen was silent.
Alice's Adventures in Wonderland, Chapter 8 —Lewis Carroll

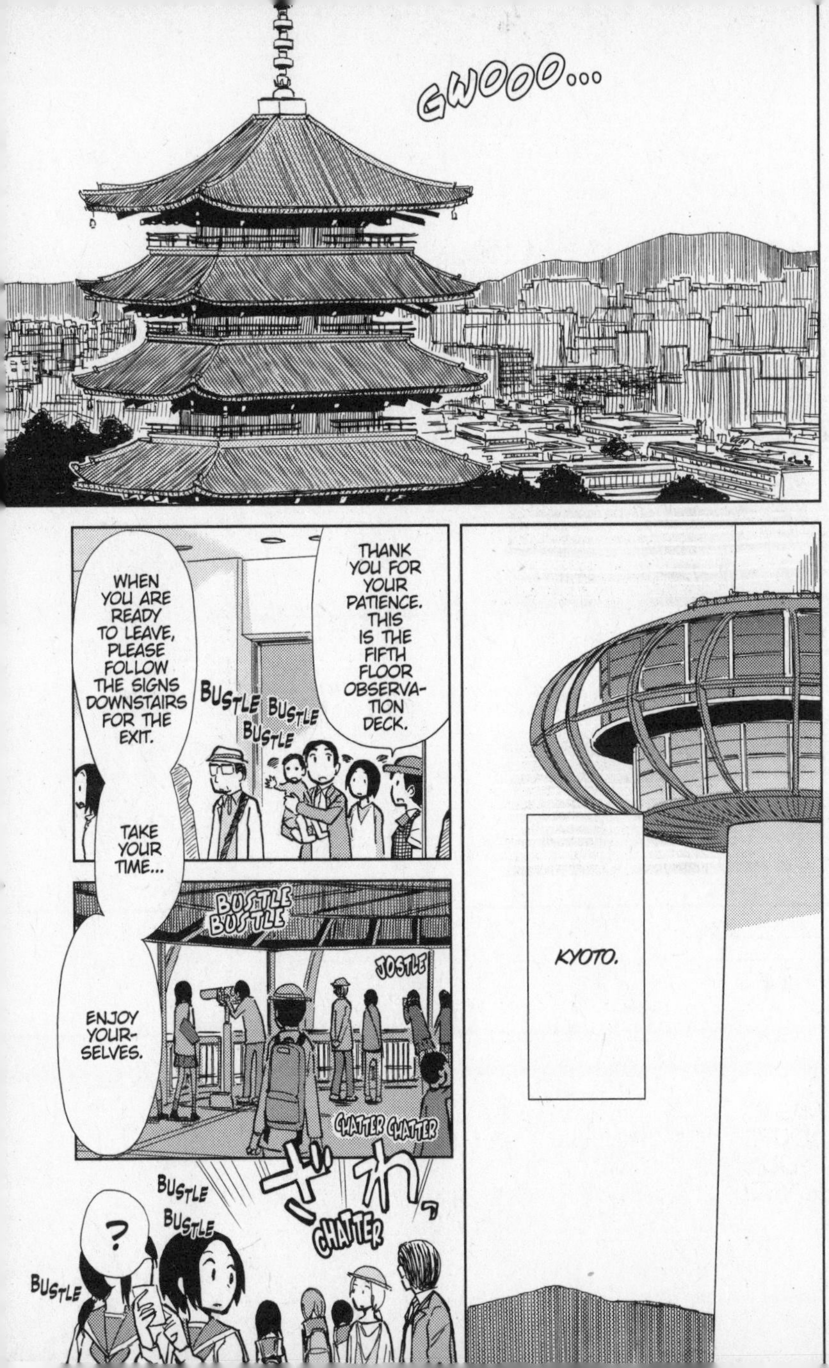
GWOOO...
KYOTO.
THANK YOU FOR YOUR PATIENCE. THIS IS THE FIFTH FLOOR OBSERVATION DECK.
WHEN YOU ARE READY TO LEAVE, PLEASE FOLLOW THE SIGNS DOWNSTAIRS FOR THE EXIT.
BUSTLE BUSTLE BUSTLE
TAKE YOUR TIME...
ENJOY YOURSELVES.
BUSTLE BUSTLE
JOSTLE
CHATTER CHATTER
ざわ
CHATTER
BUSTLE BUSTLE
?
BUSTLE

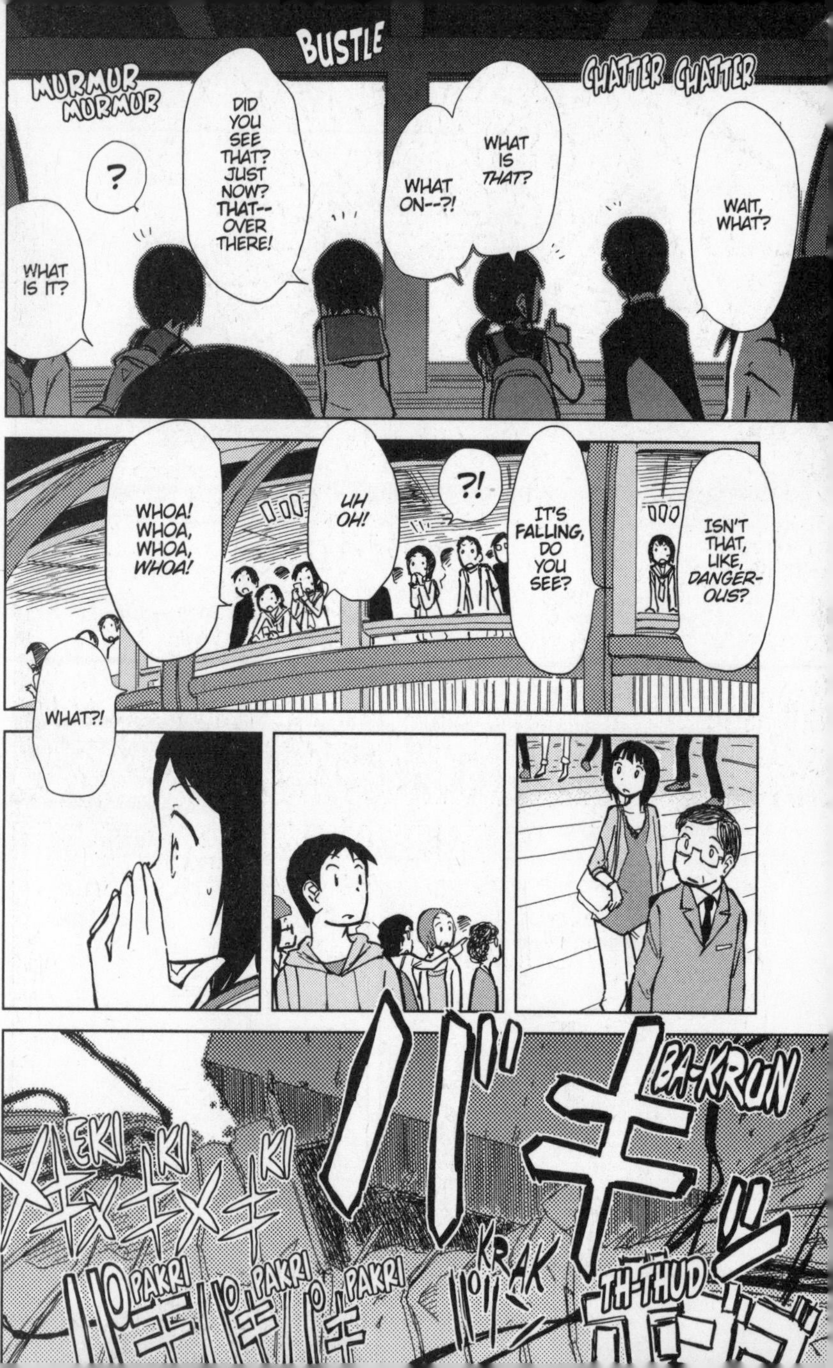
CHATTER CHATTER
WAIT, WHAT?
WHAT IS *THAT?*
WHAT ON--?!
BUSTLE
DID YOU SEE THAT? JUST NOW? THAT--OVER THERE!
?
MURMUR MURMUR
WHAT IS IT?
ISN'T THAT, LIKE, DANGER-OUS?
IT'S FALLING, DO YOU SEE?
?!
UH OH!
WHOA! WHOA, WHOA, *WHOA!*
WHAT?!
BA-KRUN
TH-THUD
KRAK
EKI KI KI
PAKRI PAKRI PAKRI

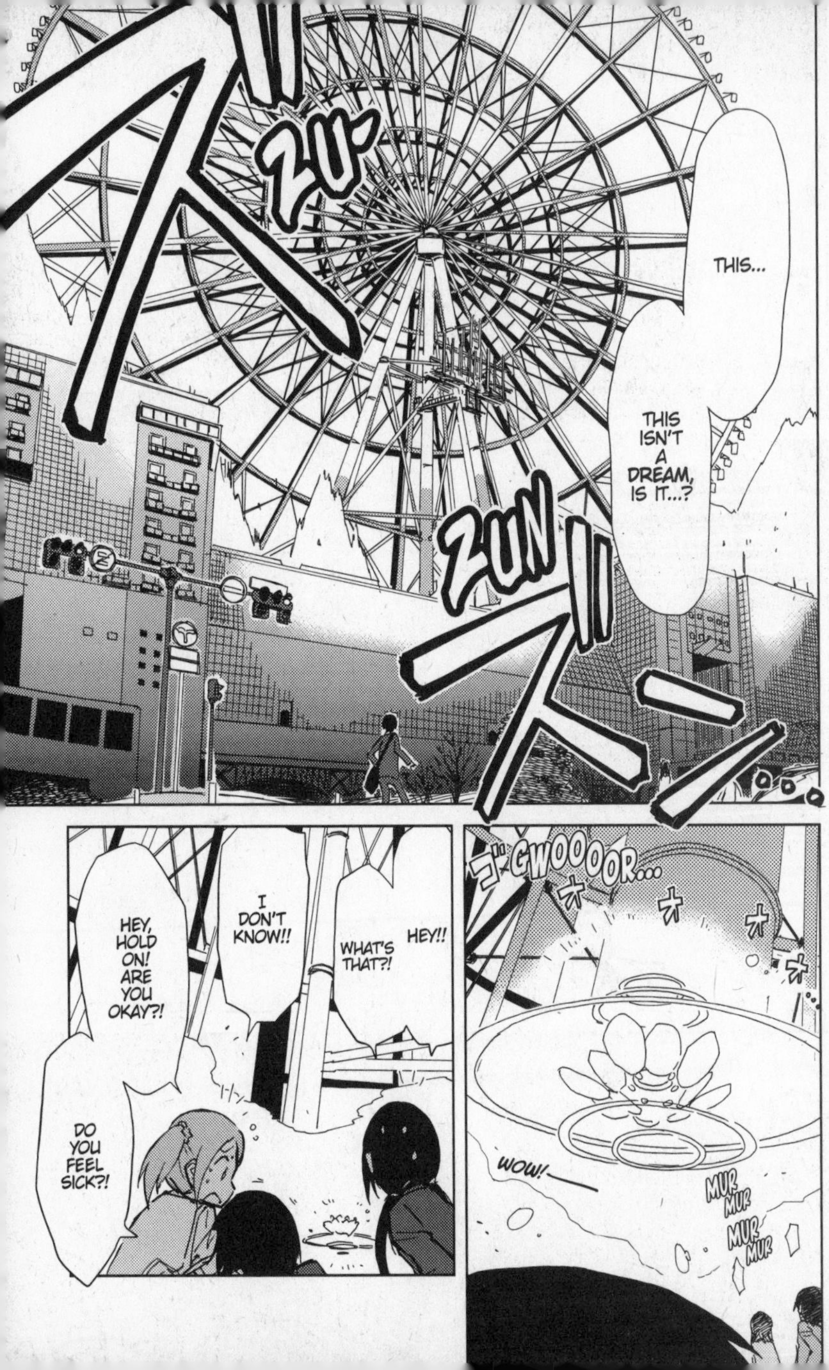
THIS...
THIS ISN'T A DREAM, IS IT...?
ZU-
ZUN
GWOOOOR...
WOW!—
MUR MUR
MUR MUR
HEY!!
WHAT'S THAT?!
I DON'T KNOW!!
HEY, HOLD ON! ARE YOU OKAY?!
DO YOU FEEL SICK?!

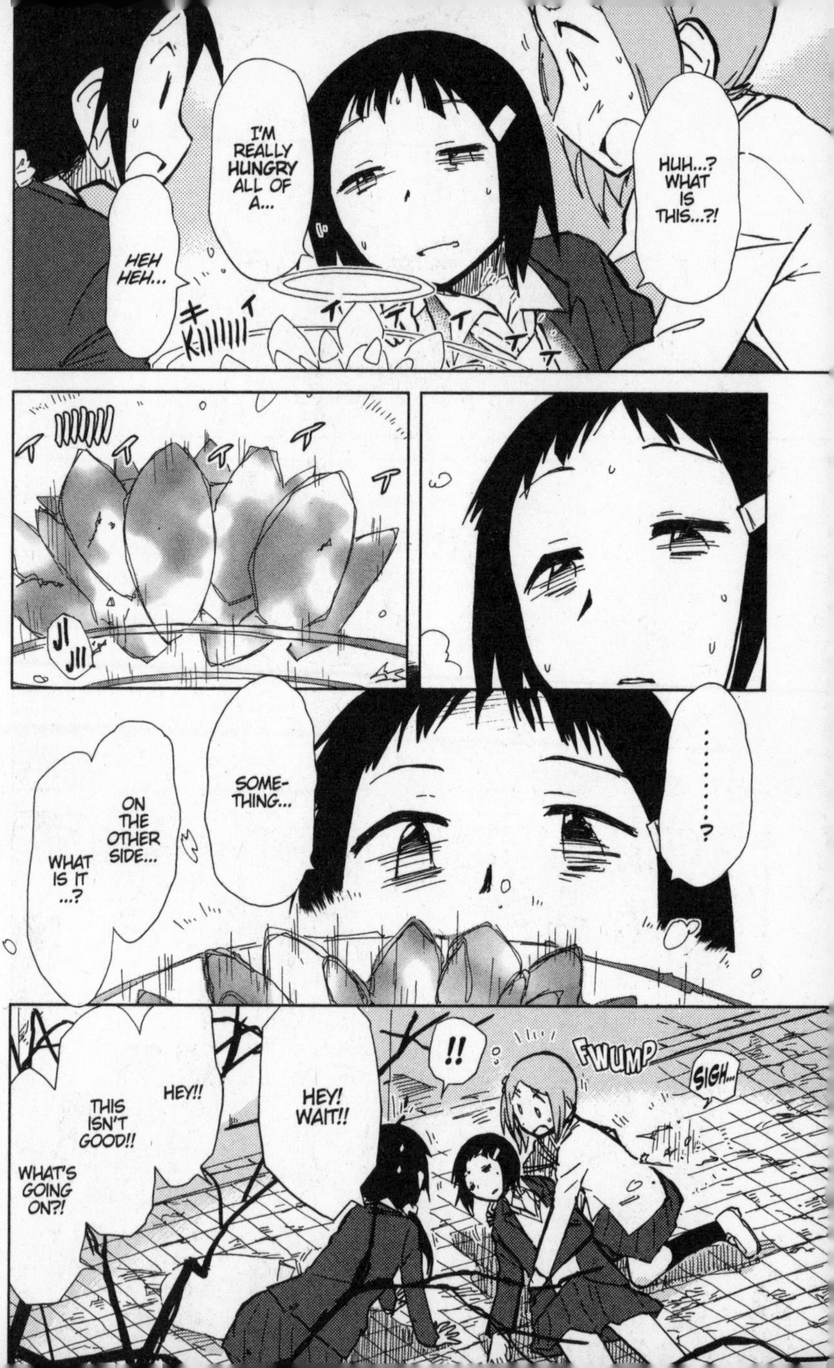
HUH...? WHAT IS THIS...?!
I'M REALLY HUNGRY ALL OF A...
HEH HEH...
KIIIIIII
JI JII
......?
SOME-THING...
ON THE OTHER SIDE...
WHAT IS IT ...?
SIGH...
FWUMP
!!
HEY! WAIT!!
HEY!!
THIS ISN'T GOOD!!
WHAT'S GOING ON?!

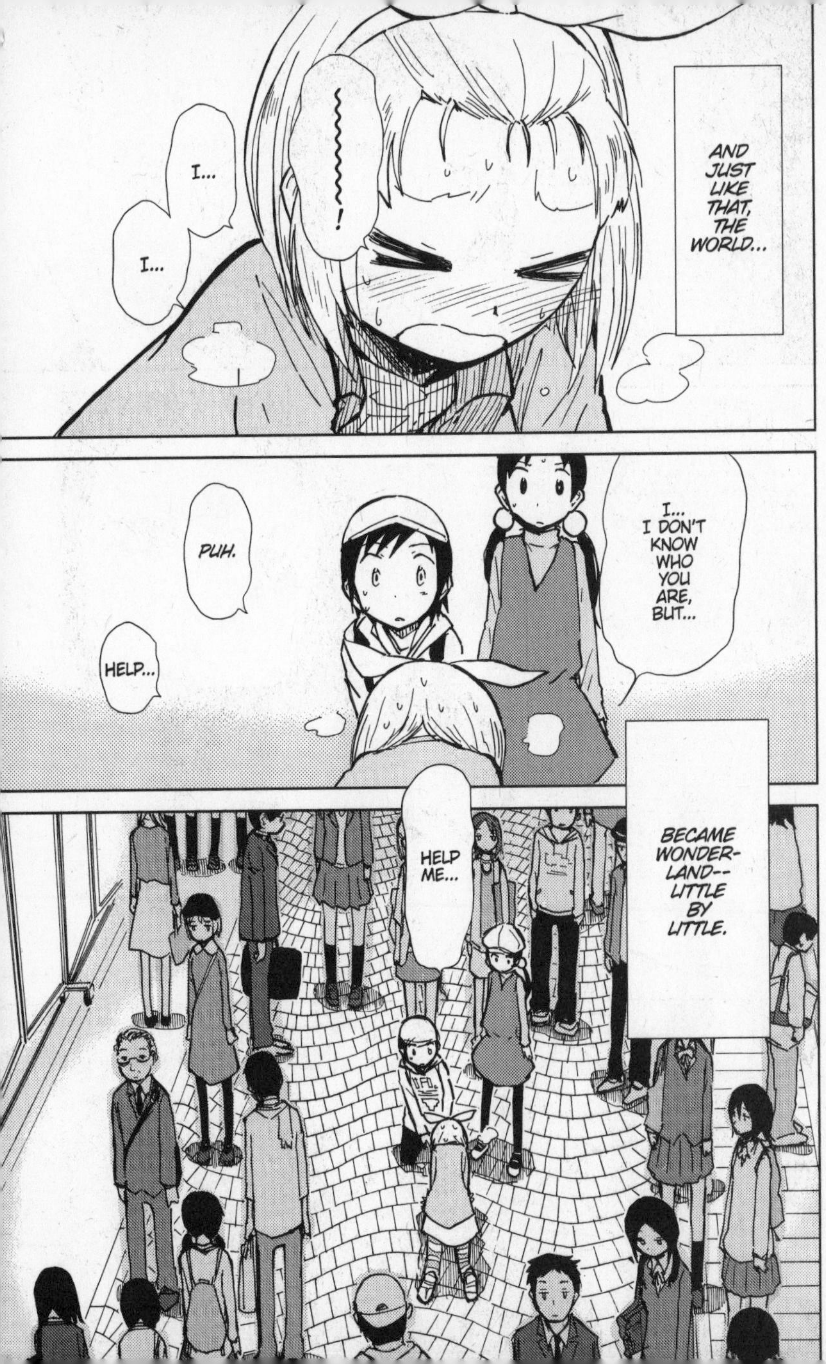
AND JUST LIKE THAT, THE WORLD...
I...
I...
I... I DON'T KNOW WHO YOU ARE, BUT...
PUH.
HELP...
BECAME WONDER-LAND-- LITTLE BY LITTLE.
HELP ME...

Chapter 13
The Day the Town Stood Still

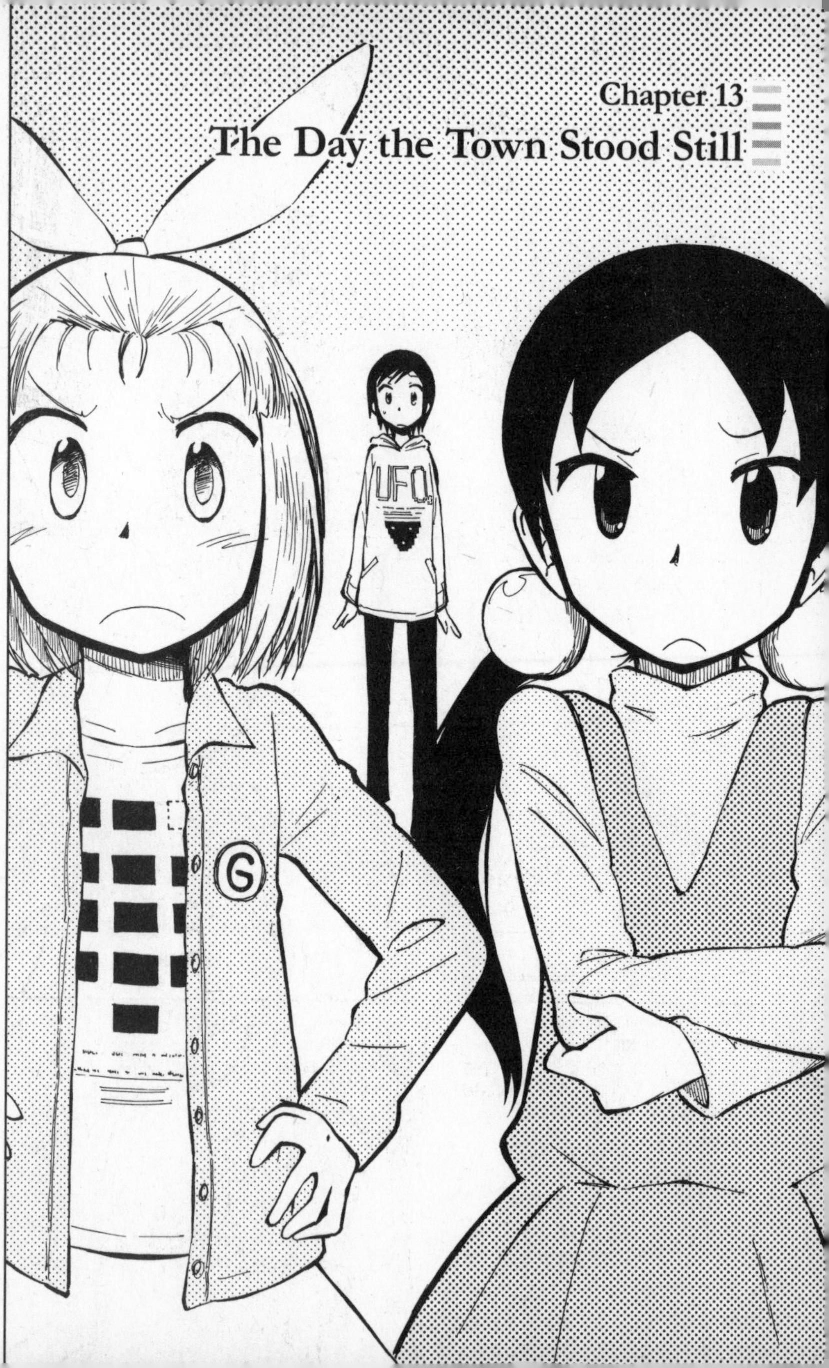
UFO

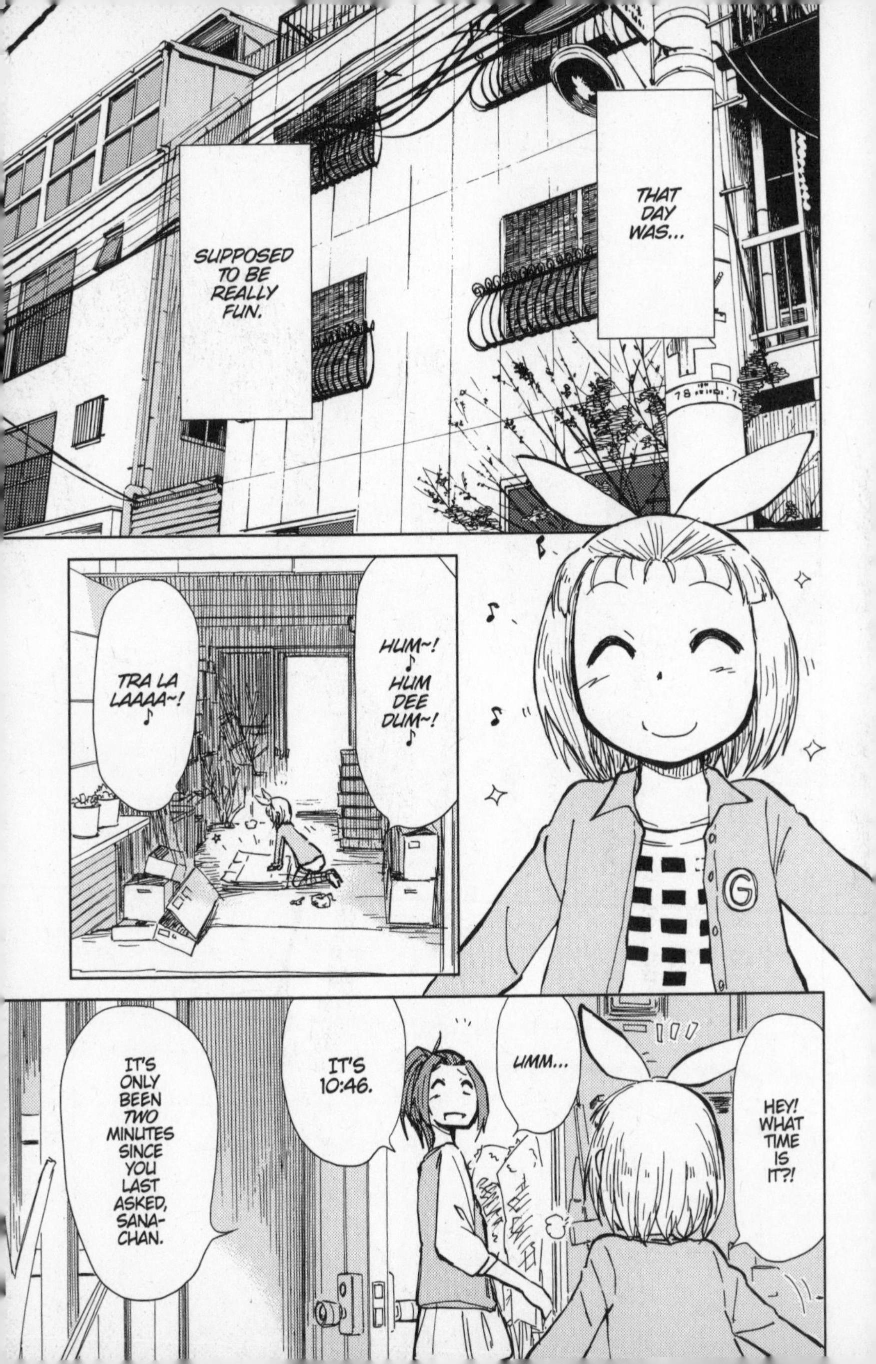
THAT DAY WAS...
SUPPOSED TO BE REALLY FUN.
HUM~! ♪ HUM DEE DUM~! ♪
TRA LA LAAAA~! ♪
HEY! WHAT TIME IS IT?!
UMM...
IT'S 10:46.
IT'S ONLY BEEN *TWO* MINUTES SINCE YOU LAST ASKED, SANA-CHAN.

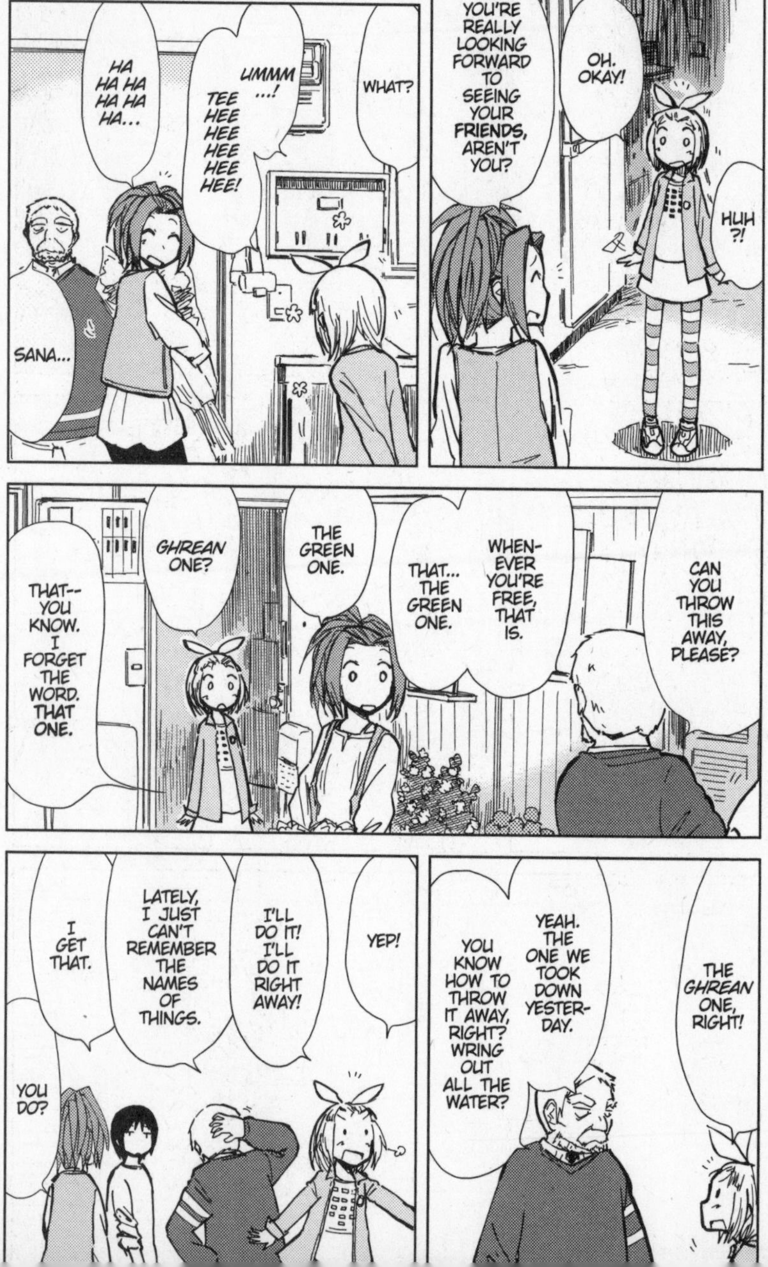
OH. OKAY!
YOU'RE REALLY LOOKING FORWARD TO SEEING YOUR FRIENDS, AREN'T YOU?
HUH?!
WHAT?
UMMM...! TEE HEE HEE HEE HEE HEE!
HA HA HA HA HA HA...
SANA...
CAN YOU THROW THIS AWAY, PLEASE?
WHENEVER YOU'RE FREE, THAT IS.
THAT... THE GREEN ONE.
THE GREEN ONE.
GHREAN ONE?
THAT--YOU KNOW. I FORGET THE WORD. THAT ONE.
THE GHREAN ONE, RIGHT!
YEAH. THE ONE WE TOOK DOWN YESTERDAY.
YOU KNOW HOW TO THROW IT AWAY, RIGHT? WRING OUT ALL THE WATER?
YEP!
I'LL DO IT! I'LL DO IT RIGHT AWAY!
LATELY, I JUST CAN'T REMEMBER THE NAMES OF THINGS.
I GET THAT.
YOU DO?

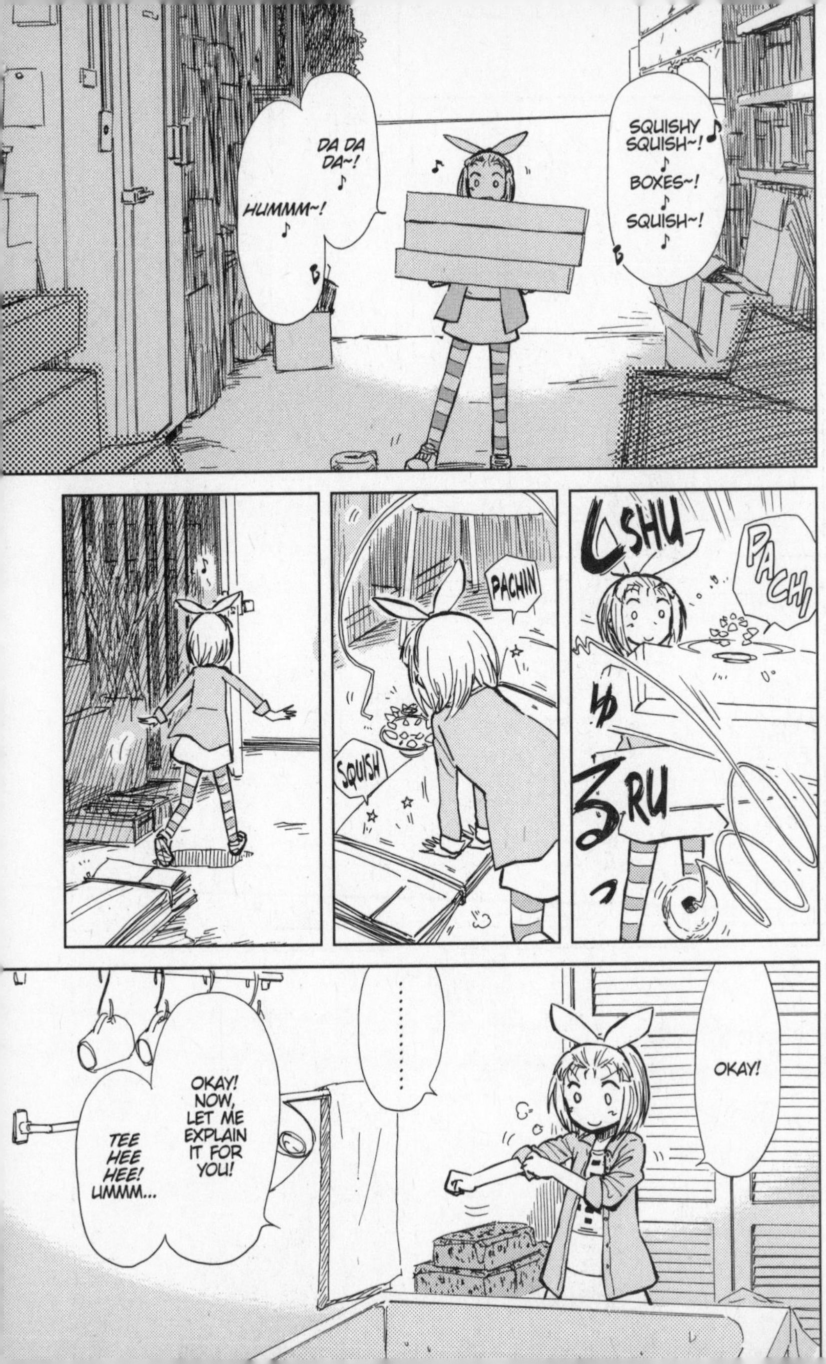
SQUISHY SQUISH~! ♪ BOXES~! ♪ SQUISH~! ♪
DA DA DA~! ♪ HUMMM~! ♪
PACHI
SHU
RU
PACHIN
SQUISH
OKAY!
......
OKAY! NOW, LET ME EXPLAIN IT FOR YOU!
TEE HEE HEE! UMMM...

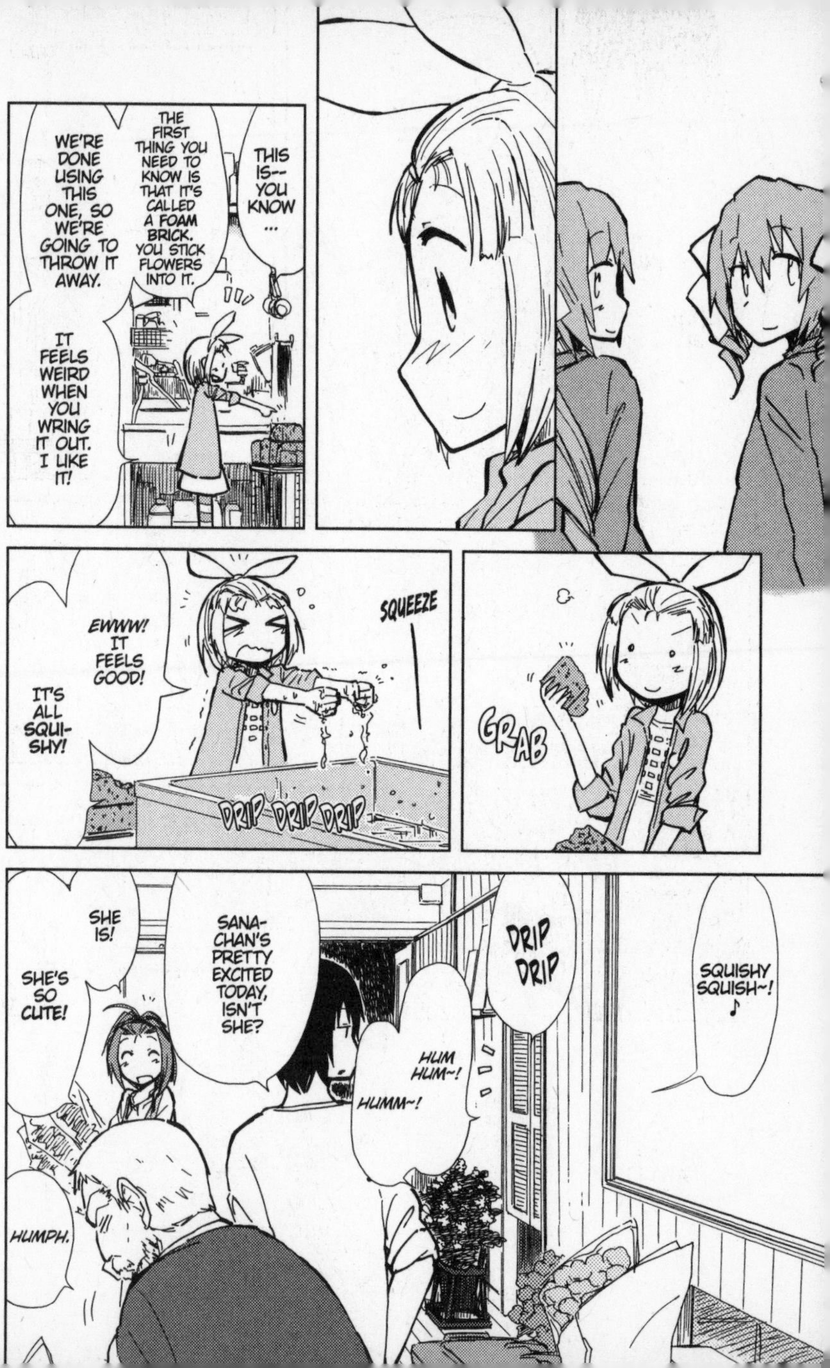
THIS IS-- YOU KNOW ...
THE FIRST THING YOU NEED TO KNOW IS THAT IT'S CALLED A FOAM BRICK. YOU STICK FLOWERS INTO IT.
WE'RE DONE USING THIS ONE, SO WE'RE GOING TO THROW IT AWAY.
IT FEELS WEIRD WHEN YOU WRING IT OUT. I LIKE IT!
GRAB
SQUEEZE
EWWW! IT FEELS GOOD!
IT'S ALL SQUISHY!
DRIP DRIP DRIP
SQUISHY SQUISH~! ♪
DRIP DRIP
HUM HUM~!
HUMM~!
SANA-CHAN'S PRETTY EXCITED TODAY, ISN'T SHE?
SHE IS!
SHE'S SO CUTE!
HUMPH.

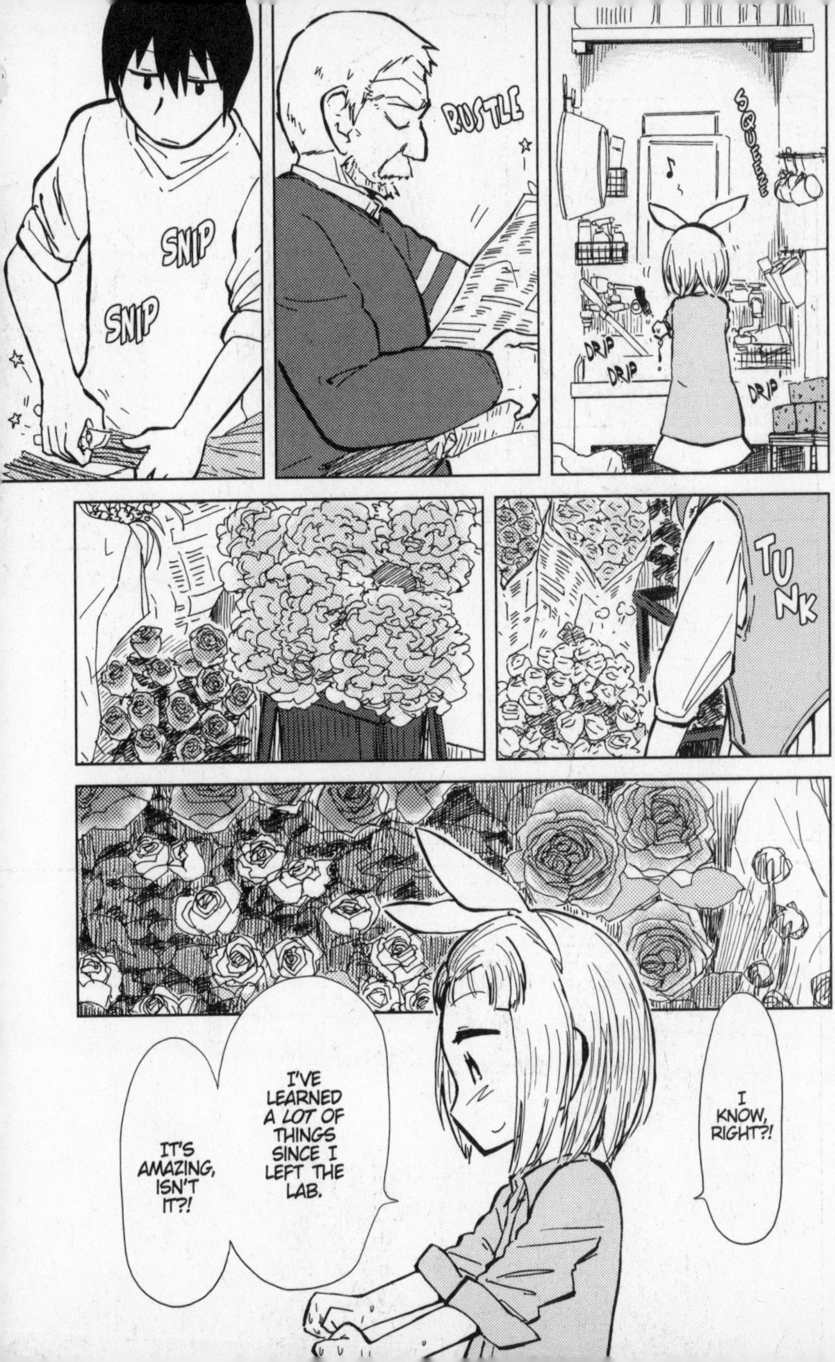
SQUEEZE
DRIP
DRIP
DRIP
RUSTLE
SNIP
SNIP
TUNK
I KNOW, RIGHT?!
I'VE LEARNED A LOT OF THINGS SINCE I LEFT THE LAB.
IT'S AMAZING, ISN'T IT?!

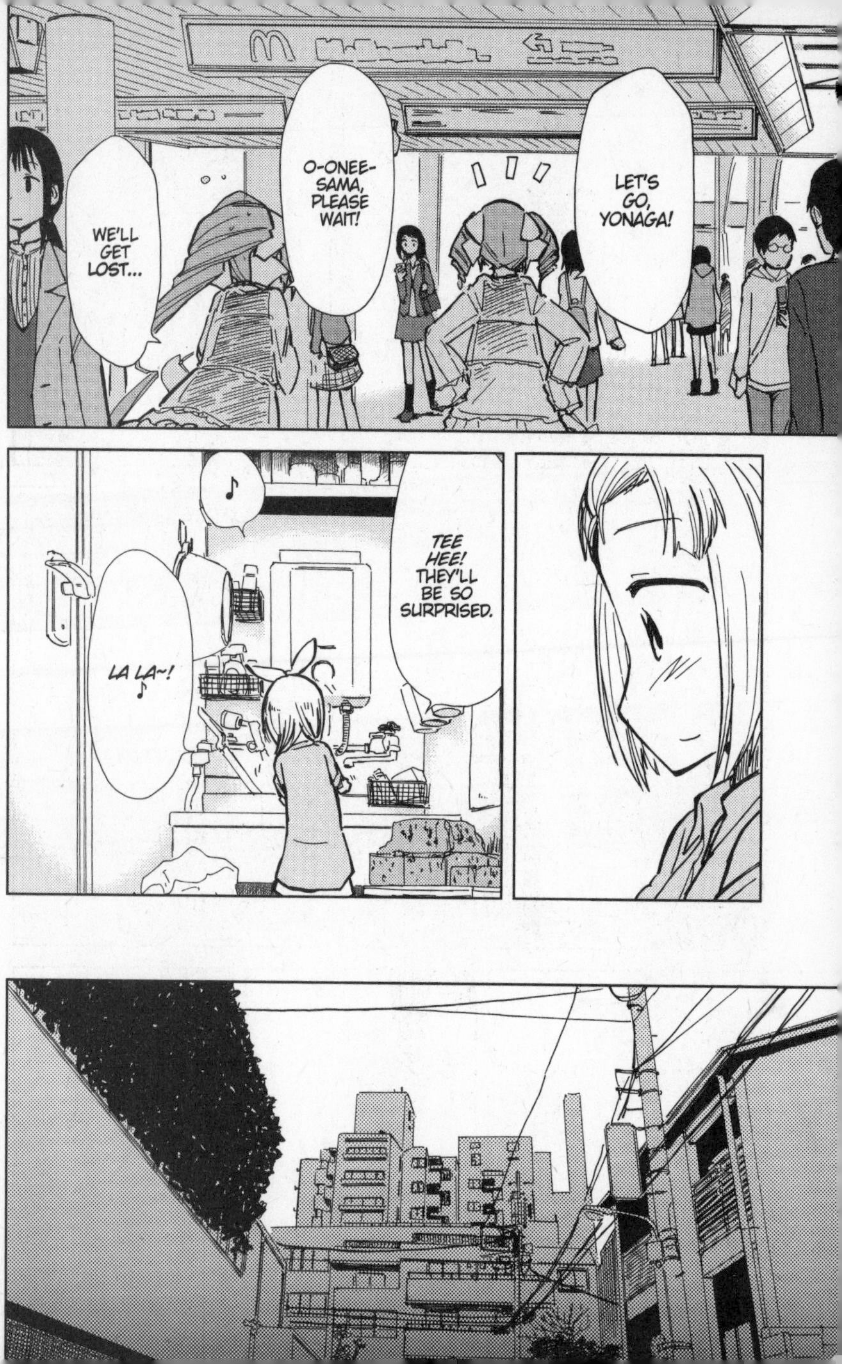
LET'S GO, YONAGA!
O-ONEE-SAMA, PLEASE WAIT!
WE'LL GET LOST...
TEE HEE! THEY'LL BE SO SURPRISED.
♪
LA LA~! ♪

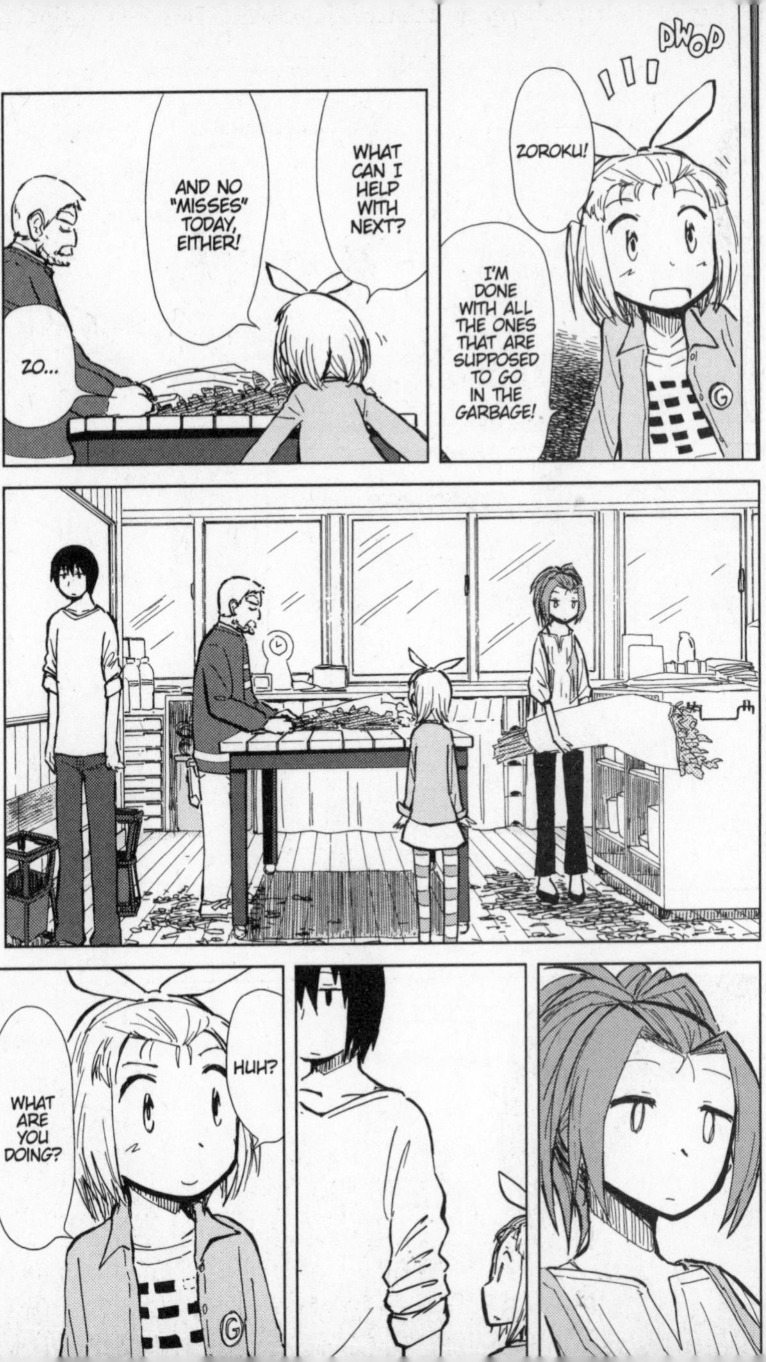
DWOP
ZOROKU!
I'M DONE WITH ALL THE ONES THAT ARE SUPPOSED TO GO IN THE GARBAGE!
WHAT CAN I HELP WITH NEXT?
AND NO "MISSES" TODAY, EITHER!
ZO...
HUH?
WHAT ARE YOU DOING?

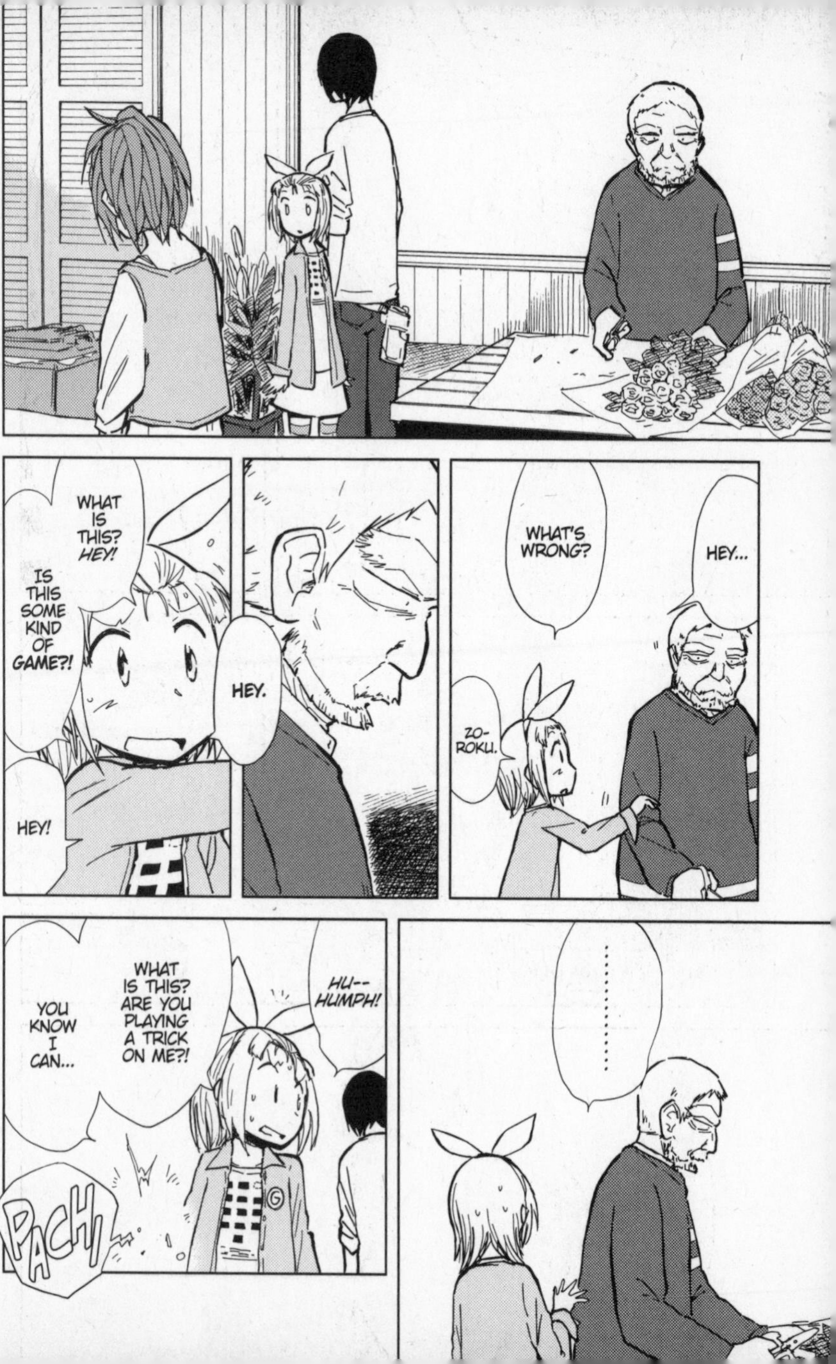
HEY...
WHAT'S WRONG?
ZO-ROKU.
HEY.
WHAT IS THIS? HEY!
IS THIS SOME KIND OF GAME?!
HEY!
......
HU--HUMPH!
WHAT IS THIS? ARE YOU PLAYING A TRICK ON ME?!
YOU KNOW I CAN...
PACHI

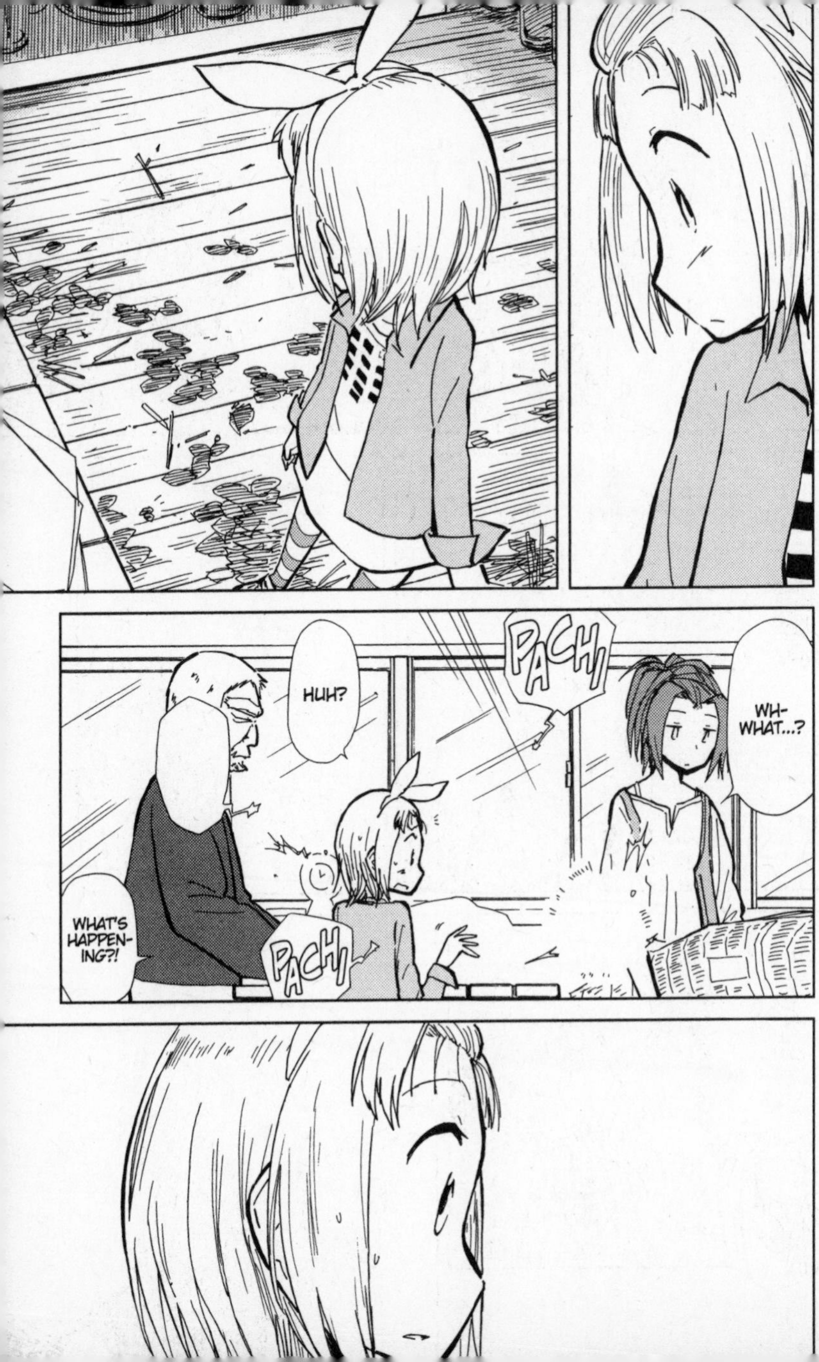
WH-
WHAT...?
PACHI
HUH?
PACHI
WHAT'S HAPPEN-ING?!

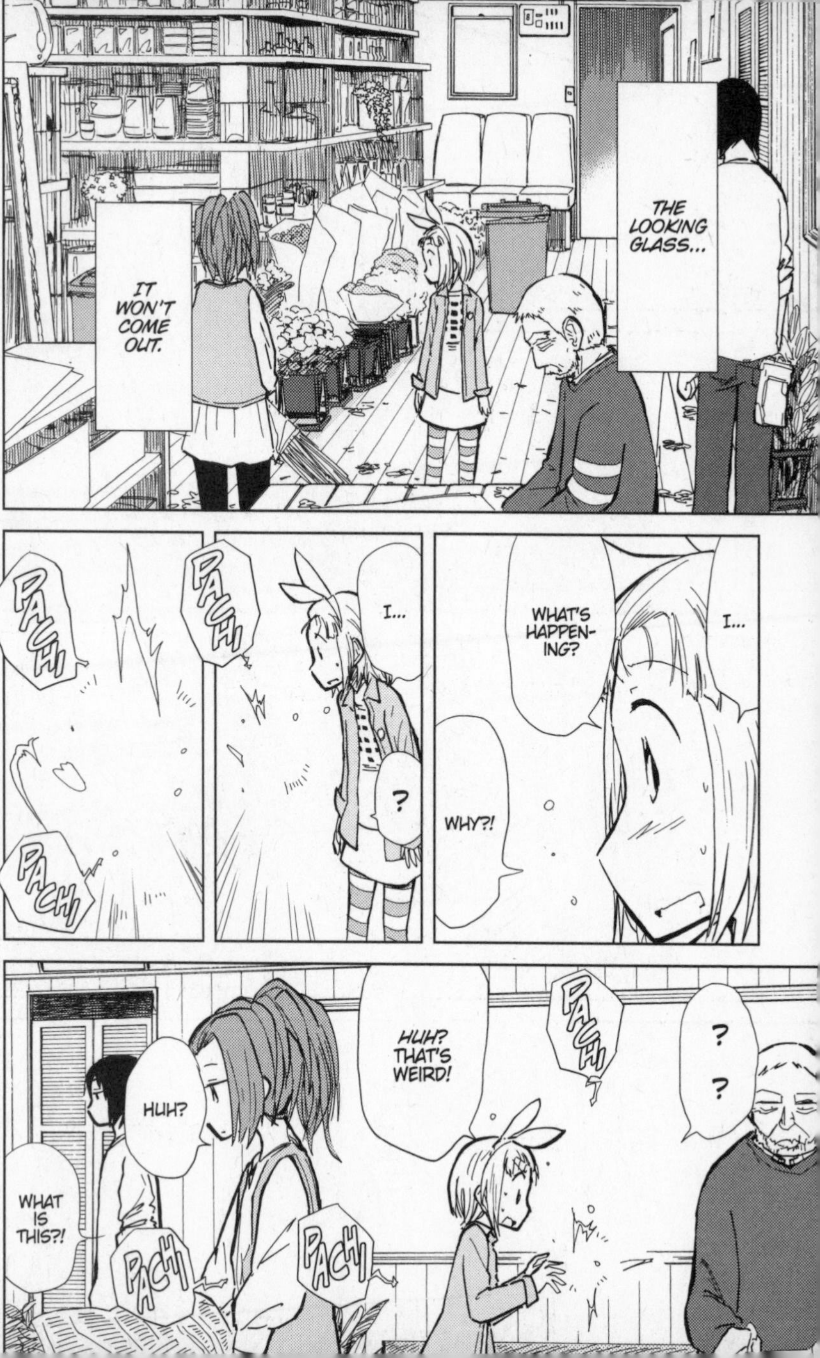
THE LOOKING GLASS...
IT WON'T COME OUT.
I...
WHAT'S HAPPEN-ING?
WHY?!
I...
?
PACHI
PACHI
PACHI
?
?
PACHI
HUH? THAT'S WEIRD!
HUH?
WHAT IS THIS?!
PACHI
PACHI

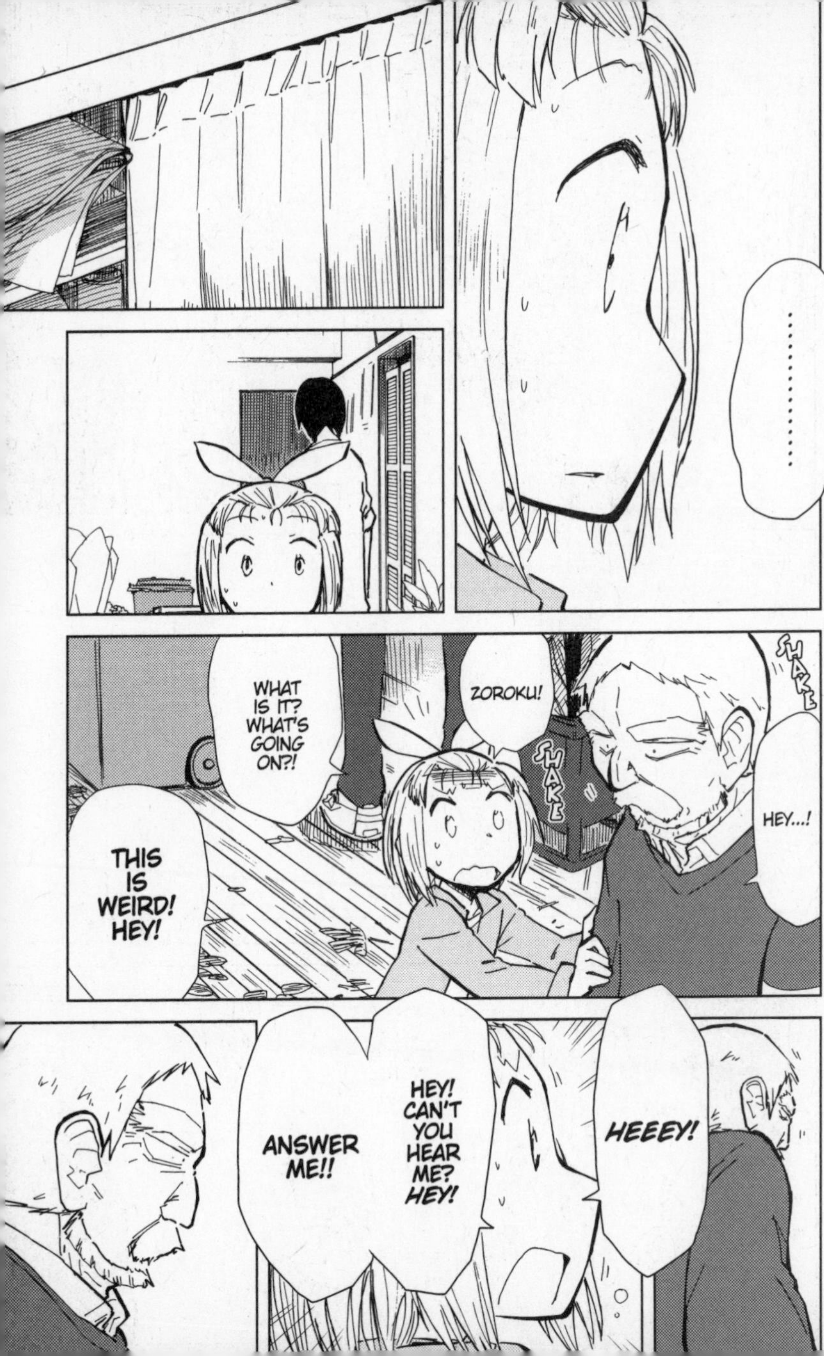
......
SHAKE
HEY...!
SHAKE
ZOROKU!
WHAT IS IT? WHAT'S GOING ON?!
THIS IS WEIRD! HEY!
HEEEY!
HEY! CAN'T YOU HEAR ME? HEY!
ANSWER ME!!

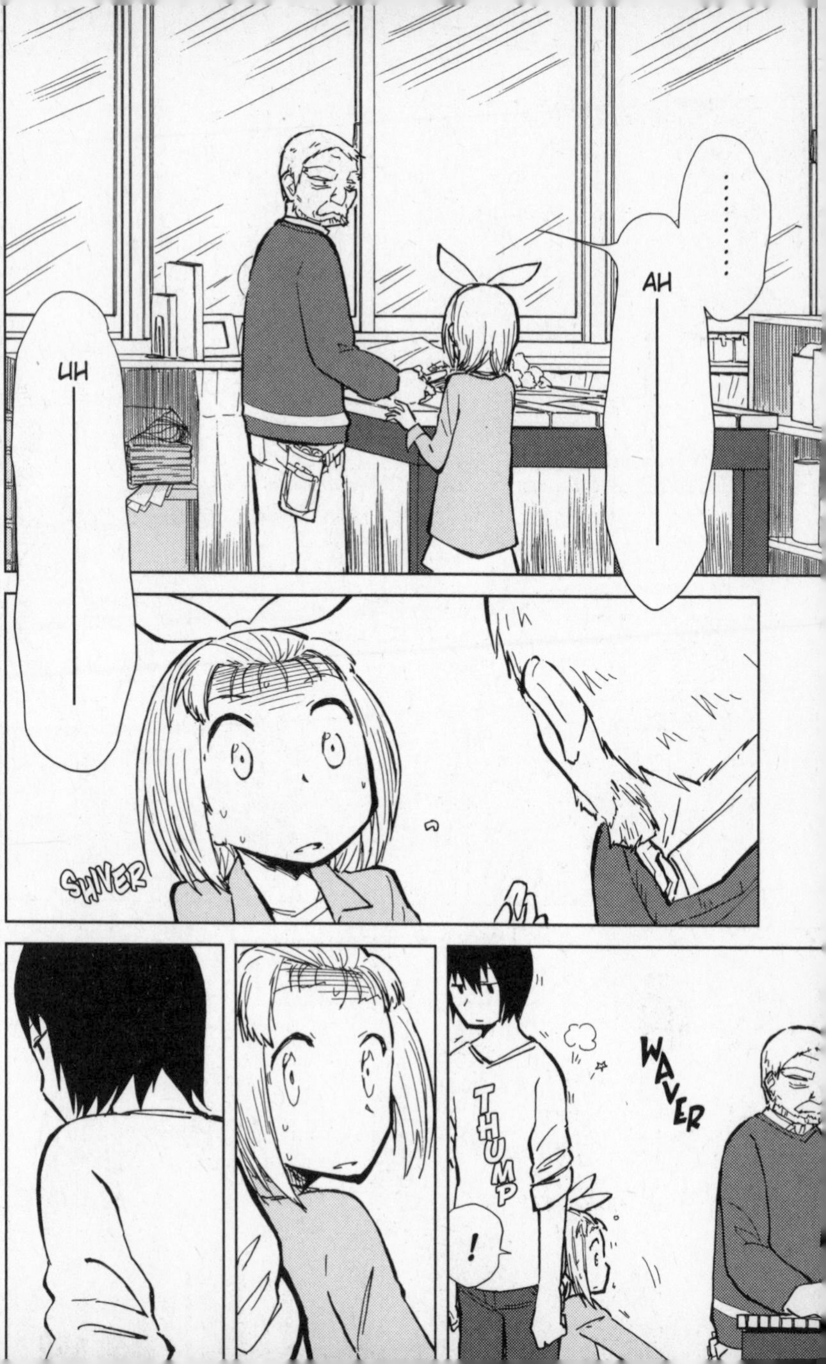
......
AH —
UH —
SHIVER
WAVER
THUMP
!

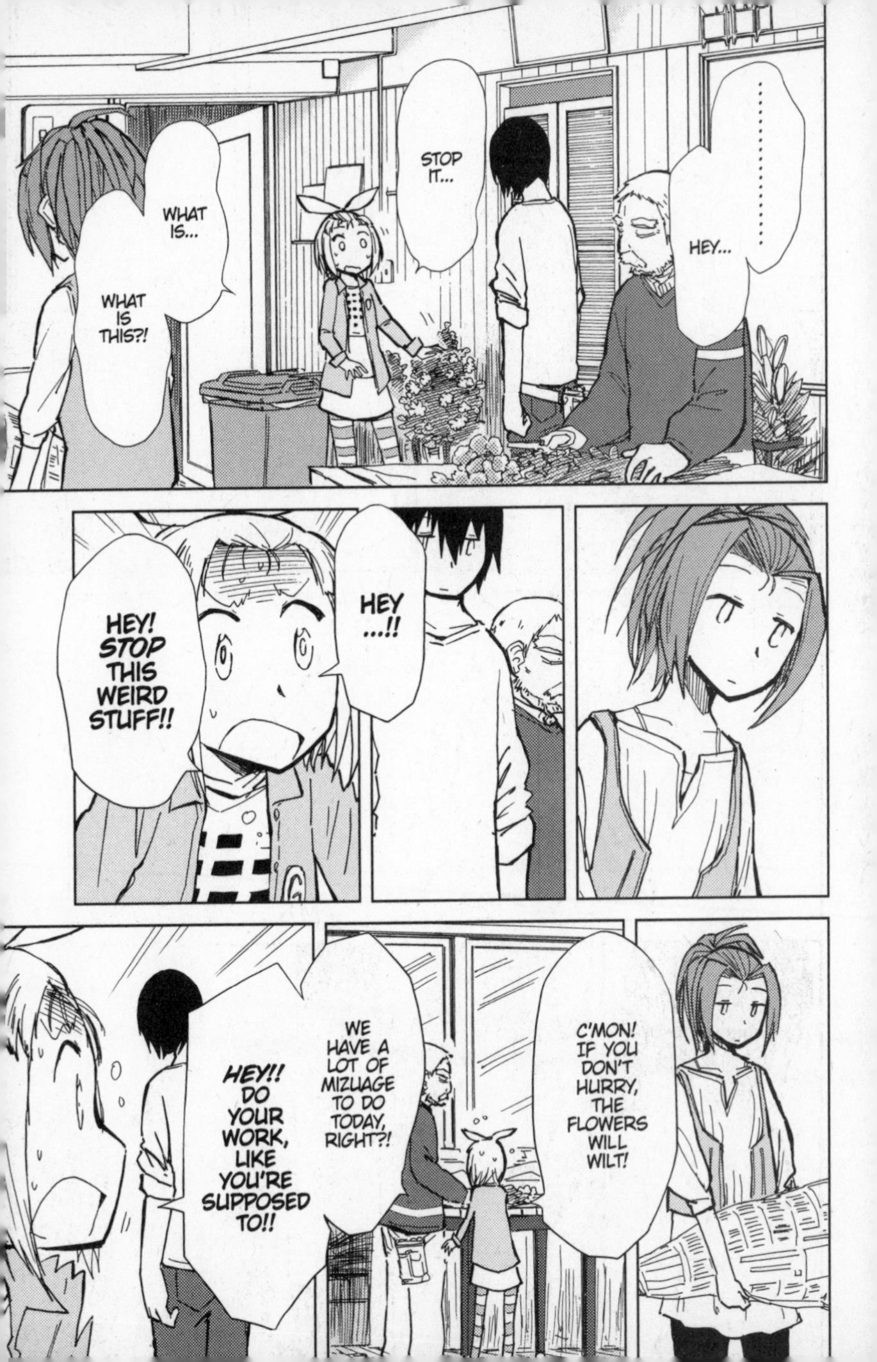
......
HEY...
STOP IT...
WHAT IS... WHAT IS THIS?!
HEY ...!!
HEY! STOP THIS WEIRD STUFF!!
C'MON! IF YOU DON'T HURRY, THE FLOWERS WILL WILT!
WE HAVE A LOT OF MIZUAGE TO DO TODAY, RIGHT?!
HEY!! DO YOUR WORK, LIKE YOU'RE SUPPOSED TO!!

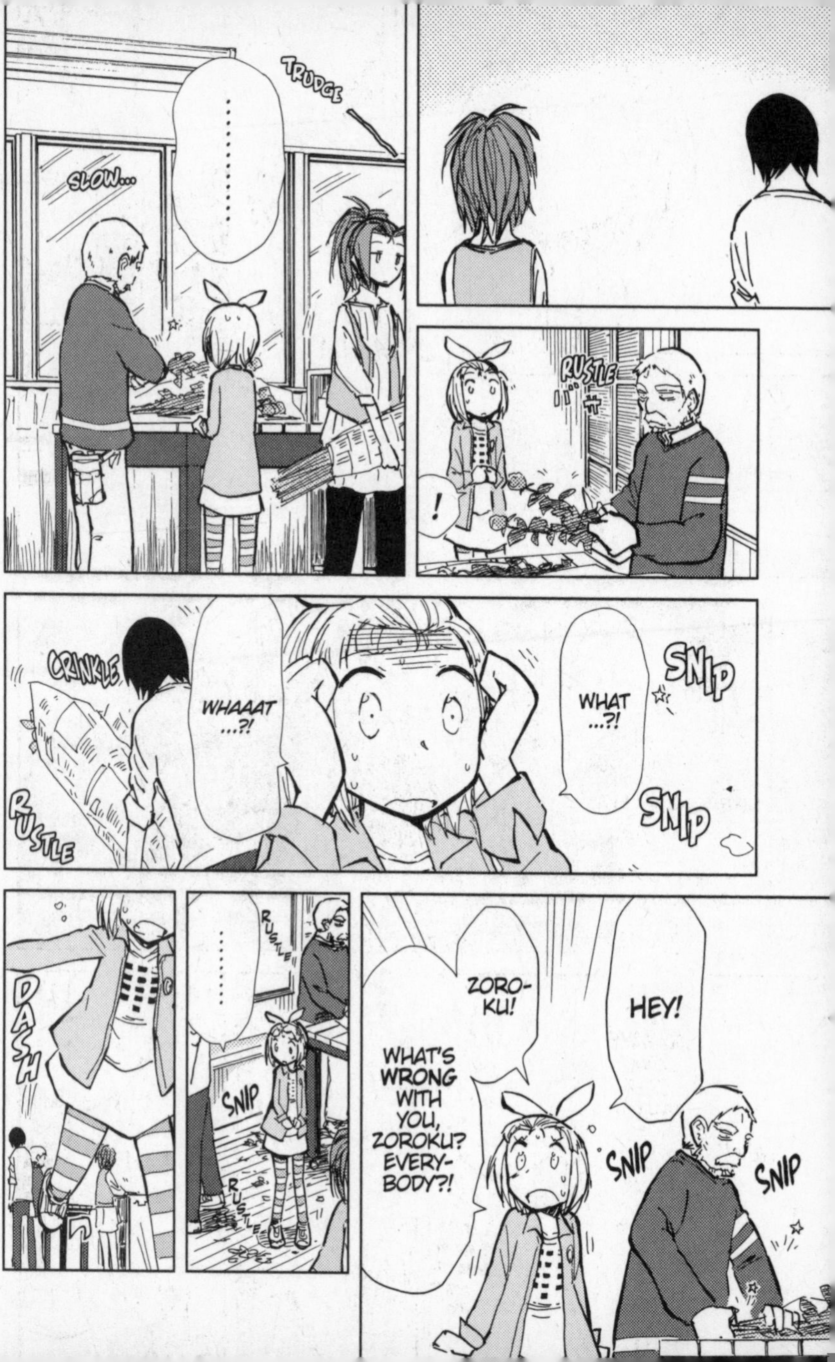
RUSTLE
!
TRUDGE
......
SLOW...
SNIP
WHAT ...?!
SNIP
WHAAAT ...?!
CRINKLE
RUSTLE
HEY!
ZOROKU!
WHAT'S WRONG WITH YOU, ZOROKU? EVERYBODY?!
SNIP
SNIP
RUSTLE
......
SNIP
RUSTLE
DASH

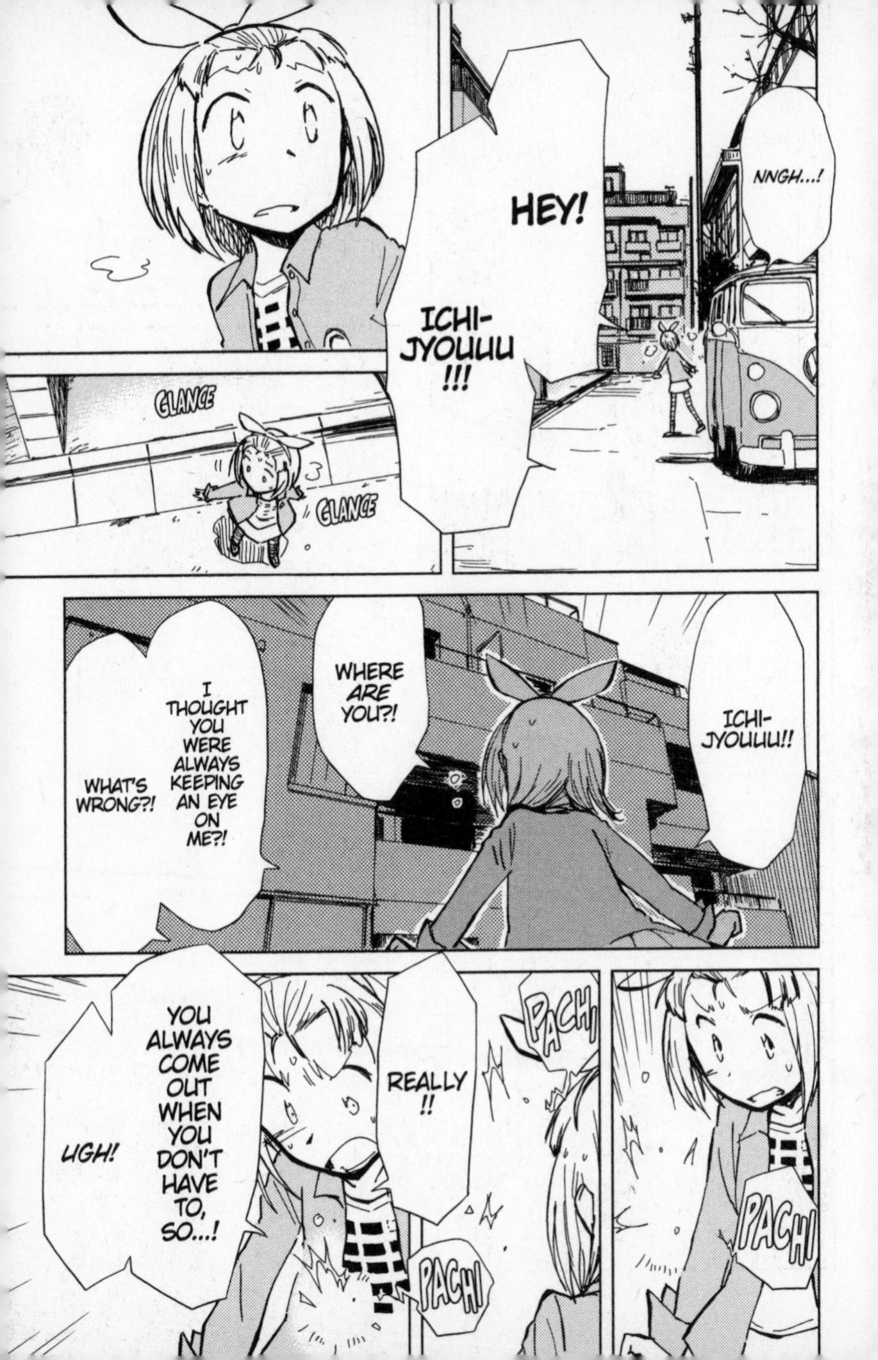
NNGH...!
HEY!
ICHI-JYOUUU!!!
GLANCE
GLANCE
ICHI-JYOUUU!!
WHERE ARE YOU?!
I THOUGHT YOU WERE ALWAYS KEEPING AN EYE ON ME?!
WHAT'S WRONG?!
PACHI
PACHI
REALLY!!
YOU ALWAYS COME OUT WHEN YOU DON'T HAVE TO, SO...!
UGH!
PACHI

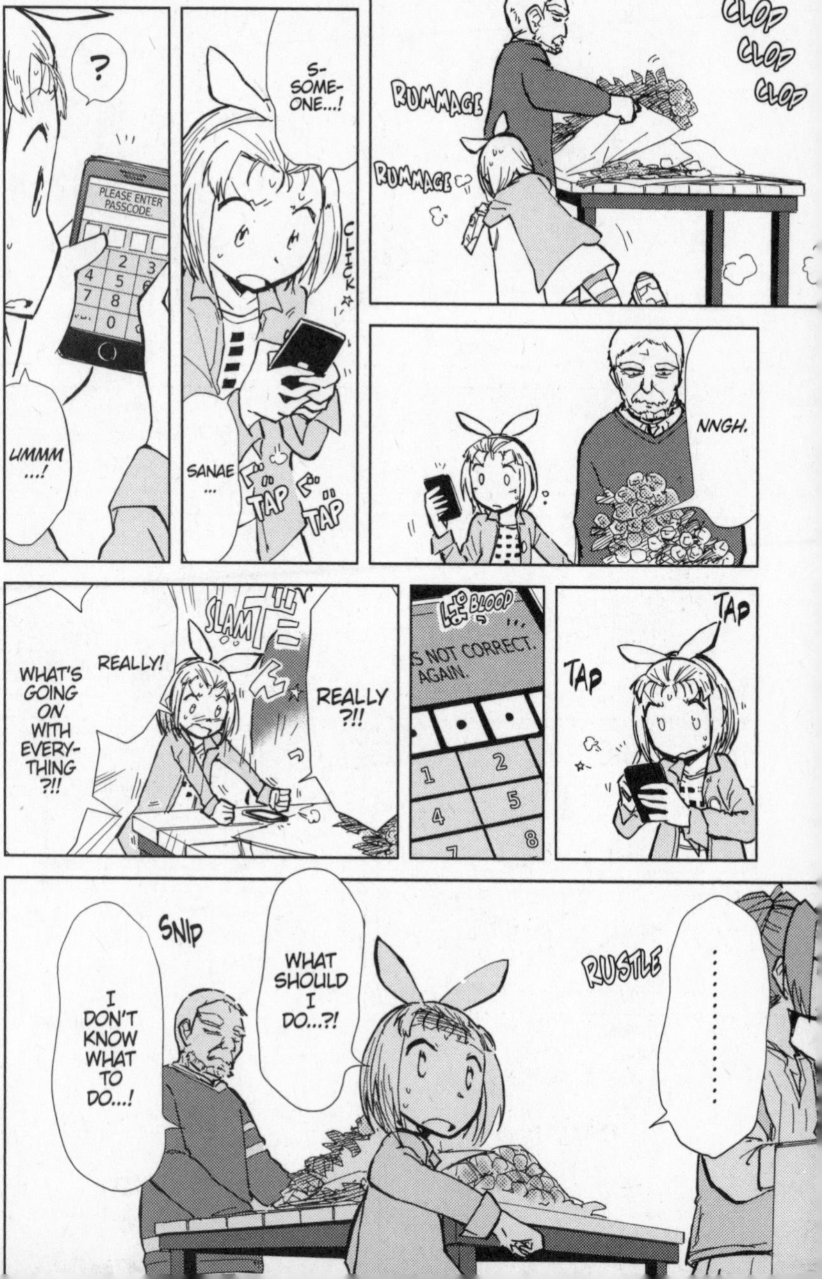
CLOP CLOP CLOP CLOP
RUMMAGE
RUMMAGE
NNGH.
S-SOMEONE...!
CLICK
SANAE...
TAP TAP
?
PLEASE ENTER PASSCODE.
UMMM...!
TAP
TAP
BLOOP
S NOT CORRECT.
AGAIN.
REALLY?!!
SLAM
REALLY!
WHAT'S GOING ON WITH EVERYTHING?!!
RUSTLE
....
WHAT SHOULD I DO...?!
SNIP
I DON'T KNOW WHAT TO DO...!

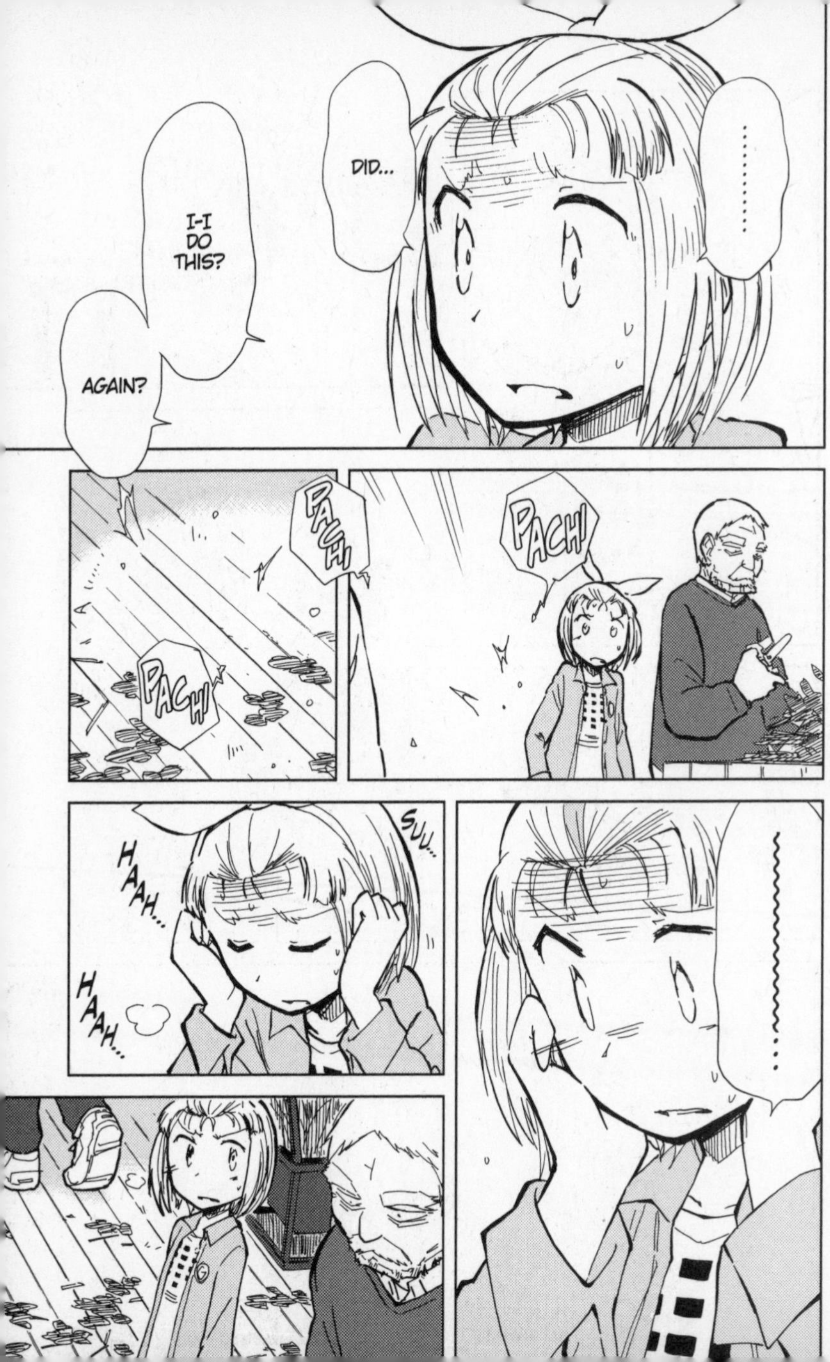
……
DID…
I-I DO THIS?
AGAIN?
PACHI
PACHI
PACHI
……
SUU…
HAAAH…
HAAAH…

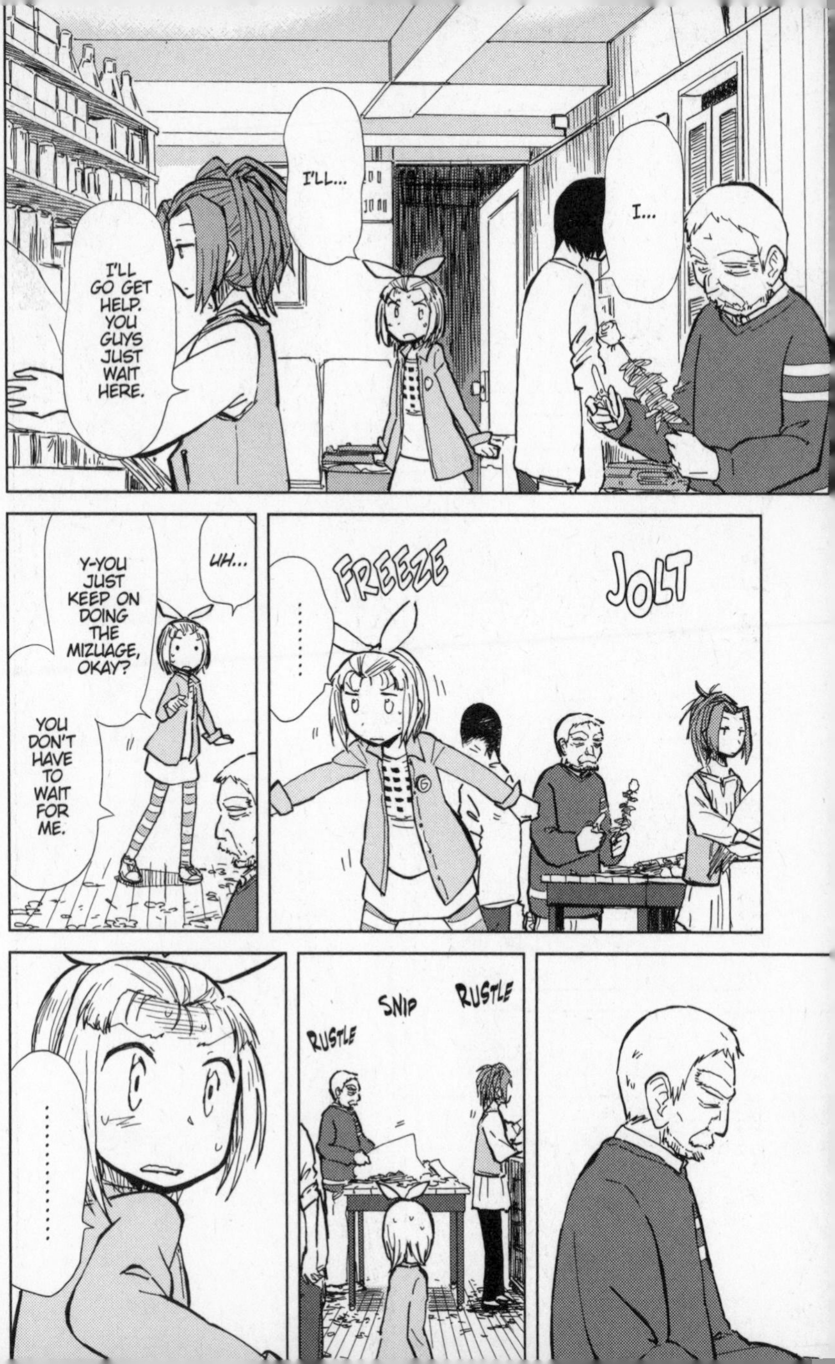
I...
I'LL...
I'LL GO GET HELP. YOU GUYS JUST WAIT HERE.
JOLT
FREEZE
......
UH...
Y-YOU JUST KEEP ON DOING THE MIZUAGE, OKAY?
YOU DON'T HAVE TO WAIT FOR ME.
RUSTLE
SNIP
RUSTLE
......

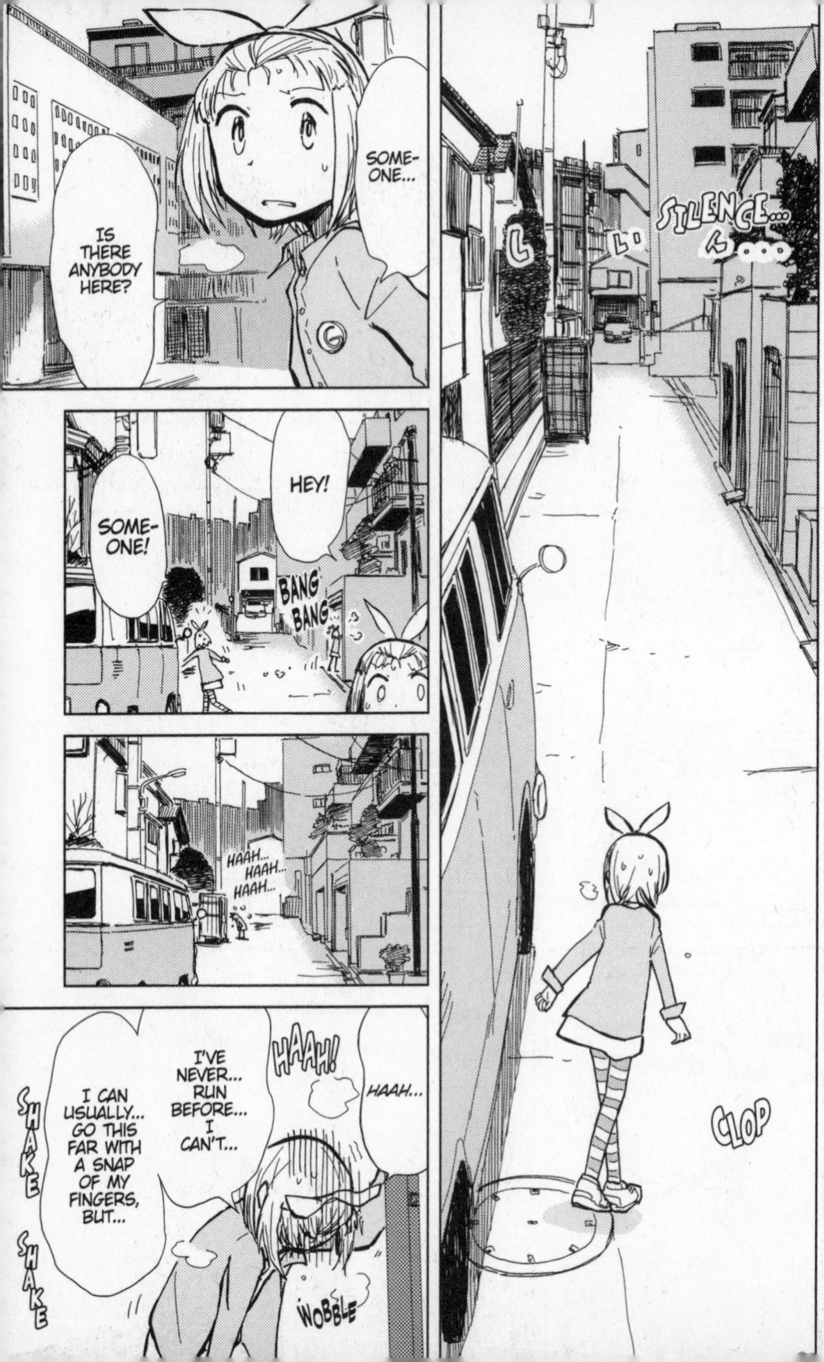
SILENCE...
CLOP
SOME-ONE...
IS THERE ANYBODY HERE?
HEY!
SOME-ONE!
BANG BANG
HAAH... HAAH... HAAH...
HAAH!
HAAH...
I'VE NEVER... RUN BEFORE... I CAN'T...
I CAN USUALLY... GO THIS FAR WITH A SNAP OF MY FINGERS, BUT...
SHAKE
SHAKE
WOBBLE

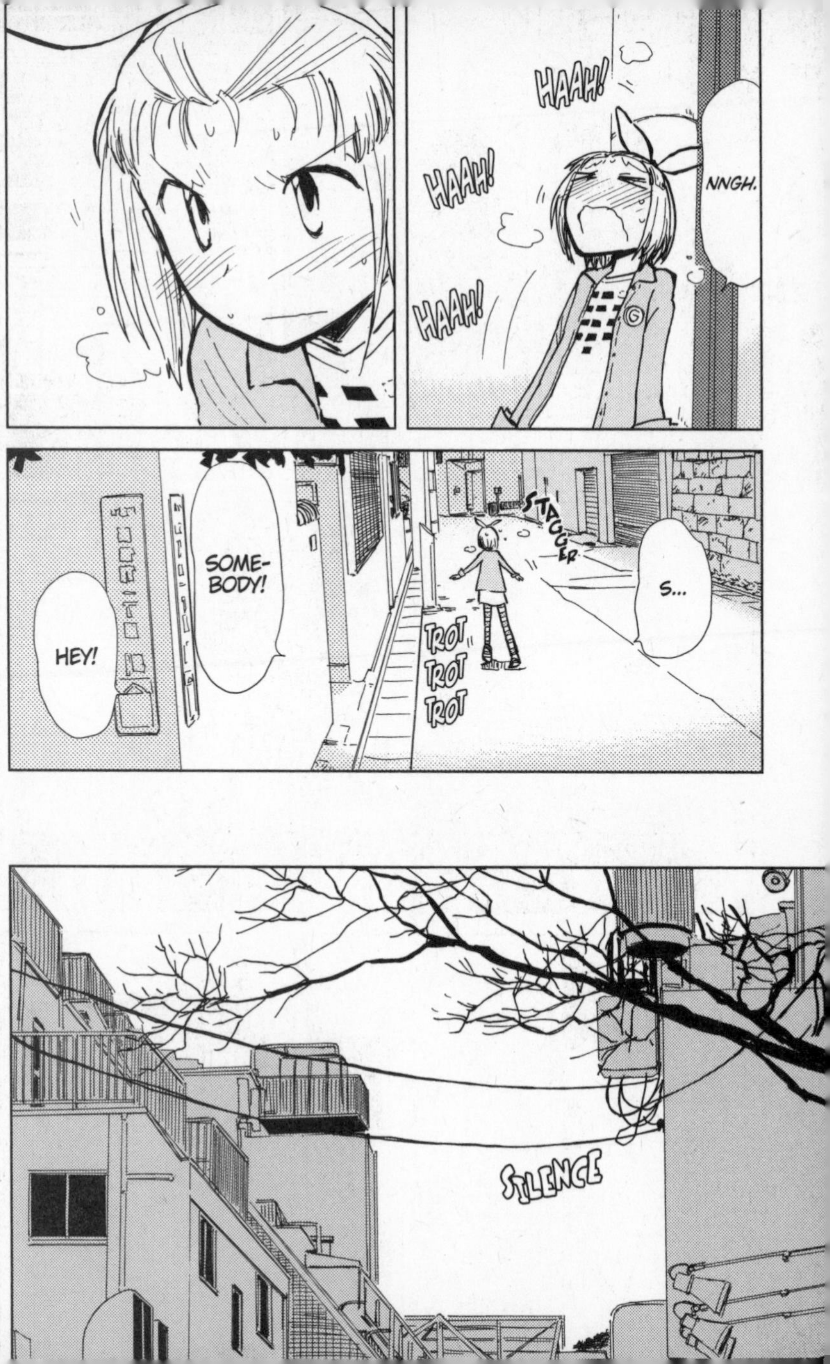
HAAH!
NNGH.
HAAH!
HAAH!
S...
STAGGER
TROT TROT TROT
SOME-BODY!
HEY!
SILENCE

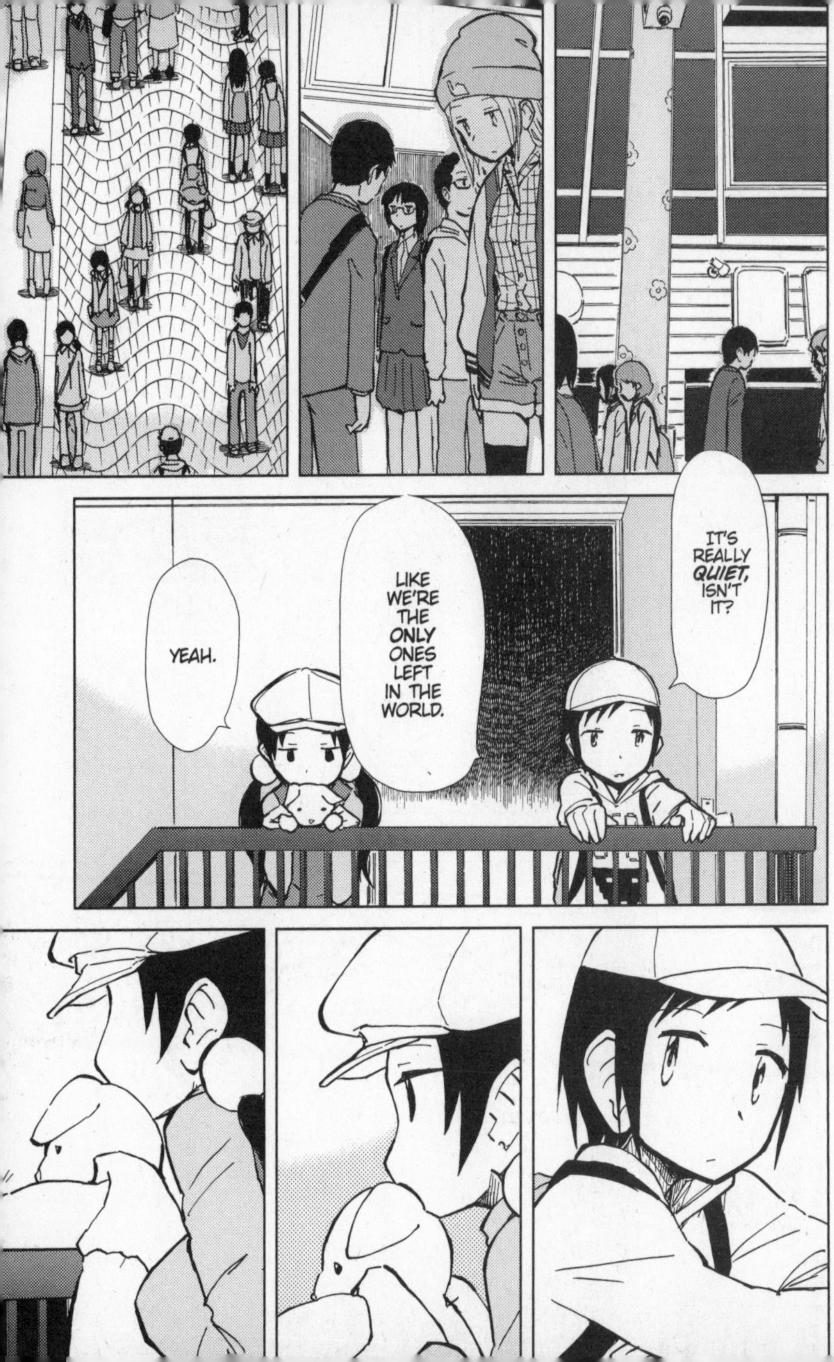
IT'S REALLY *QUIET,* ISN'T IT?
LIKE WE'RE THE ONLY ONES LEFT IN THE WORLD.
YEAH.

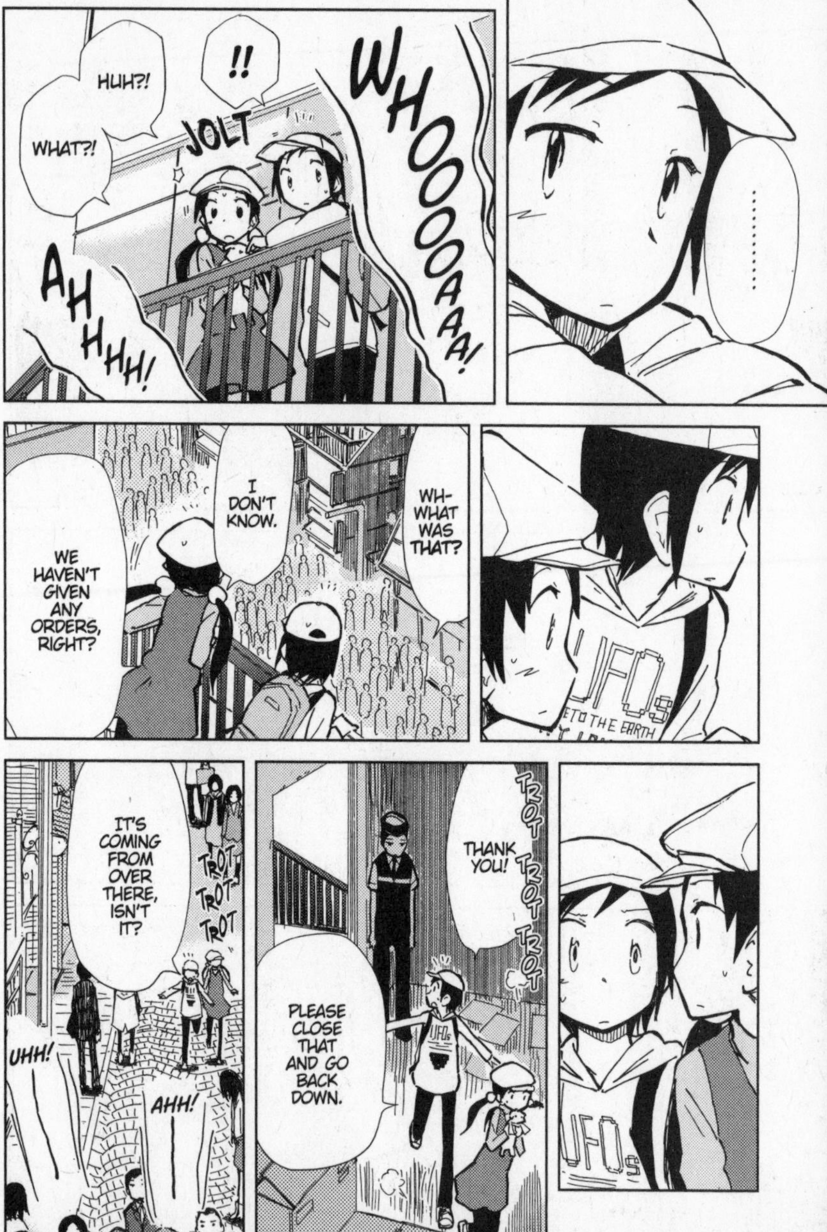
......
WHOOOOAAA!
AHHHHH!
!!
HUH?!
JOLT
WHAT?!
UFOs
TO THE EARTH
WH-WHAT WAS THAT?
I DON'T KNOW.
WE HAVEN'T GIVEN ANY ORDERS, RIGHT?
UFOs
TROT TROT TROT TROT
THANK YOU!
PLEASE CLOSE THAT AND GO BACK DOWN.
UFOs
TROT TROT TROT
IT'S COMING FROM OVER THERE, ISN'T IT?
UHH!
AHH!

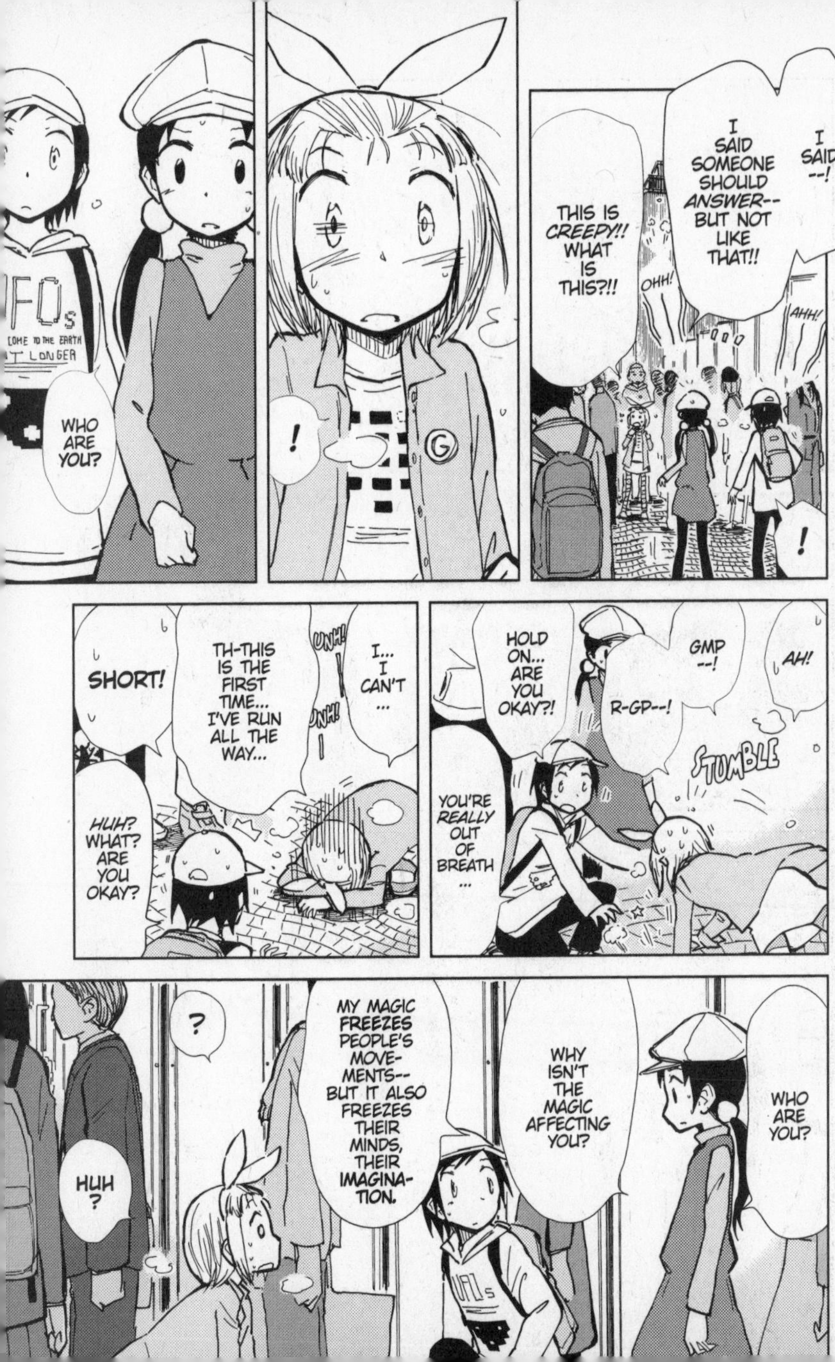
I SAID --!
I SAID SOMEONE SHOULD ANSWER-- BUT NOT LIKE THAT!!
THIS IS CREEPY!! WHAT IS THIS?!!
OHH!
AHH!
!
!
WHO ARE YOU?
AH!
GMP --!
R-GP--!
STUMBLE
HOLD ON... ARE YOU OKAY?!
YOU'RE REALLY OUT OF BREATH ...
I... I CAN'T ...
UNH!
UNH!
TH-THIS IS THE FIRST TIME... I'VE RUN ALL THE WAY...
SHORT!
HUH? WHAT? ARE YOU OKAY?
WHO ARE YOU?
WHY ISN'T THE MAGIC AFFECTING YOU?
MY MAGIC FREEZES PEOPLE'S MOVEMENTS-- BUT IT ALSO FREEZES THEIR MINDS, THEIR IMAGINATION.
?
HUH ?

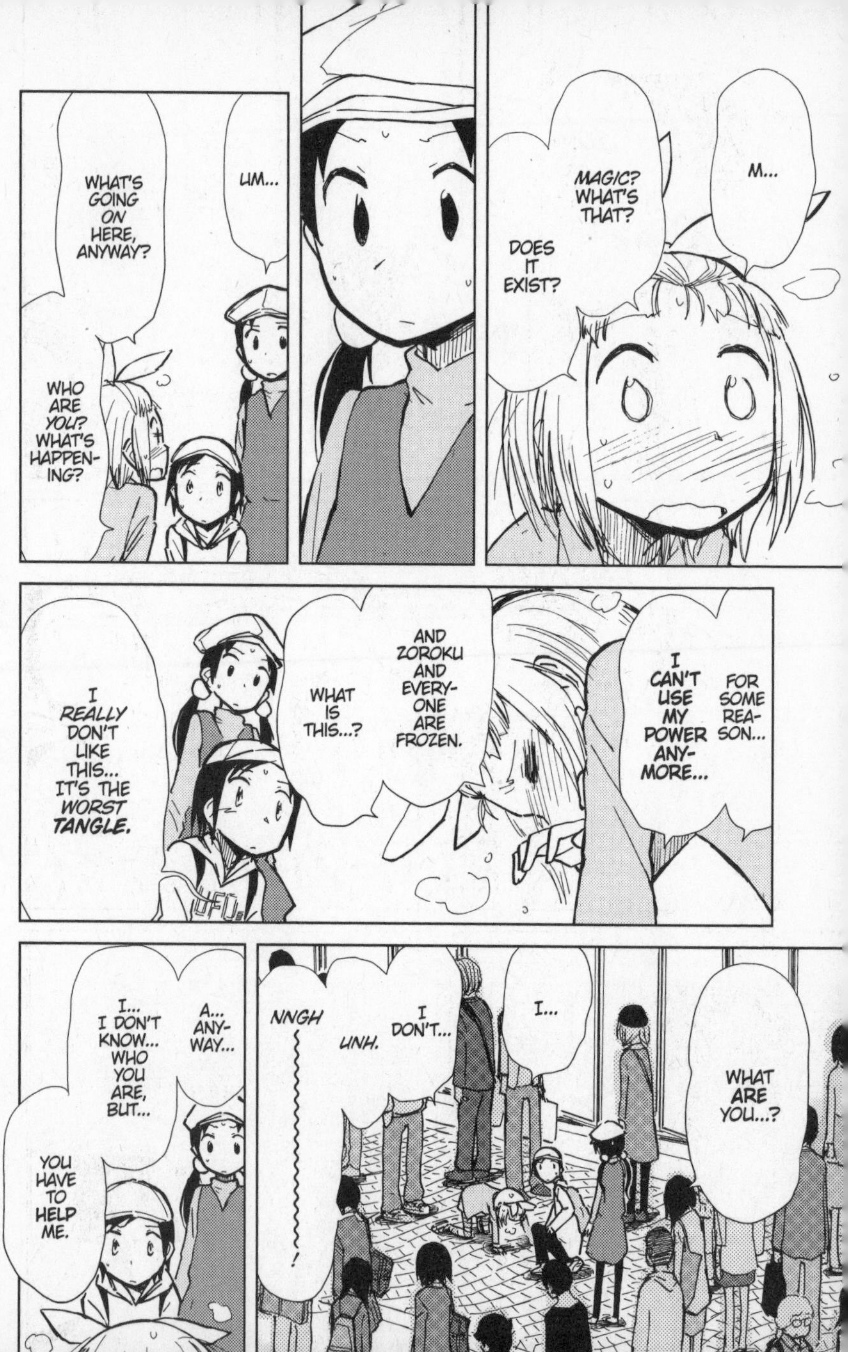
M...
MAGIC? WHAT'S THAT?
DOES IT EXIST?
UM...
WHAT'S GOING *ON* HERE, ANYWAY?
WHO ARE *YOU?* WHAT'S HAPPENING?
FOR SOME REASON...
I CAN'T USE MY POWER ANYMORE...
AND ZOROKU AND EVERYONE ARE FROZEN.
WHAT IS THIS...?
I *REALLY* DON'T LIKE THIS... IT'S THE *WORST* ***TANGLE.***
WHAT ARE YOU...?
I...
I DON'T...
UNH.
NNGH
!
A... ANYWAY...
I... I DON'T KNOW... WHO YOU ARE, BUT...
YOU HAVE TO HELP ME.

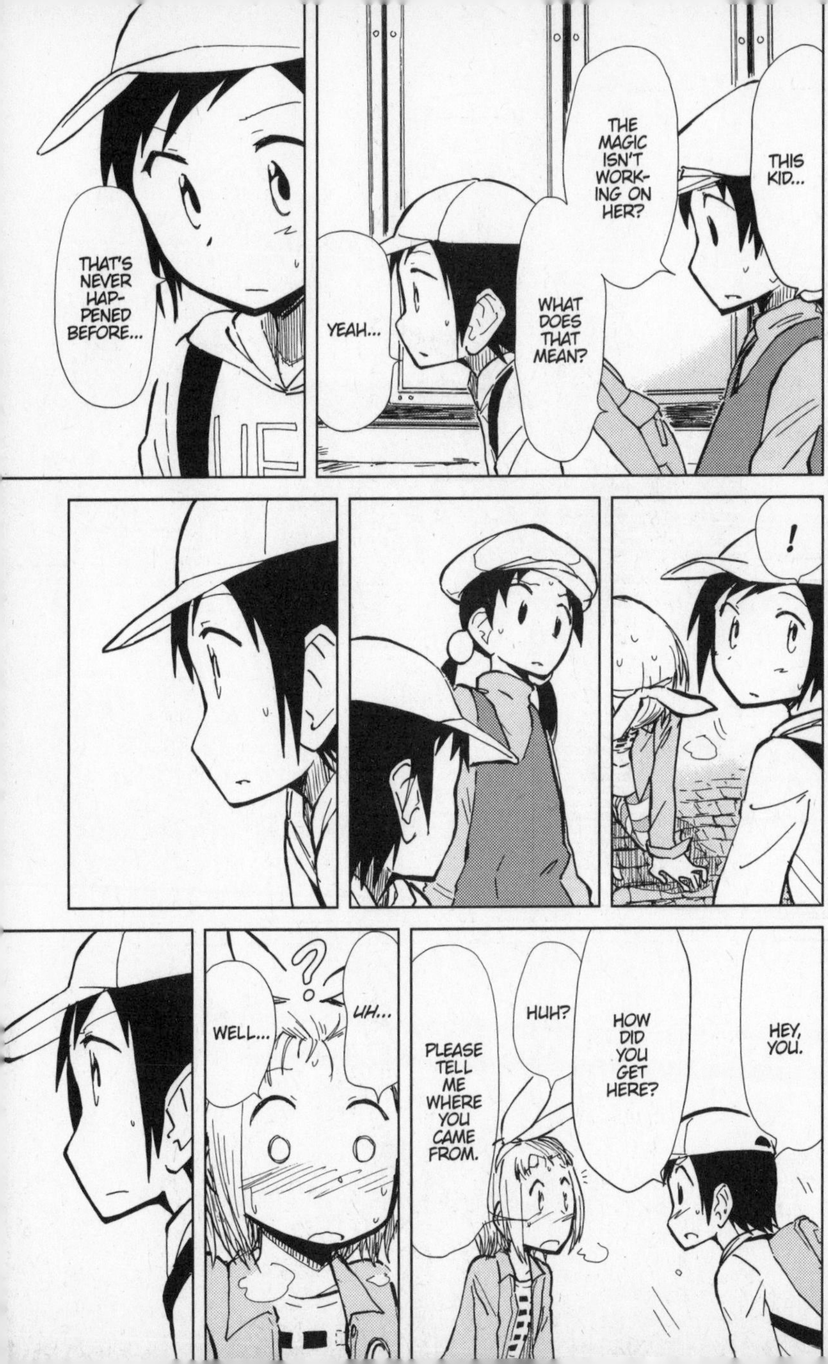
THIS KID...
THE MAGIC ISN'T WORK-ING ON HER?
WHAT DOES THAT MEAN?
YEAH...
THAT'S NEVER HAP-PENED BEFORE...
!
HEY, YOU.
HOW DID YOU GET HERE?
HUH?
PLEASE TELL ME WHERE YOU CAME FROM.
UH...
?
WELL...

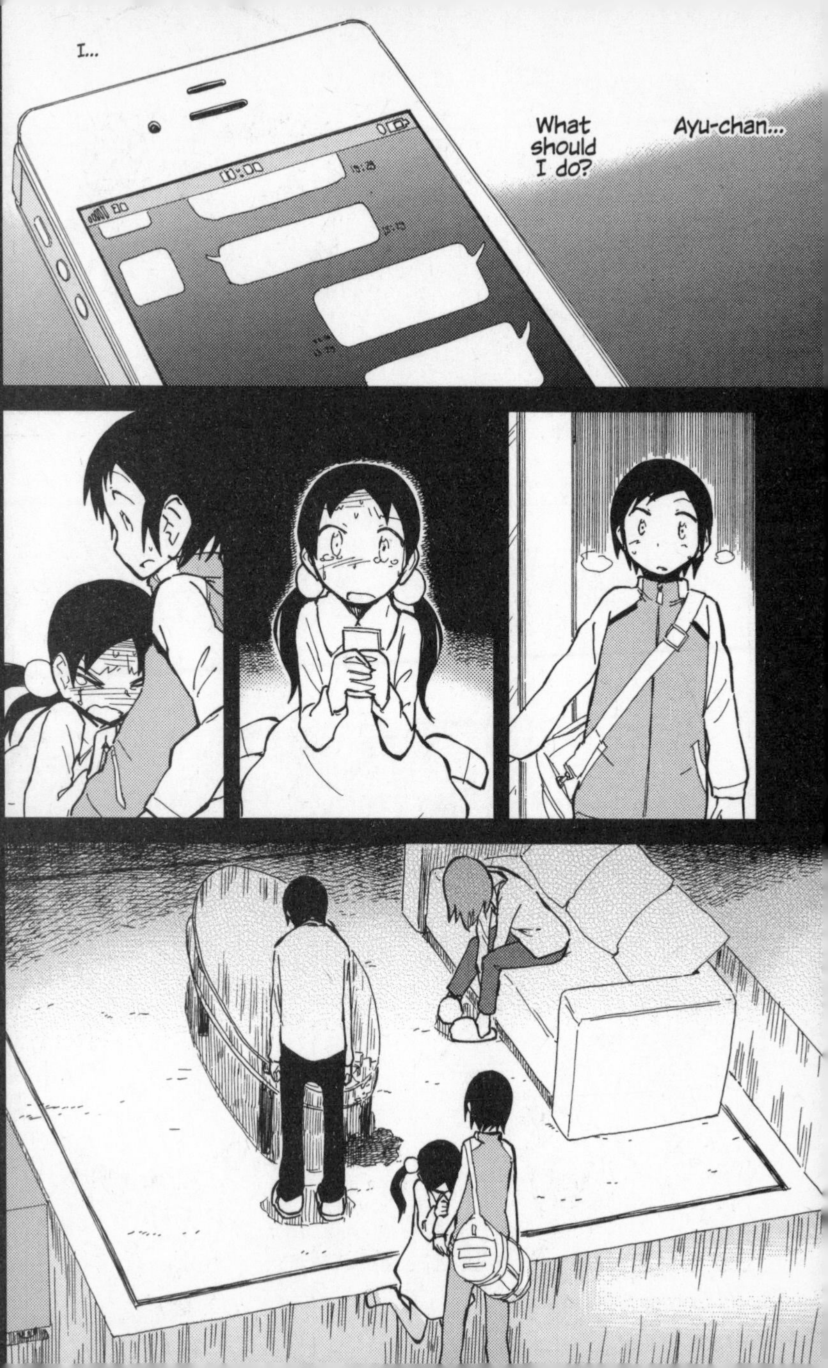
Ayu-chan...
What should I do?
I...

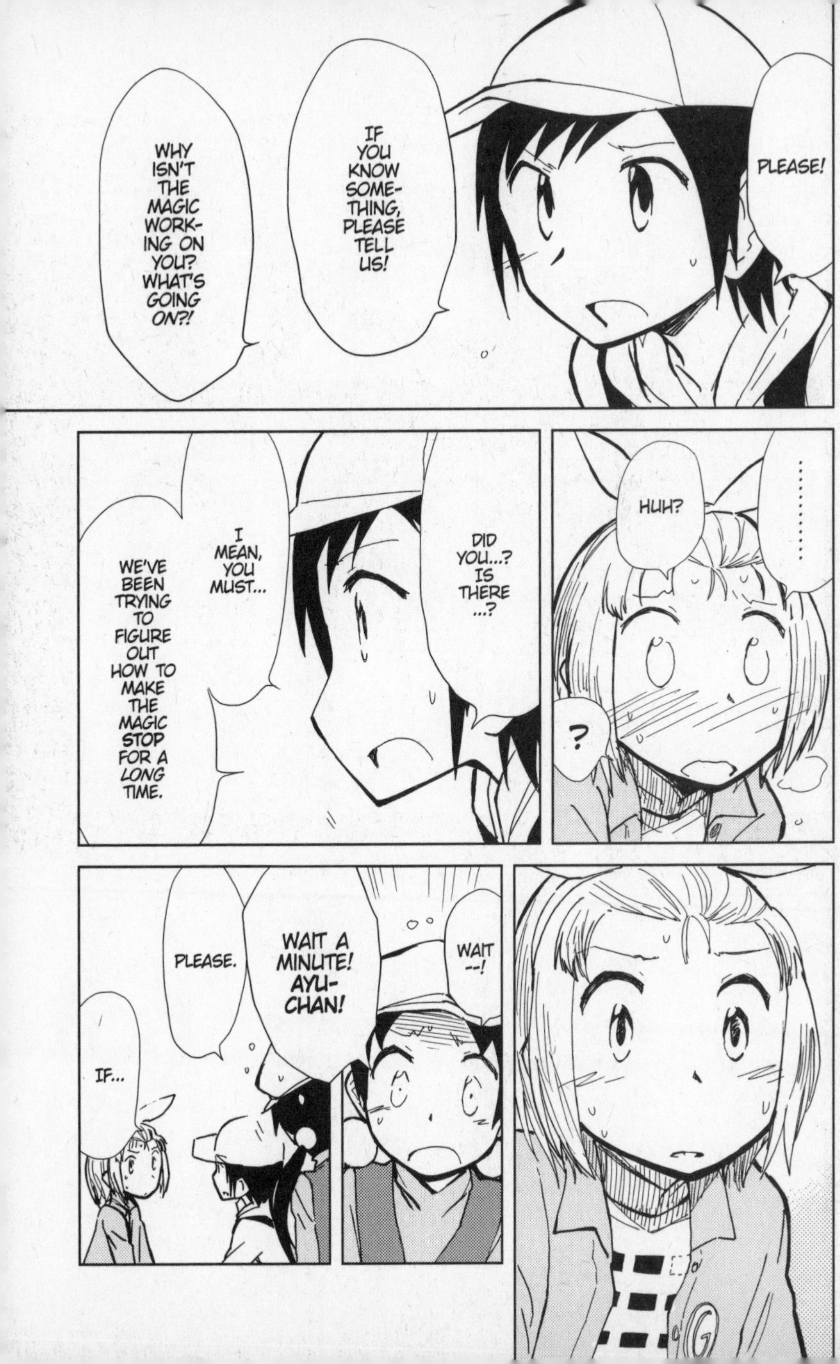
PLEASE!
IF YOU KNOW SOMETHING, PLEASE TELL US!
WHY ISN'T THE MAGIC WORKING ON YOU? WHAT'S GOING ON?!
......
HUH?
?
DID YOU...? IS THERE ...?
I MEAN, YOU MUST...
WE'VE BEEN TRYING TO FIGURE OUT HOW TO MAKE THE MAGIC STOP FOR A LONG TIME.
WAIT --!
WAIT A MINUTE! AYU-CHAN!
PLEASE.
IF...

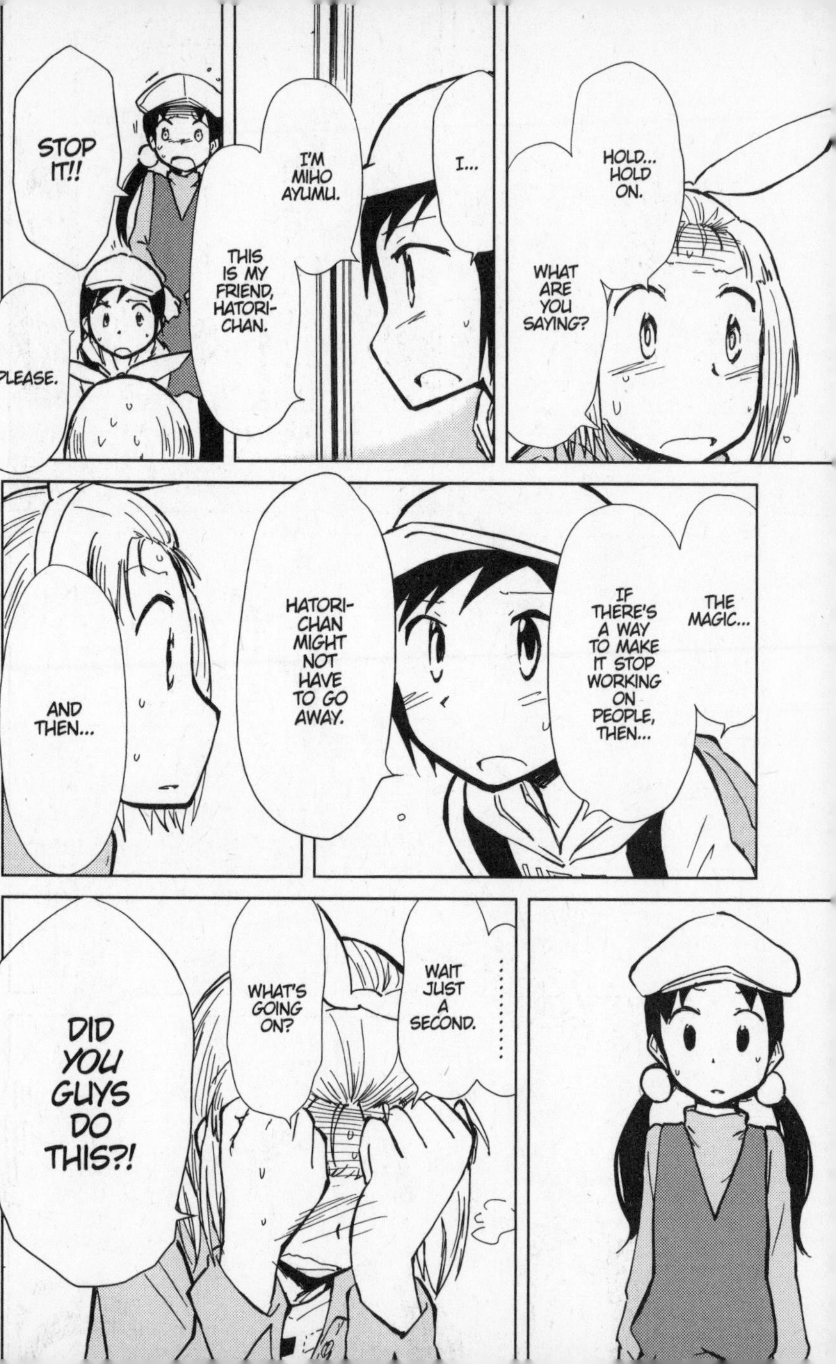
HOLD... HOLD ON.
WHAT ARE YOU SAYING?
I...
I'M MIHO AYUMU.
THIS IS MY FRIEND, HATORI-CHAN.
STOP IT!!
PLEASE.
THE MAGIC...
IF THERE'S A WAY TO MAKE IT STOP WORKING ON PEOPLE, THEN...
HATORI-CHAN MIGHT NOT HAVE TO GO AWAY.
AND THEN...
......
WAIT JUST A SECOND.
WHAT'S GOING ON?
DID YOU GUYS DO THIS?!

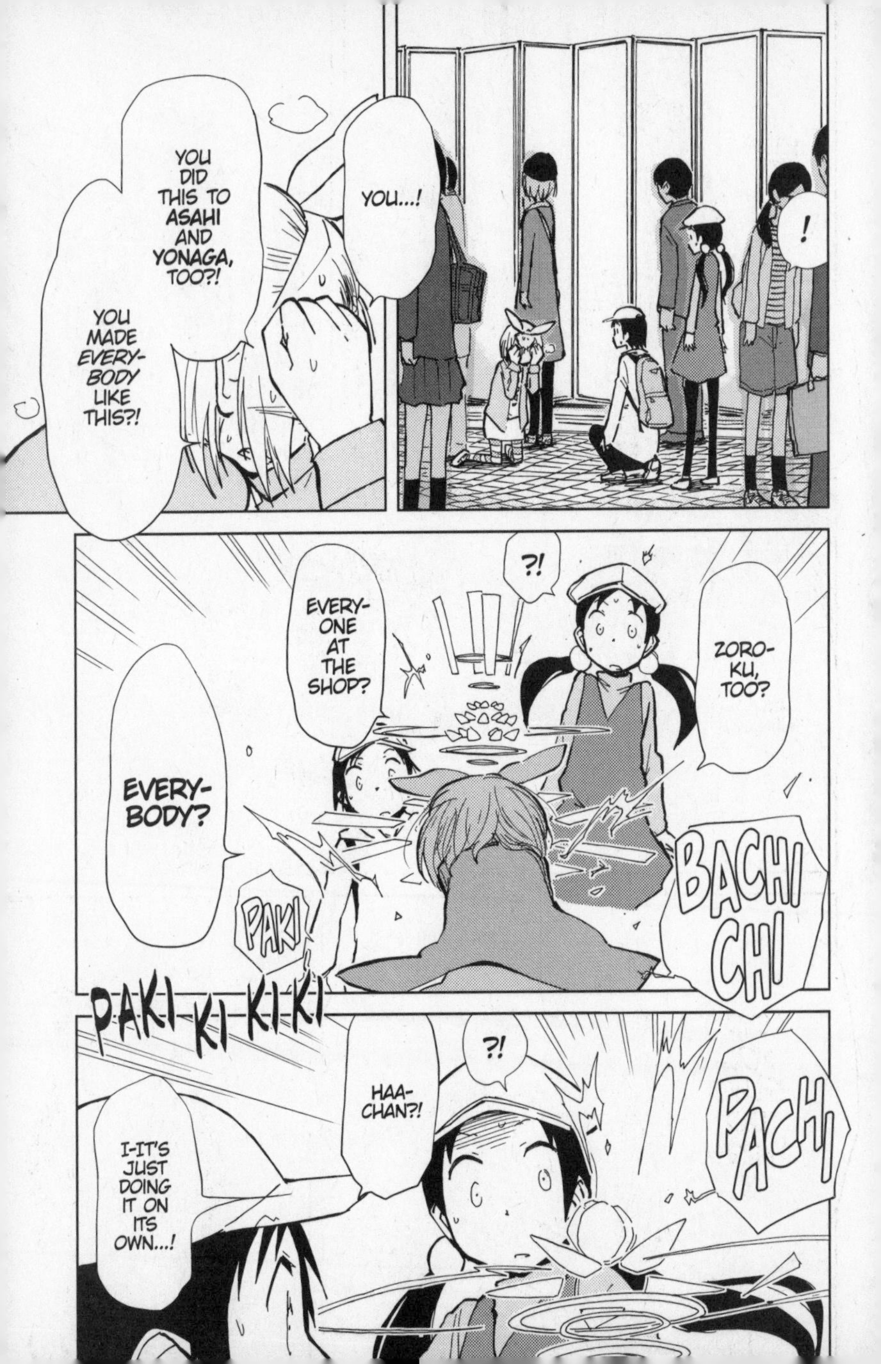
!
YOU...!
YOU DID THIS TO ASAHI AND YONAGA, TOO?!
YOU MADE EVERYBODY LIKE THIS?!
?!
ZOROKU, TOO?
EVERYONE AT THE SHOP?
EVERYBODY?
BACHI CHI
PAKI
PAKI KI KI KI
PACHI
?!
HAA-CHAN?!
I-IT'S JUST DOING IT ON ITS OWN...!

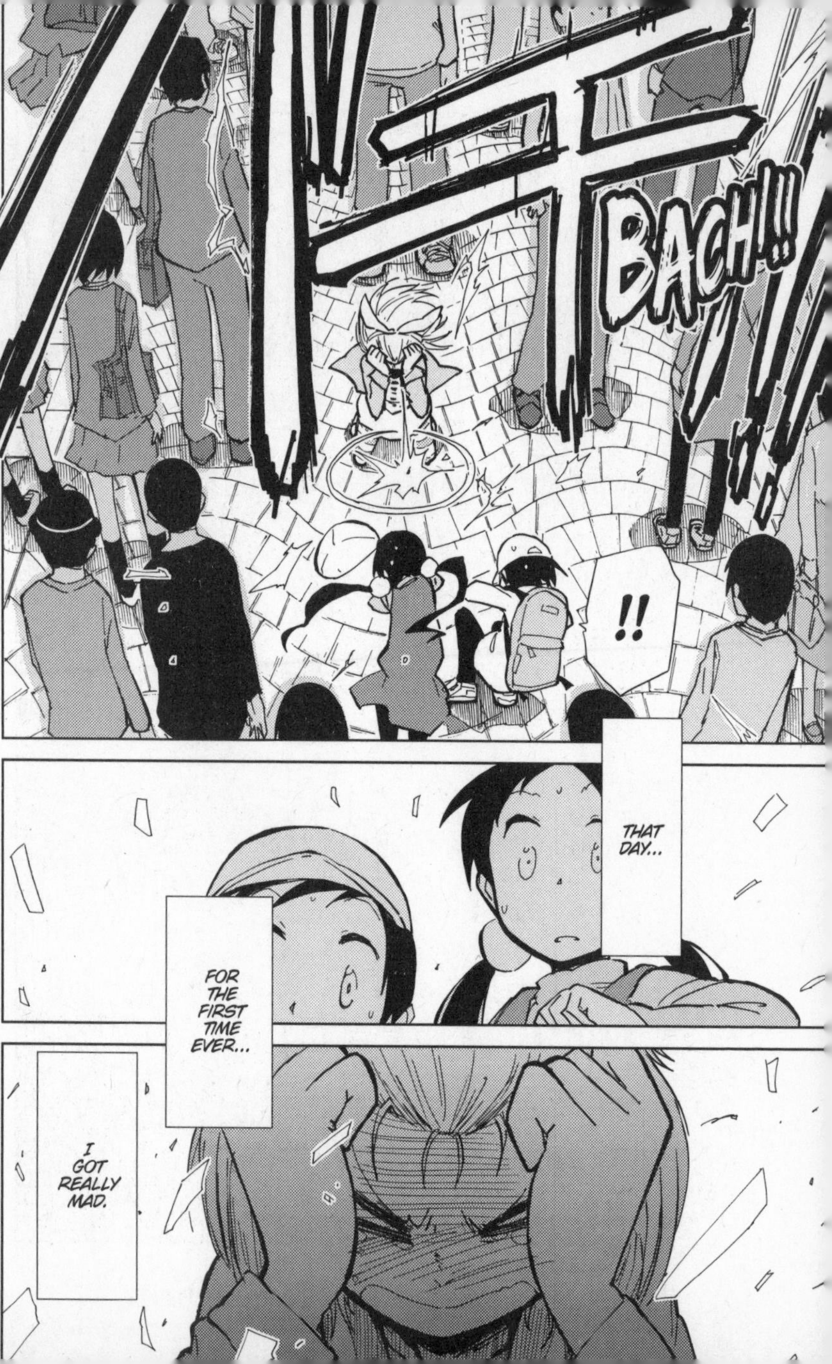
BACH!!!
!!
THAT DAY...
FOR THE FIRST TIME EVER...
I GOT REALLY MAD.

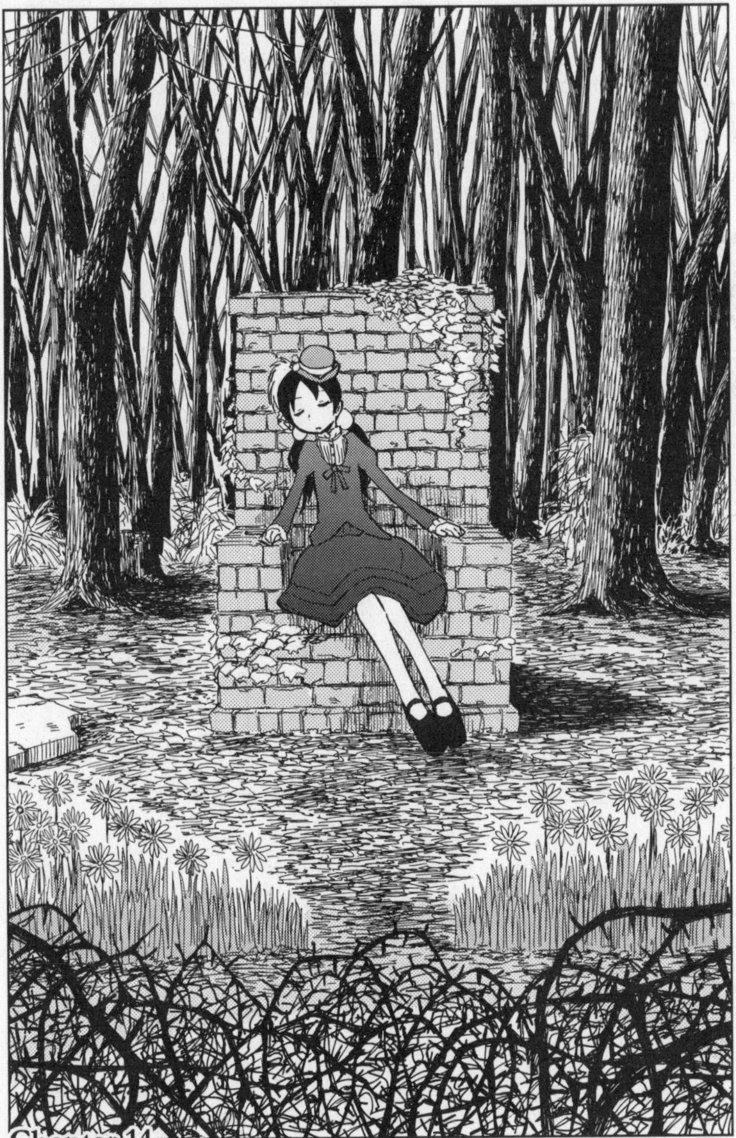

Chapter 14

An Encounter with Dee and Dum

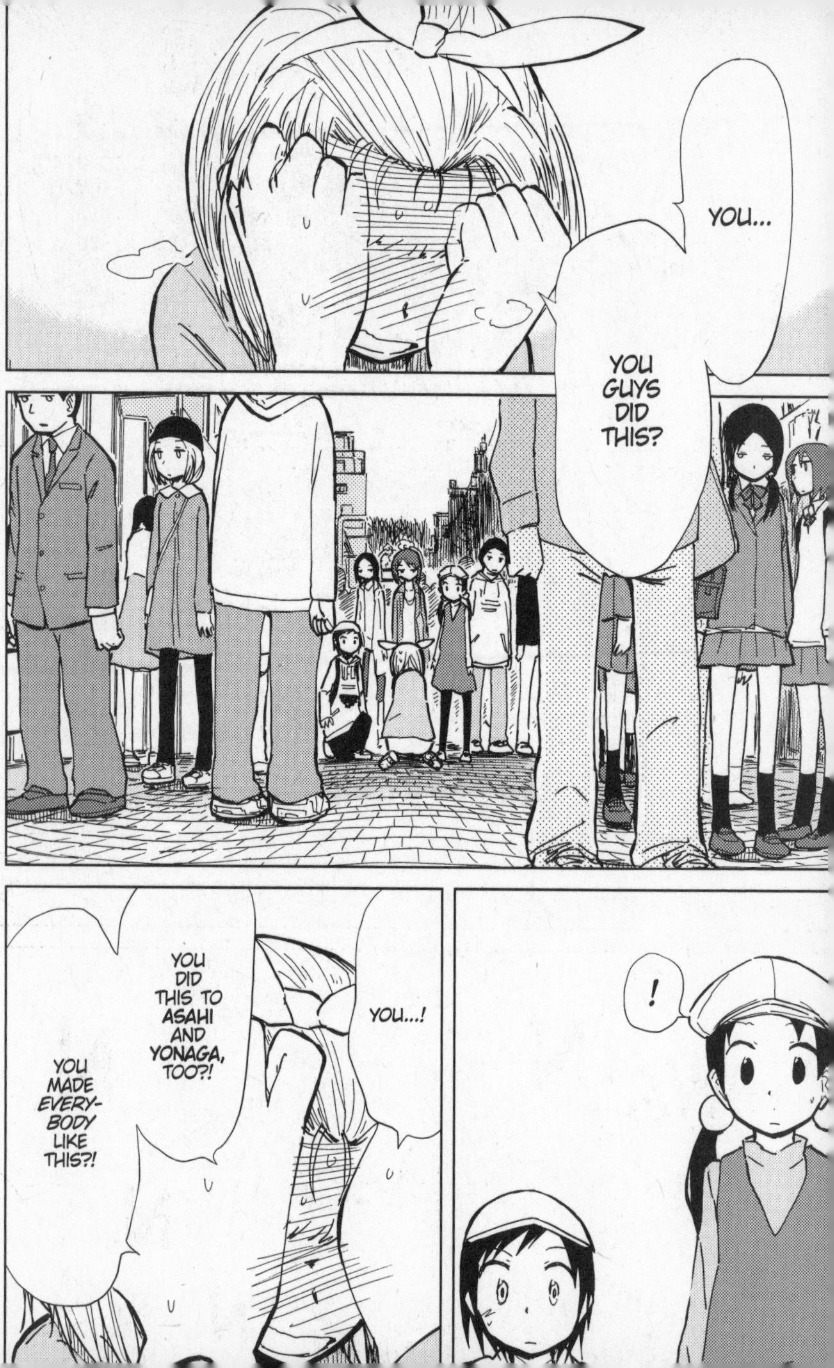
YOU...
YOU GUYS DID THIS?
!
YOU...!
YOU DID THIS TO ASAHI AND YONAGA, TOO?!
YOU MADE EVERY-BODY LIKE THIS?!

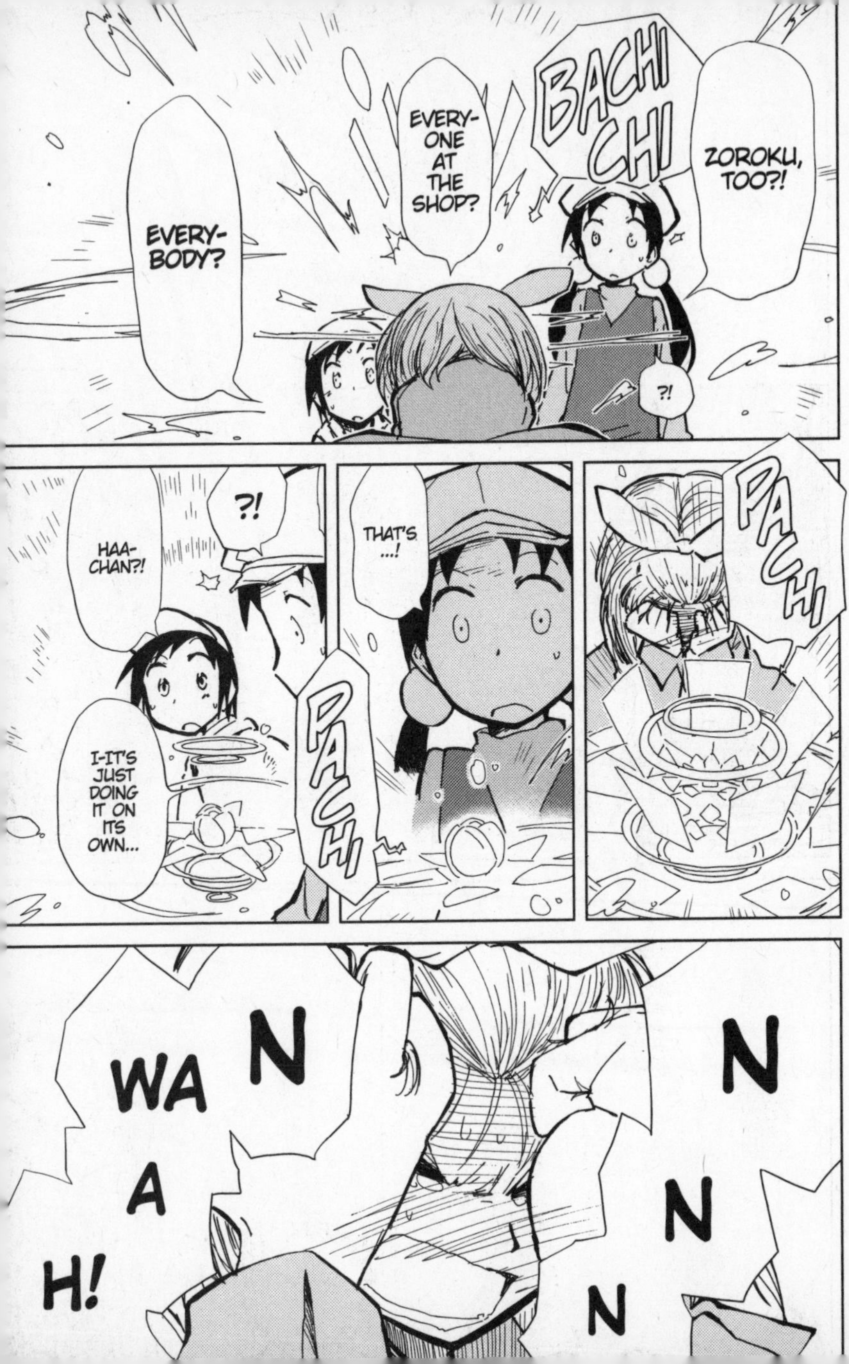
ZOROKU, TOO?!
BACHI CHI
EVERY-ONE AT THE SHOP?
?!
EVERY-BODY?
PACHI
THAT'S ...!
PACHI
?!
HAA-CHAN?!
I-IT'S JUST DOING IT ON ITS OWN...
WA A H!
N N N N N

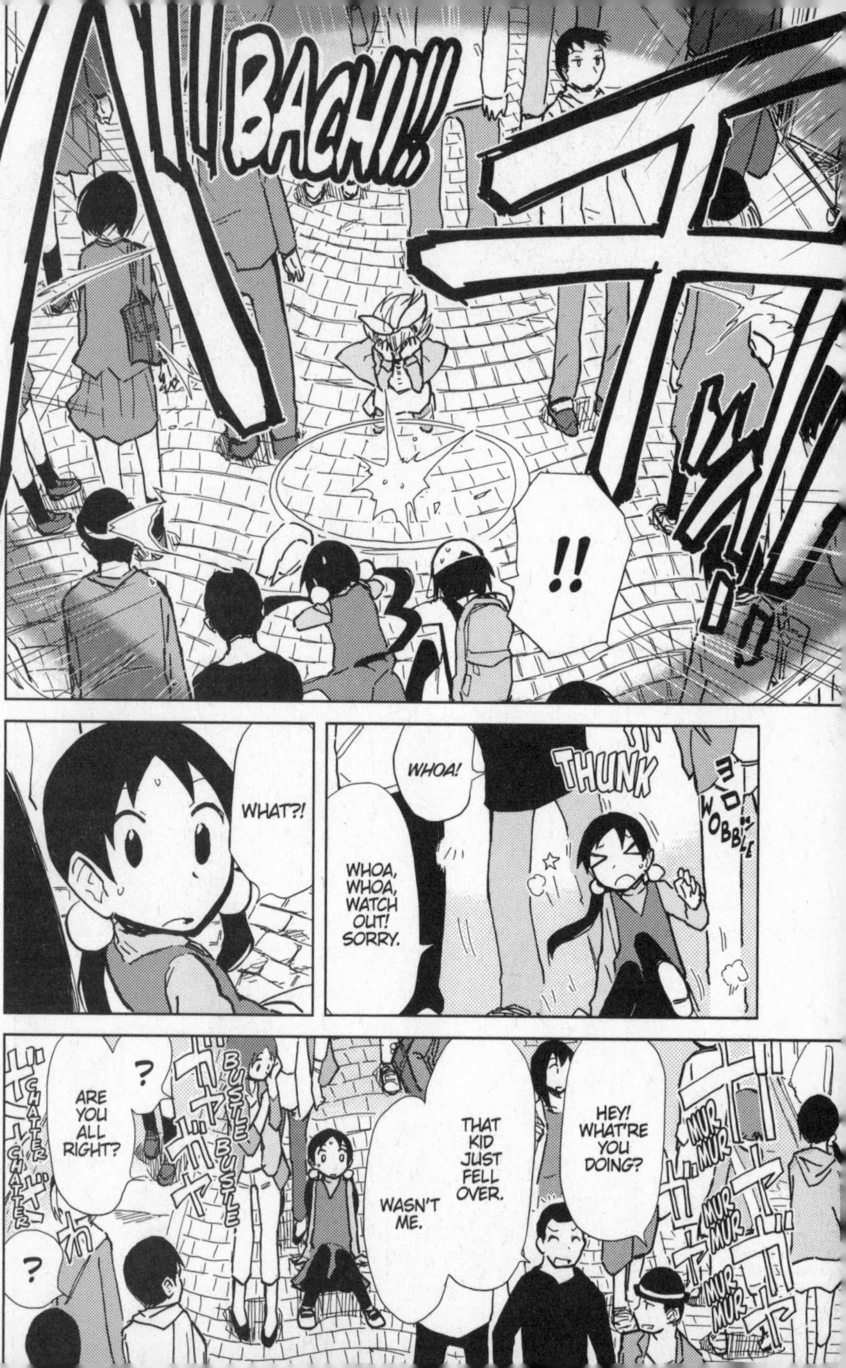
BACH!!!
!!
WHOA!
WHOA, WHOA, WATCH OUT! SORRY.
THUNK
WOBBLE
WHAT?!
MUR MUR
MUR MUR
MUR MUR
HEY! WHAT'RE YOU DOING?
THAT KID JUST FELL OVER.
WASN'T ME.
BUSTLE BUSTLE
?
ARE YOU ALL RIGHT?
CHATTER CHATTER
?

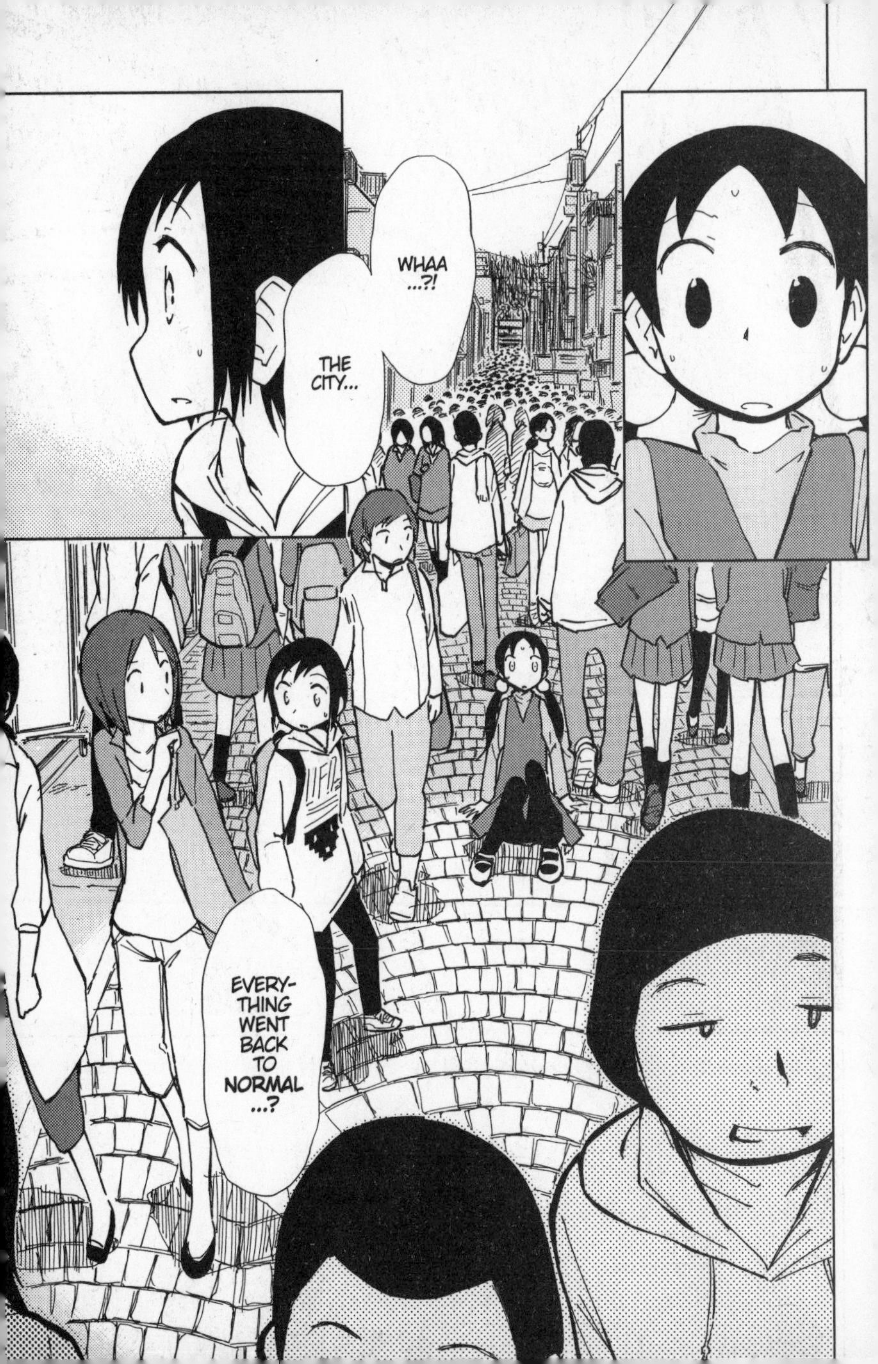
WHAA ...?!
THE CITY...
EVERY-THING WENT BACK TO NORMAL ...?

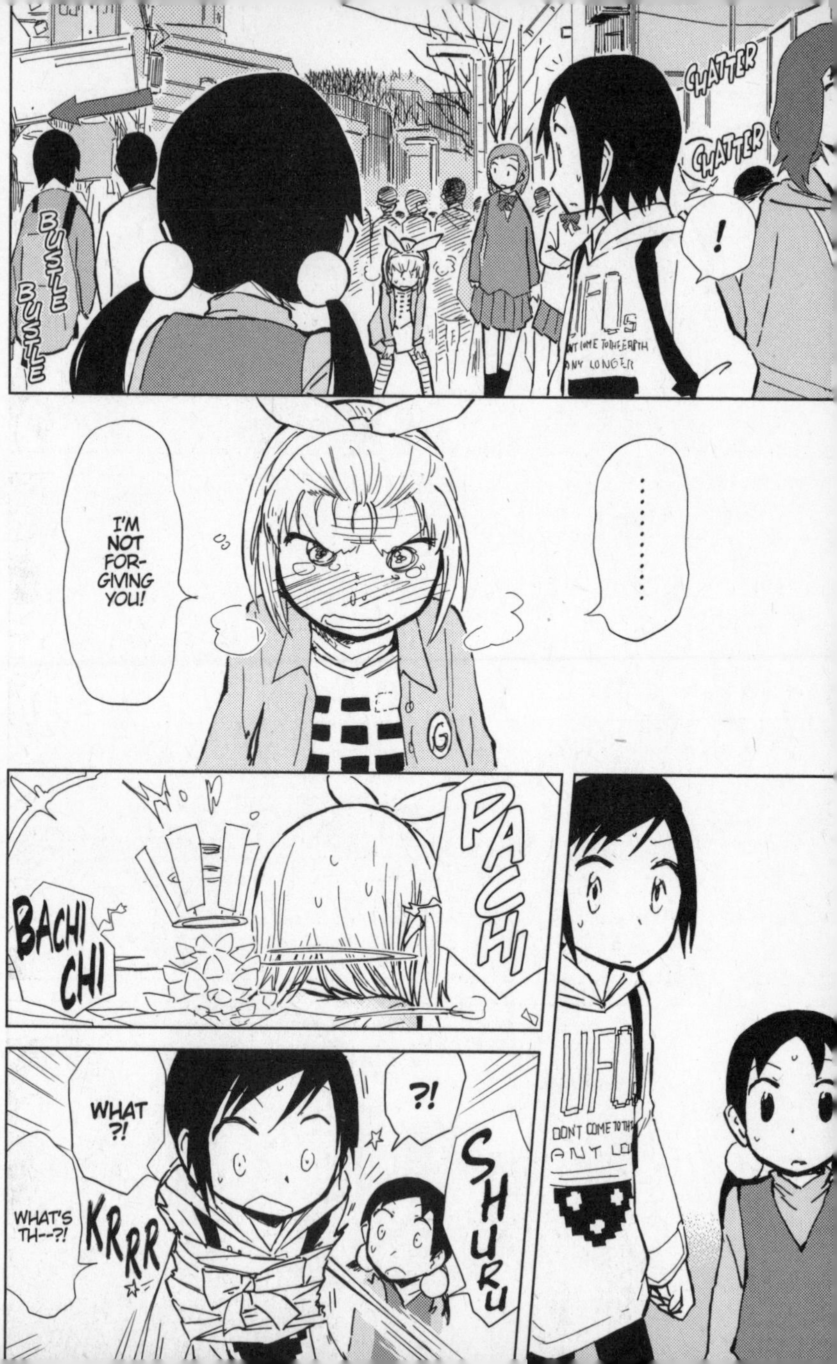
CHATTER
CHATTER
!
BUSTLE BUSTLE
......
I'M NOT FOR-GIVING YOU!
PACHI
BACHI CHI
?!
SHURU
WHAT ?!
KRRR
WHAT'S TH--?!

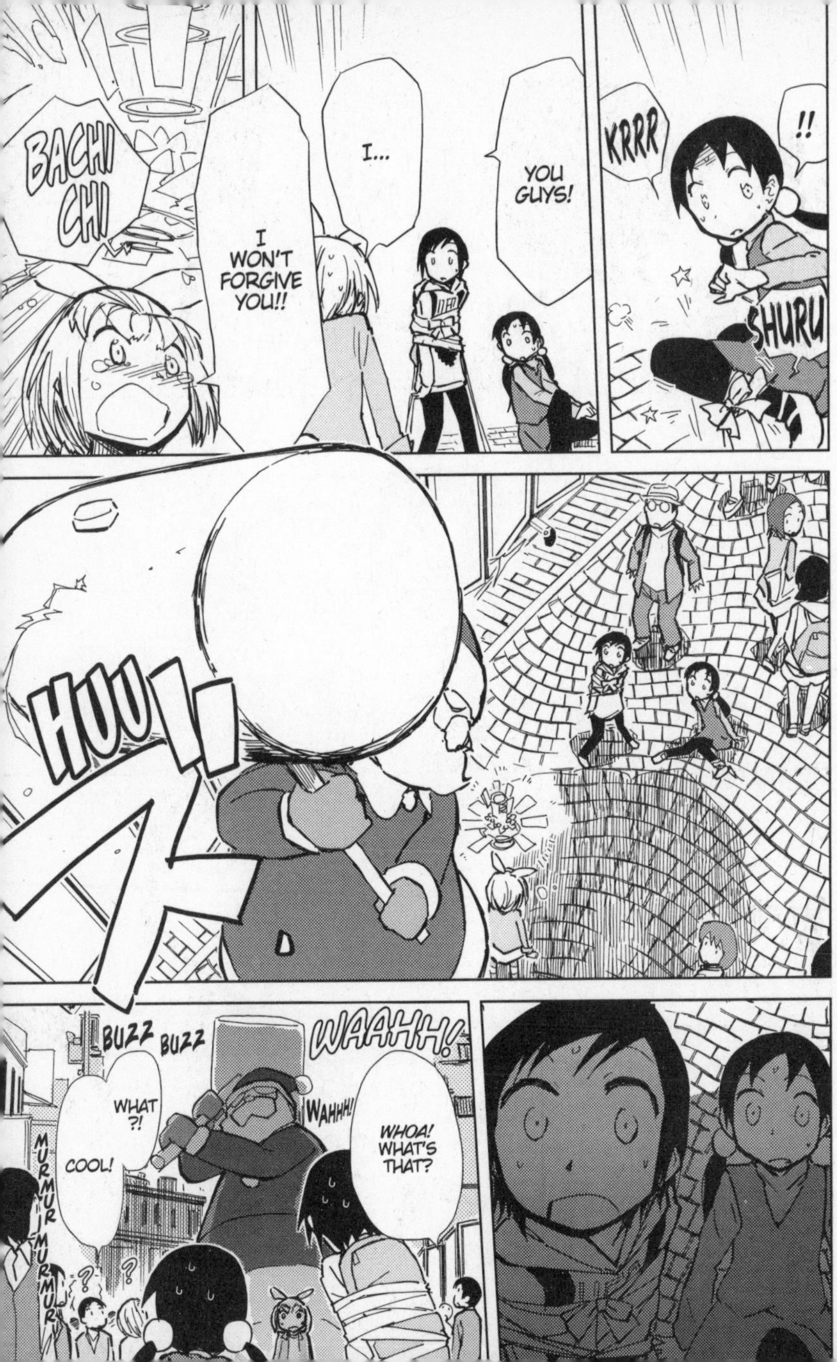
!!
KRRR
SHURU
YOU GUYS!
I...
I WON'T FORGIVE YOU!!
BACHI CHI
HUU!!
WAAHH!
WAHHH!
WHOA! WHAT'S THAT?
BUZZ BUZZ
WHAT?!
COOL!
MURMUR MURMUR
?
?

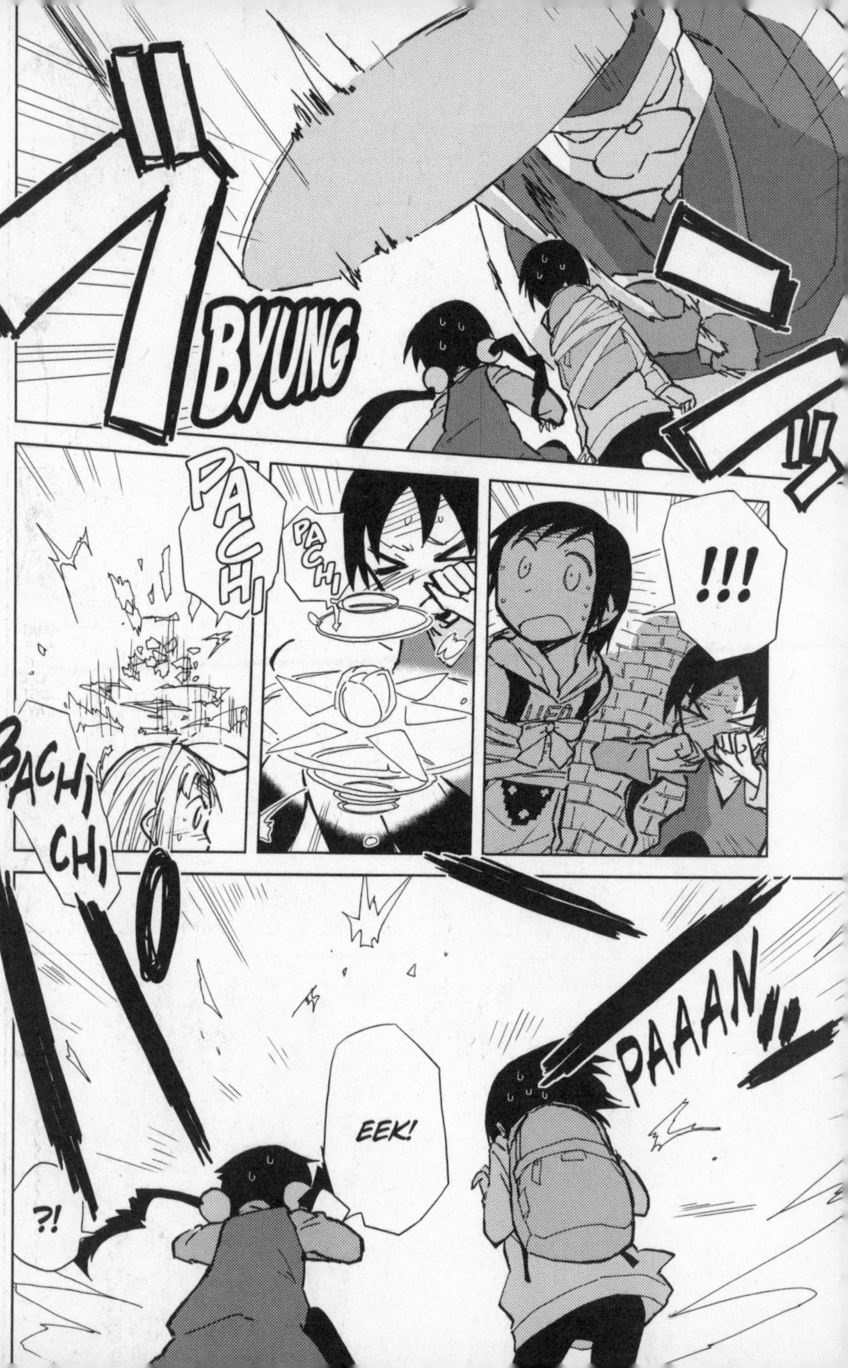
BYUNG
!!!
PACHI
PACHI
BACHI CHI
PAAAN!!
EEK!
?!

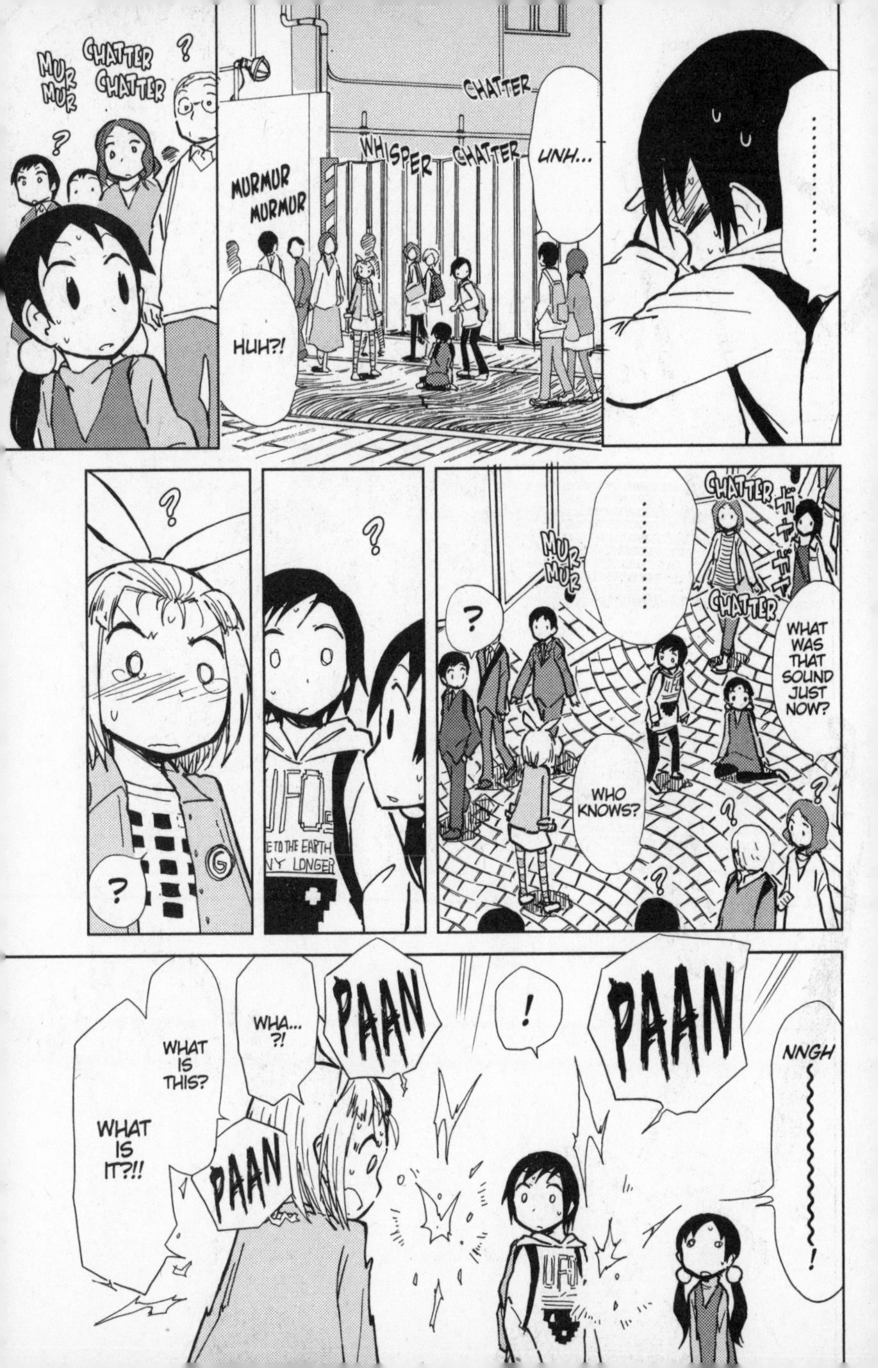
……
CHATTER
WHISPER
CHATTER
UNH…
MURMUR MURMUR
HUH?!
MUR MUR
CHATTER CHATTER
?
?
CHATTER
ガヤガヤ
CHATTER
……
MUR MUR
?
WHAT WAS THAT SOUND JUST NOW?
WHO KNOWS?
?
?
?
?
?
NNGH~!
PAAN
!
PAAN
WHA… ?!
WHAT IS THIS?
WHAT IS IT?!!
PAAN

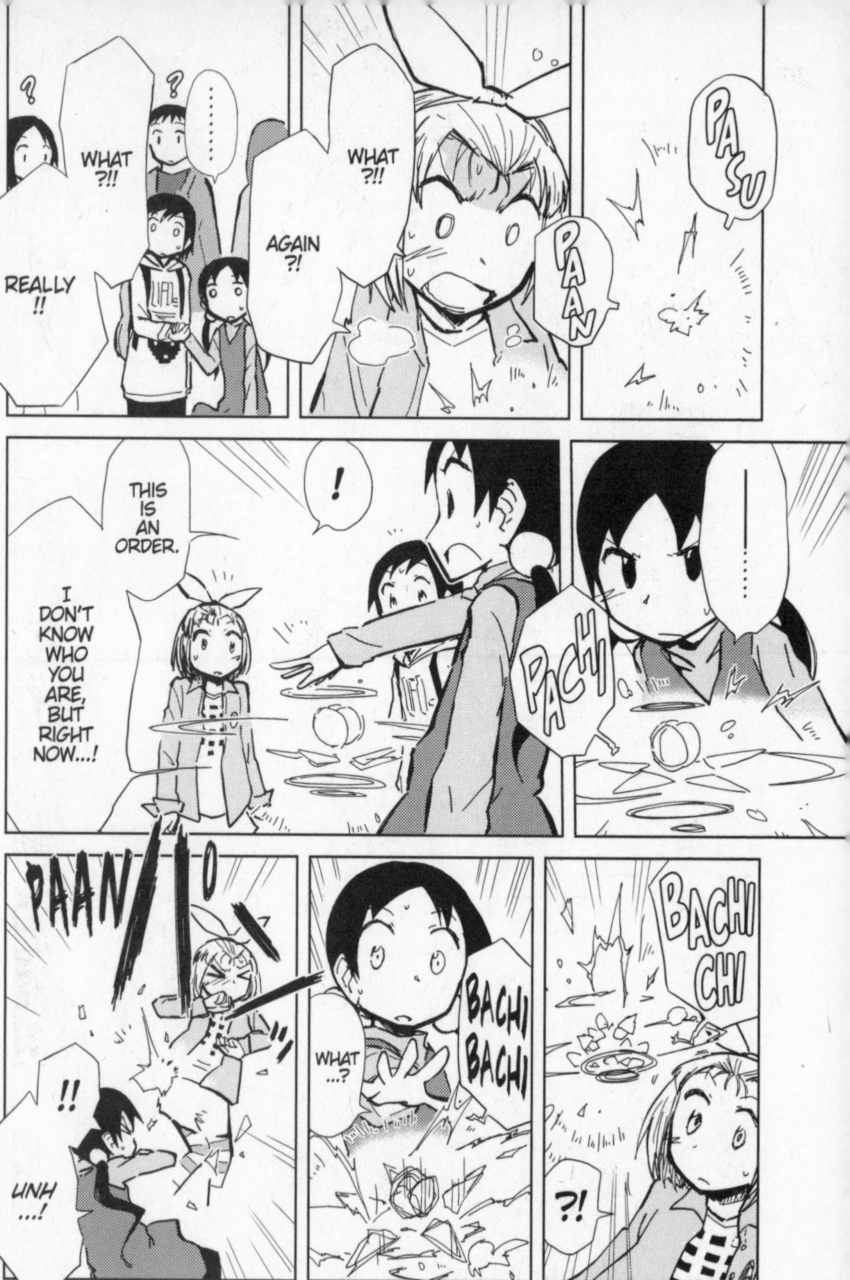
PASU
PAAN
WHAT ?!!
AGAIN ?!
......
WHAT ?!!
REALLY !!
......
PACHI
!
THIS IS AN ORDER.
I DON'T KNOW WHO YOU ARE, BUT RIGHT NOW...!
BACHI CHI
?!
BACHI BACHI
WHAT ...?
PAAN
!!
UNH ...!

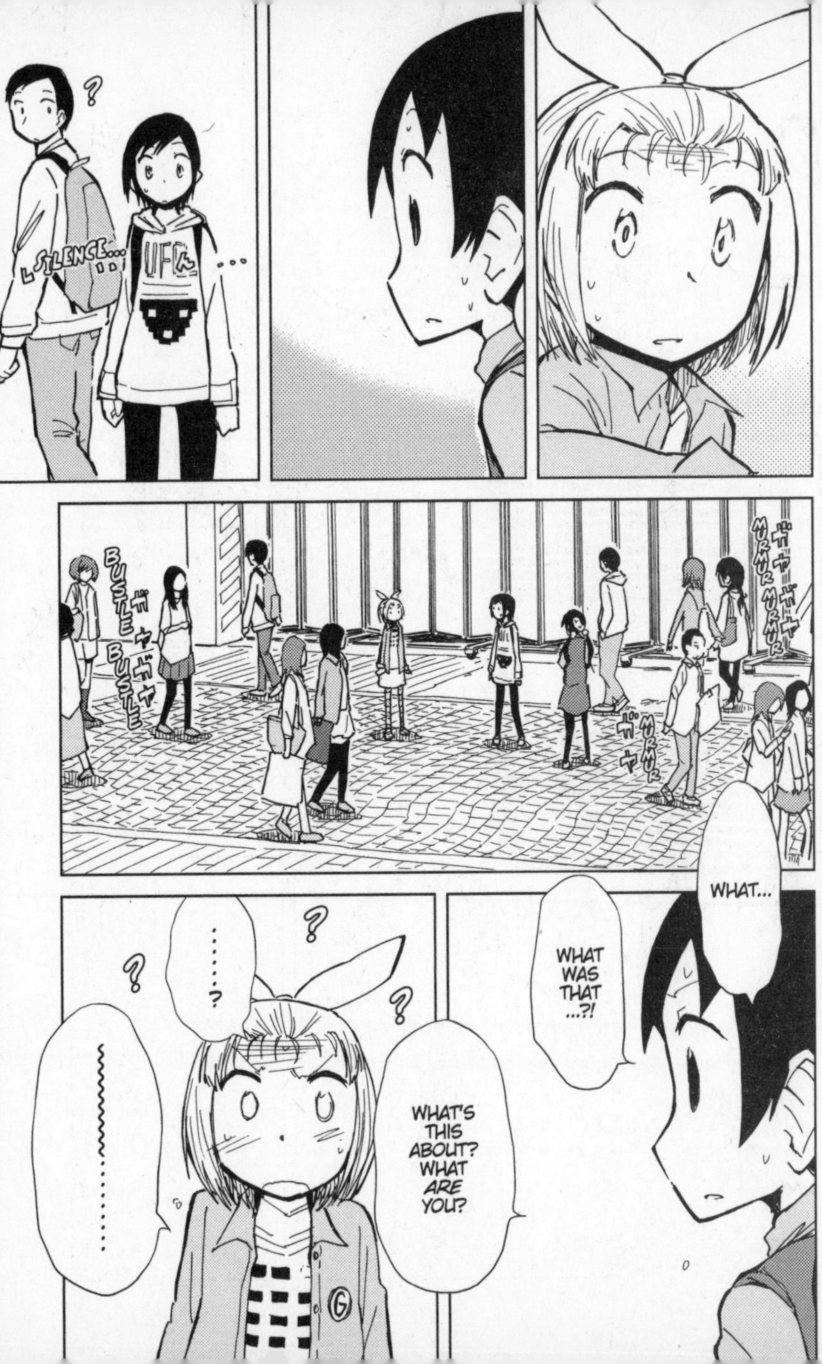
?
SILENCE...
...
MURMUR MURMUR
BUSTLE BUSTLE
MURMUR
WHAT...
WHAT WAS THAT ...?!
WHAT'S THIS ABOUT? WHAT ARE YOU?
...?
......

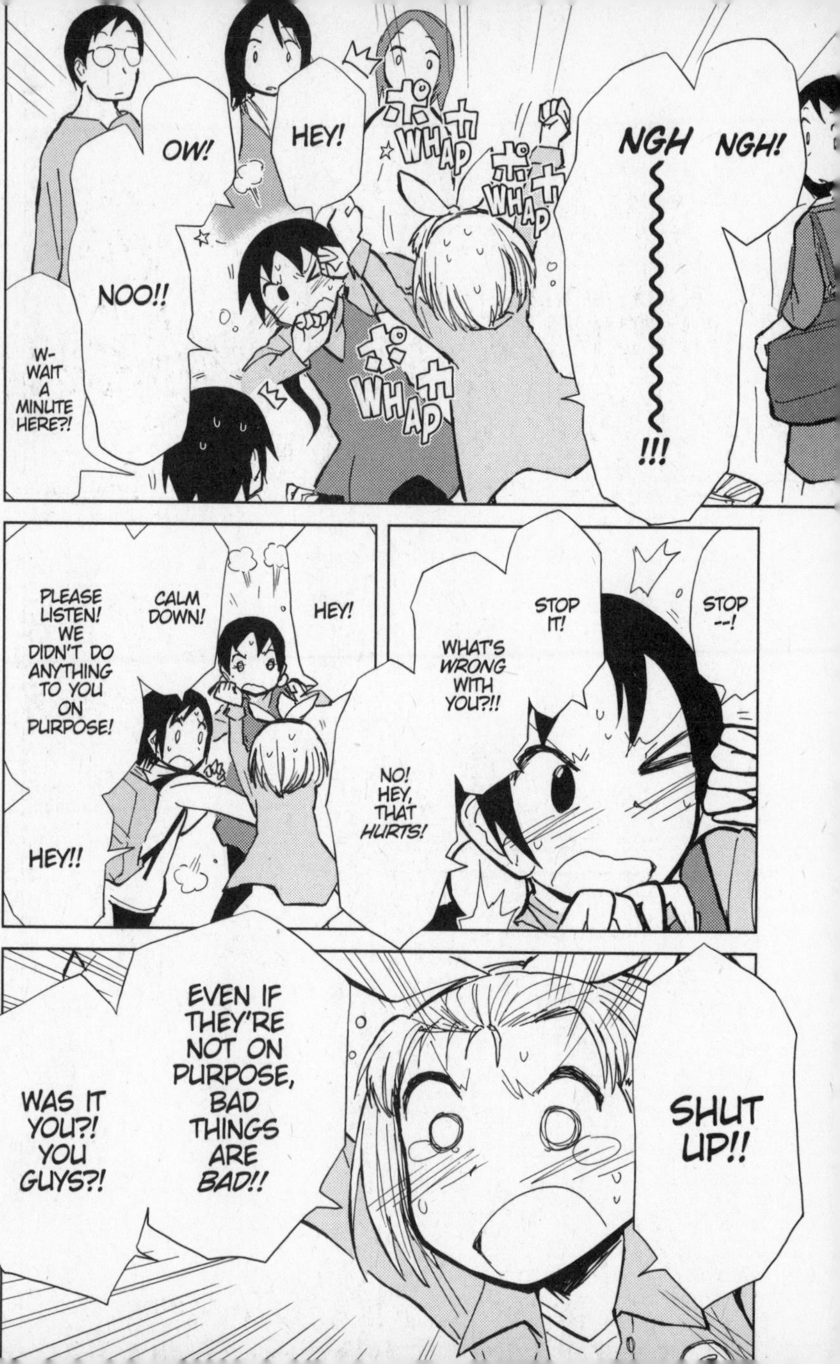
NGH NGH!
!!!
ポカ WHAP
ポカ WHAP
HEY!
OW!
ポカ WHAP
NOO!!
W-WAIT A MINUTE HERE?!
STOP --!
STOP IT!
WHAT'S WRONG WITH YOU?!!
NO! HEY, THAT HURTS!
HEY!
CALM DOWN!
PLEASE LISTEN! WE DIDN'T DO ANYTHING TO YOU ON PURPOSE!
HEY!!
SHUT UP!!
EVEN IF THEY'RE NOT ON PURPOSE, BAD THINGS ARE BAD!!
WAS IT YOU?! YOU GUYS?!

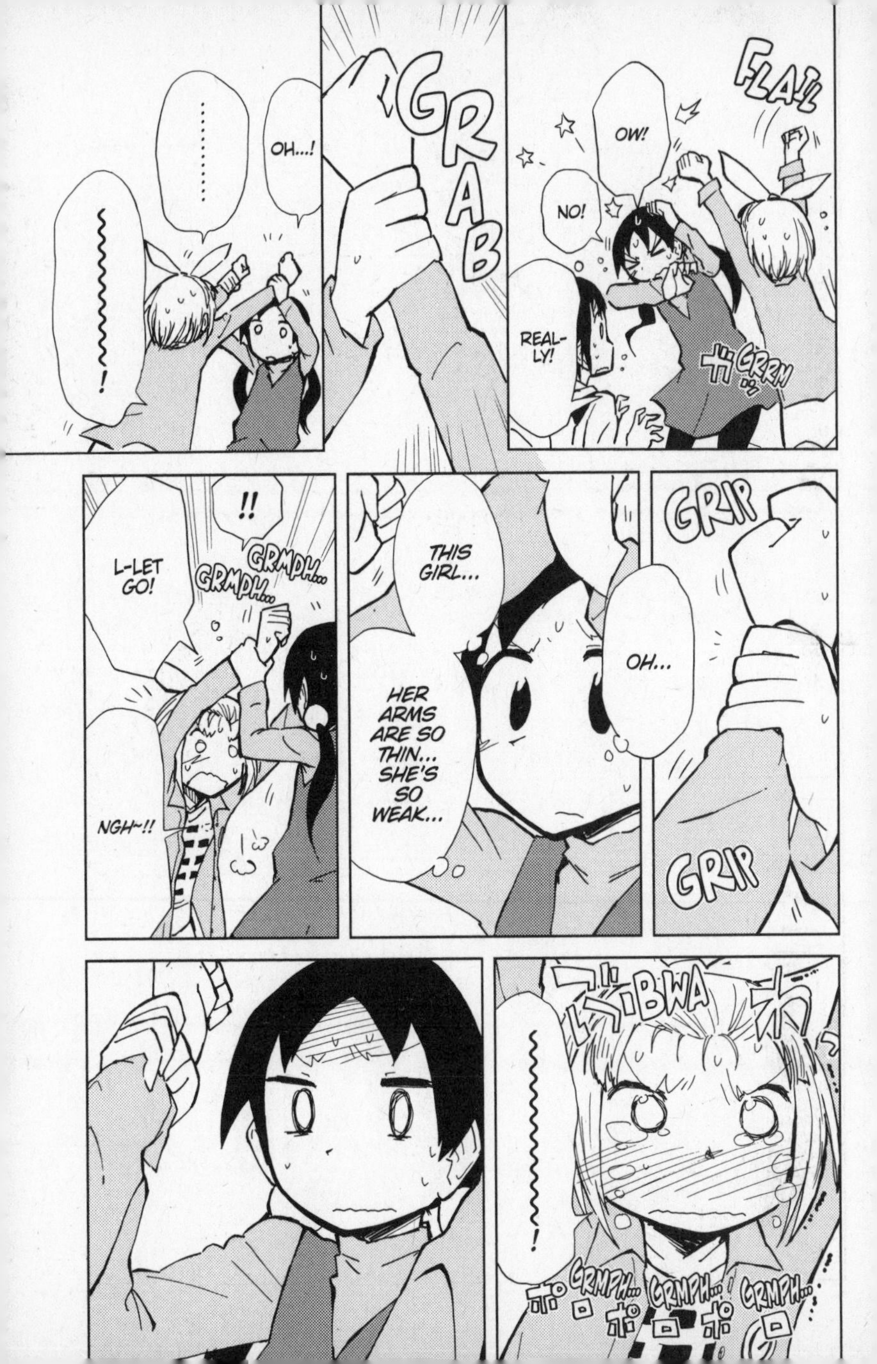
FLAIL
OW!
NO!
REAL-LY!
GRRM
GRAB
OH...!
......
~~~~~~~~!
GRIP
OH...
GRIP
THIS GIRL...
HER ARMS ARE SO THIN... SHE'S SO WEAK...
!!
GRMPH...
GRMPH...
L-LET GO!
NGH~!!
BWA
~~~~~~~~!
GRMPH...
GRMPH...
GRMPH...

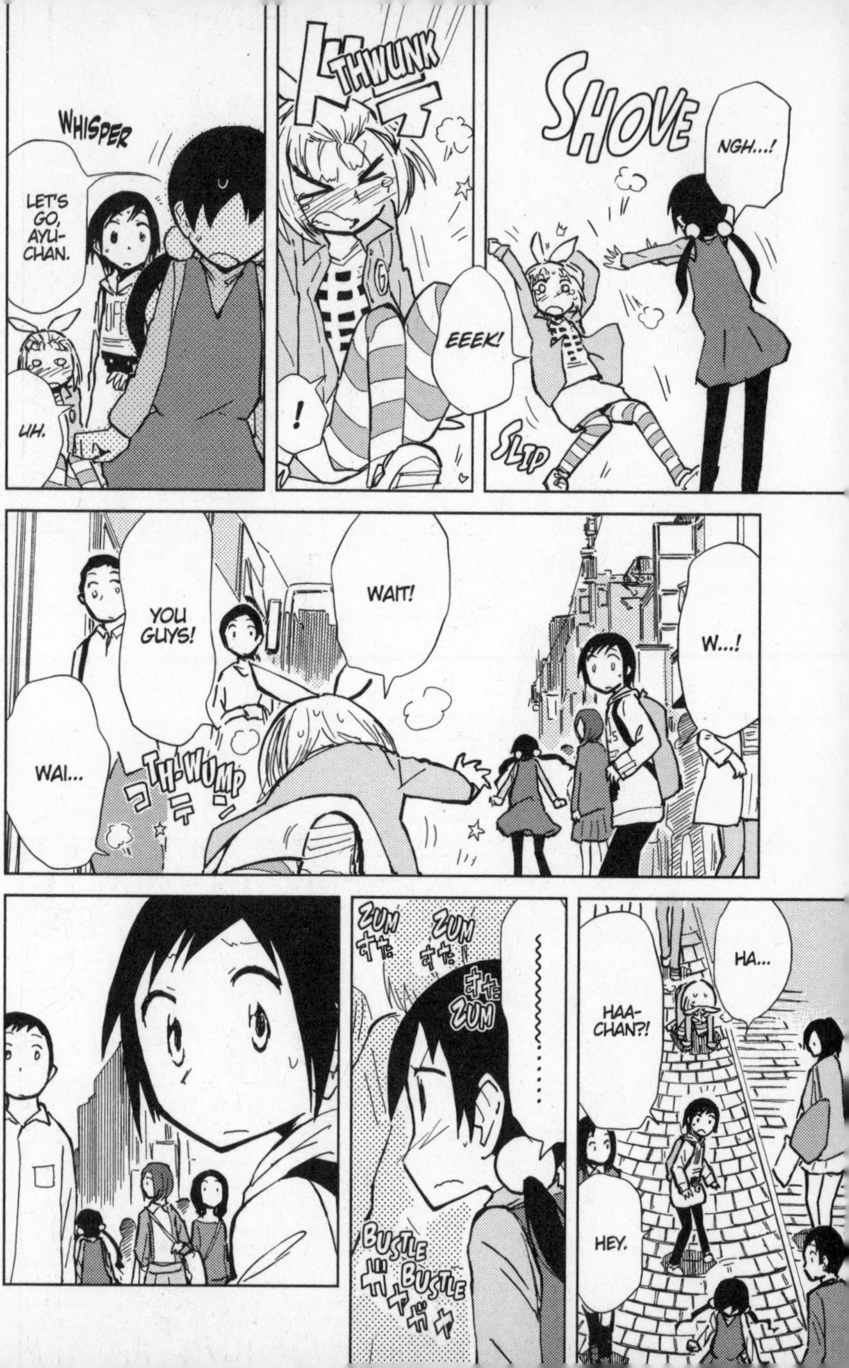
SHOVE
NGH...!
EEEK!
SLIP
THWUNK
!
WHISPER
LET'S GO, AYU-CHAN.
UH.
W...!
WAIT!
YOU GUYS!
TH-WUMP
WAI...
HA...
HAA-CHAN?!
HEY.
ZUM
ZUM
ZUM
......
BUSTLE
BUSTLE

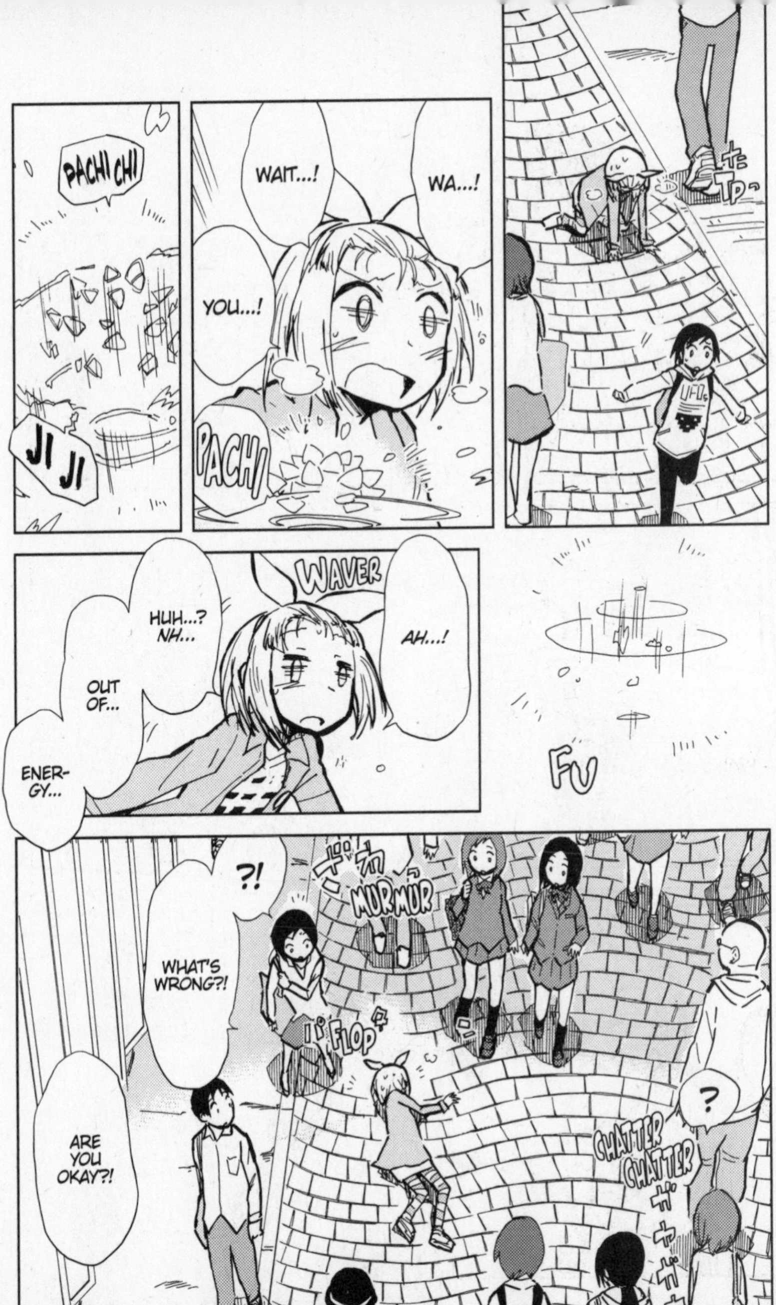
TP
WA...!
WAIT...!
YOU...!
PACHI
PACHI CHI
JI JI
FU
WAVER
AH...!
HUH...? NH...
OUT OF...
ENER-GY...
?
CHATTER CHATTER
MURMUR
?!
WHAT'S WRONG?!
FLOP
ARE YOU OKAY?!

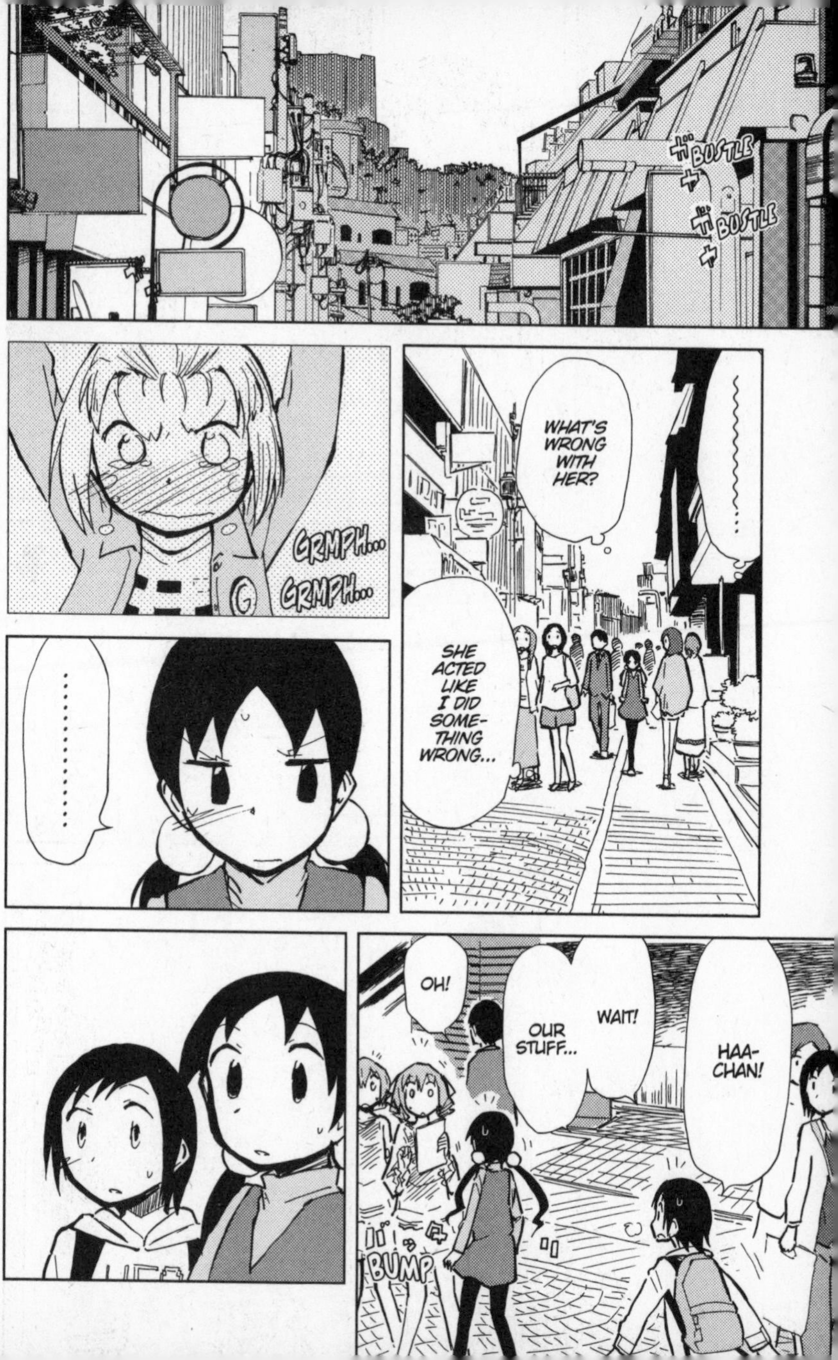
BUSTLE
BUSTLE
~~~…
WHAT'S WRONG WITH HER?
SHE ACTED LIKE I DID SOMETHING WRONG...
GRMPH...
GRMPH...
……
HAA-CHAN!
WAIT!
OUR STUFF...
OH!
BUMP
~~~

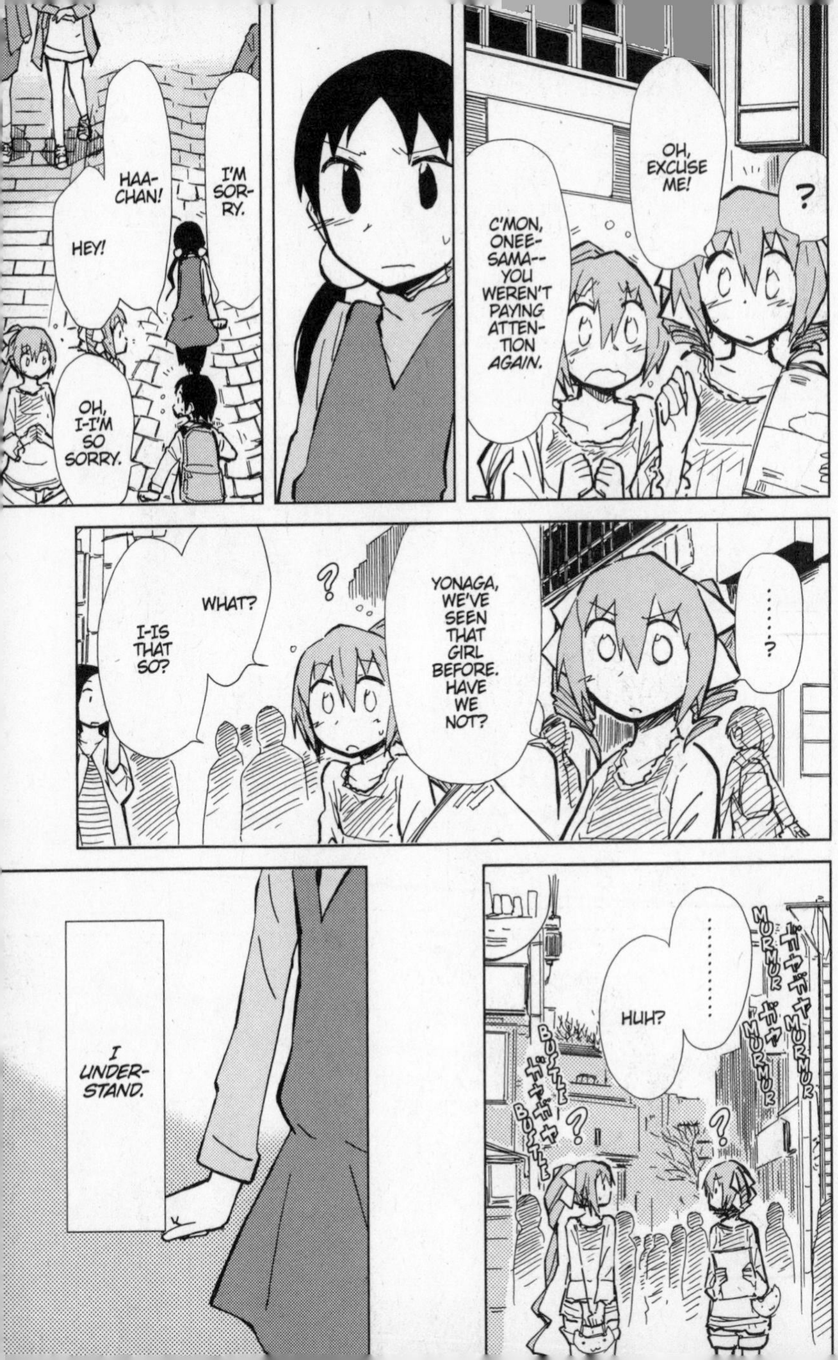
OH, EXCUSE ME!
?
C'MON, ONEE-SAMA--YOU WEREN'T PAYING ATTENTION AGAIN.
I'M SORRY.
HAA-CHAN!
HEY!
OH, I-I'M SO SORRY.
......?
YONAGA, WE'VE SEEN THAT GIRL BEFORE. HAVE WE NOT?
?
WHAT?
I-IS THAT SO?
ガヤガヤ MURMUR
ガヤガヤ MURMUR
......
HUH?
ガヤガヤ BUSTLE
ガヤガヤ BUSTLE
?
?
I UNDERSTAND.

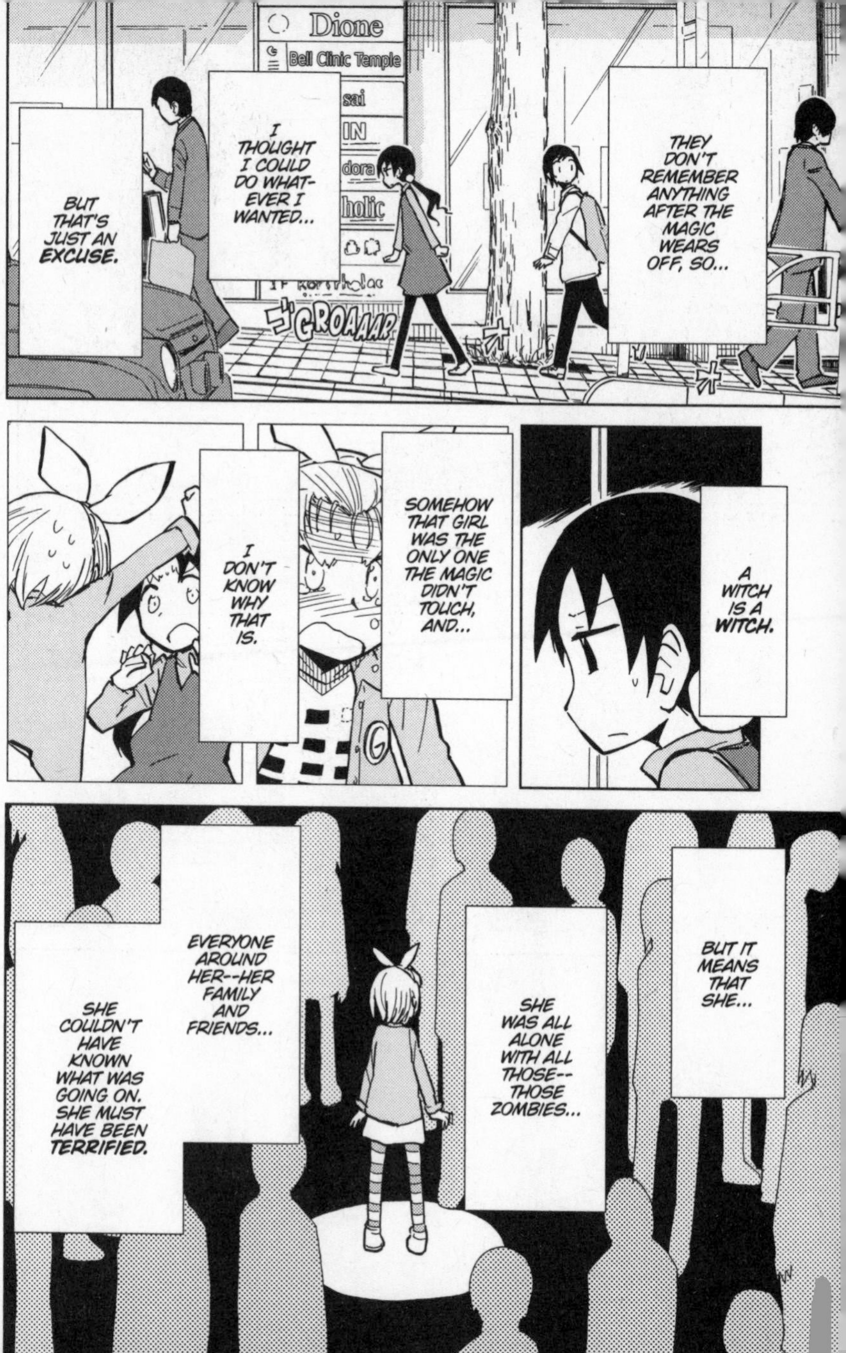
Dione
Bell Clinic Temple
sai
IN
dora
holic
THEY DON'T REMEMBER ANYTHING AFTER THE MAGIC WEARS OFF, SO...
I THOUGHT I COULD DO WHAT-EVER I WANTED...
BUT THAT'S JUST AN EXCUSE.
GROAAAR
A WITCH IS A WITCH.
SOMEHOW THAT GIRL WAS THE ONLY ONE THE MAGIC DIDN'T TOUCH, AND...
I DON'T KNOW WHY THAT IS.
BUT IT MEANS THAT SHE...
SHE WAS ALL ALONE WITH ALL THOSE-- THOSE ZOMBIES...
EVERYONE AROUND HER--HER FAMILY AND FRIENDS...
SHE COULDN'T HAVE KNOWN WHAT WAS GOING ON. SHE MUST HAVE BEEN TERRIFIED.

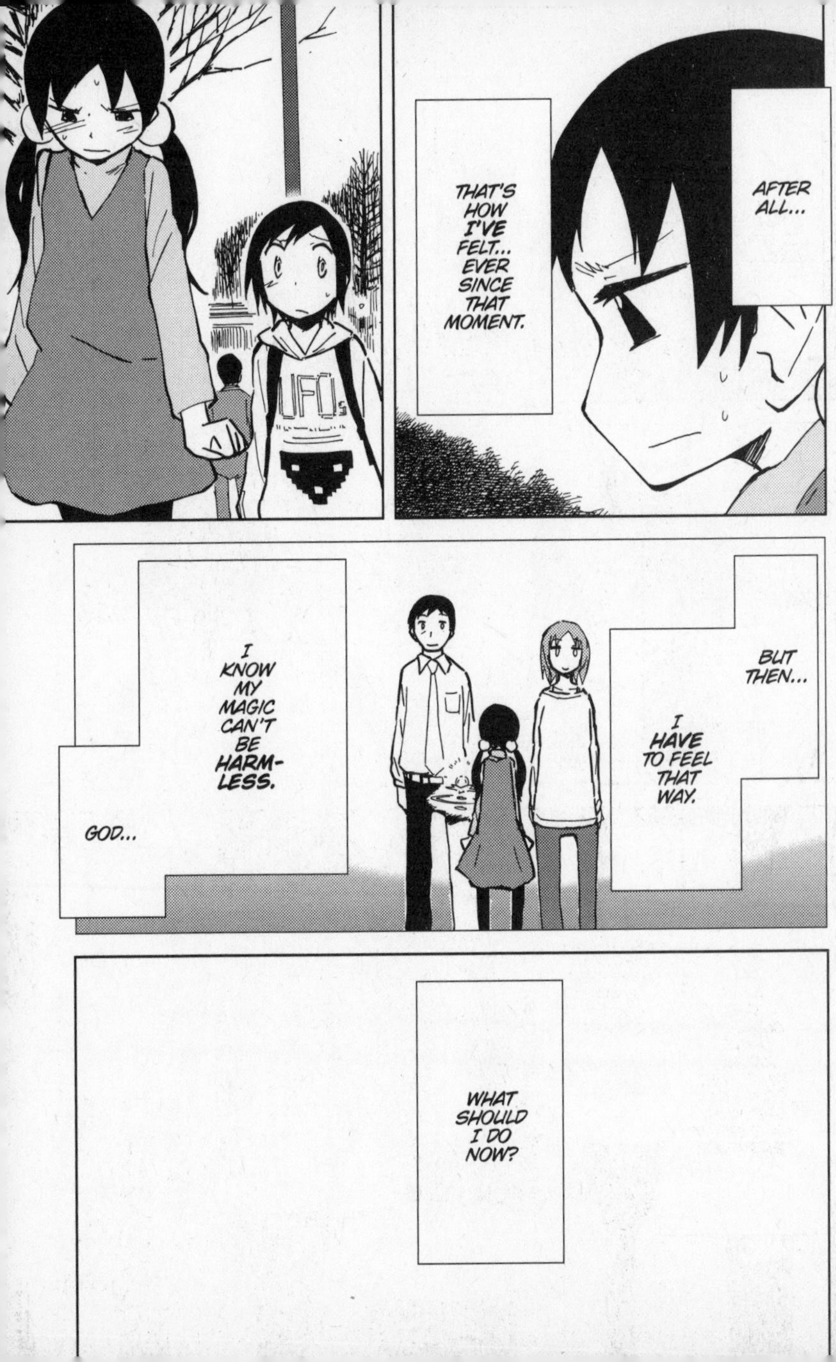
AFTER ALL...
THAT'S HOW I'VE FELT... EVER SINCE THAT MOMENT.
BUT THEN...
I HAVE TO FEEL THAT WAY.
I KNOW MY MAGIC CAN'T BE HARMLESS.
GOD...
WHAT SHOULD I DO NOW?

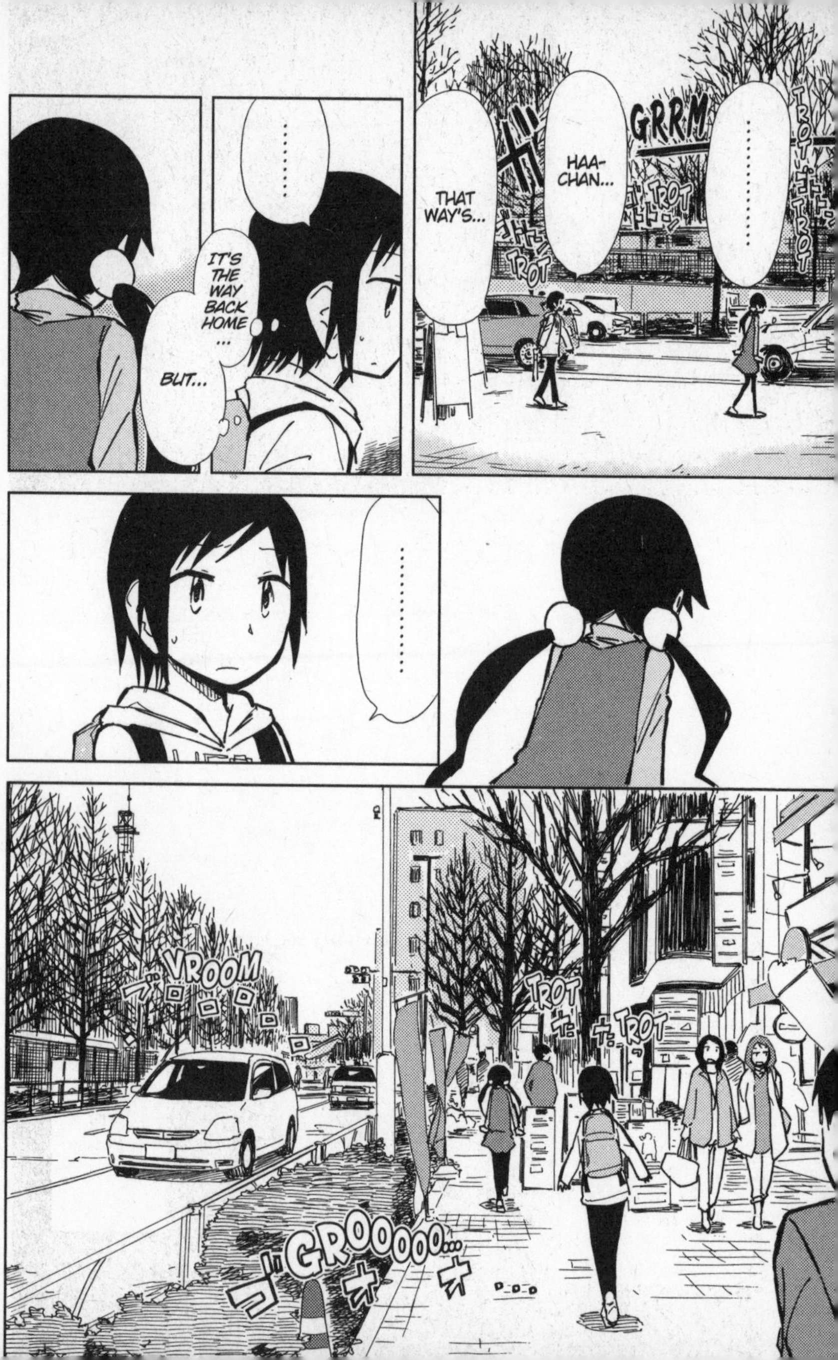
GRRM
TROT TROT
……
TROT
HAA-CHAN…
THAT WAY'S…
……
IT'S THE WAY BACK HOME …
BUT…
……
TROT
TROT
VROOM
GROOOOOO…

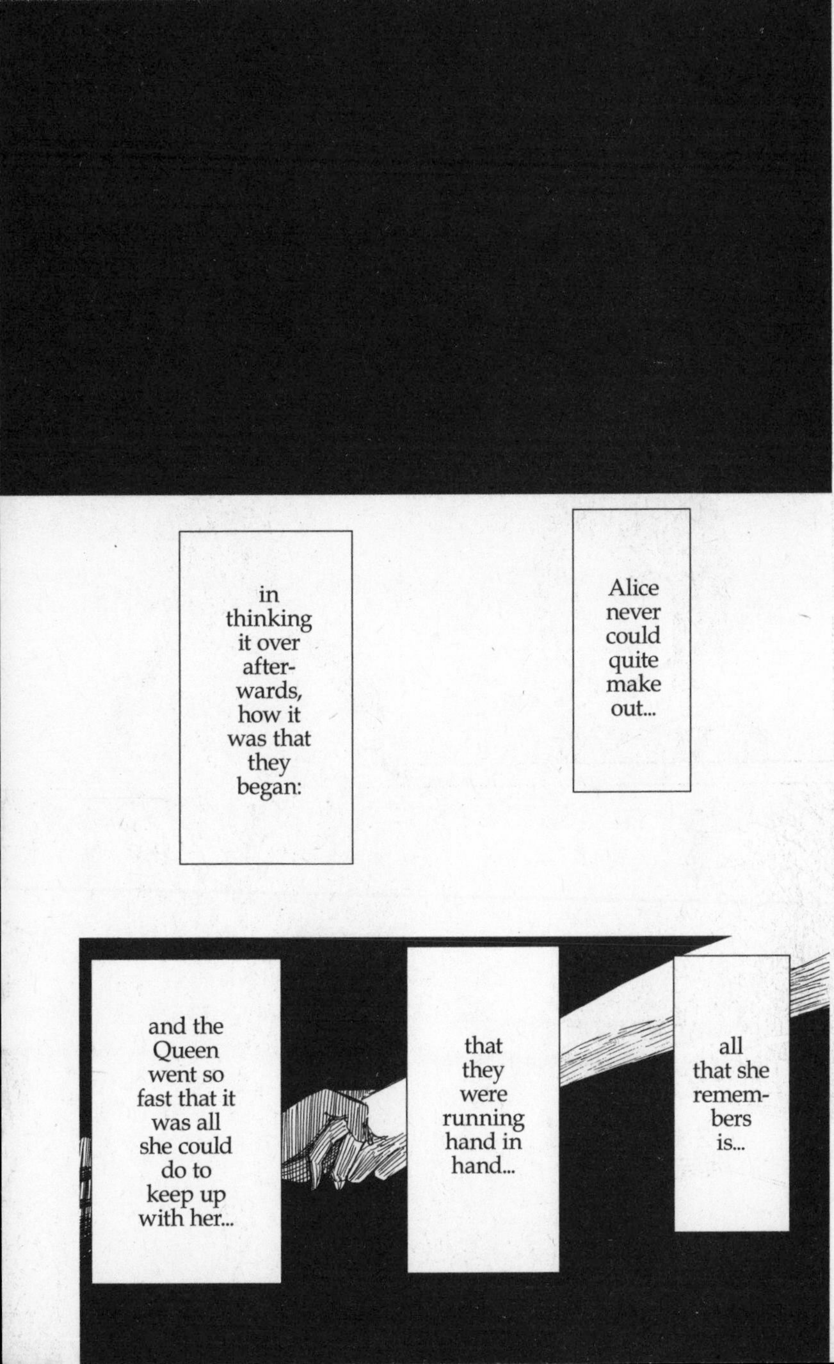
Alice never could quite make out...
in thinking it over after-wards, how it was that they began:
all that she remem-bers is...
that they were running hand in hand...
and the Queen went so fast that it was all she could do to keep up with her...

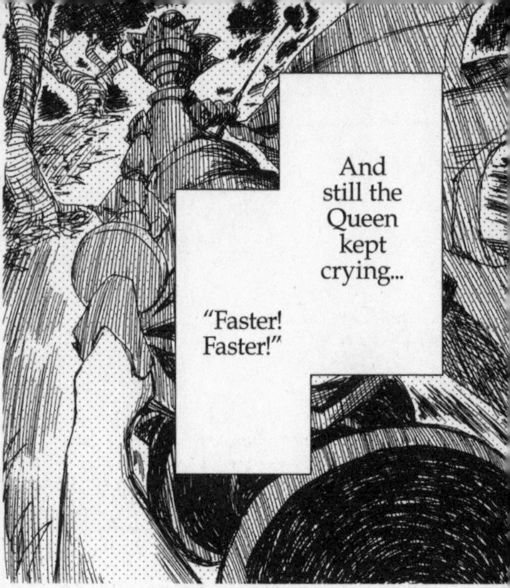
And still the Queen kept crying...
"Faster! Faster!"

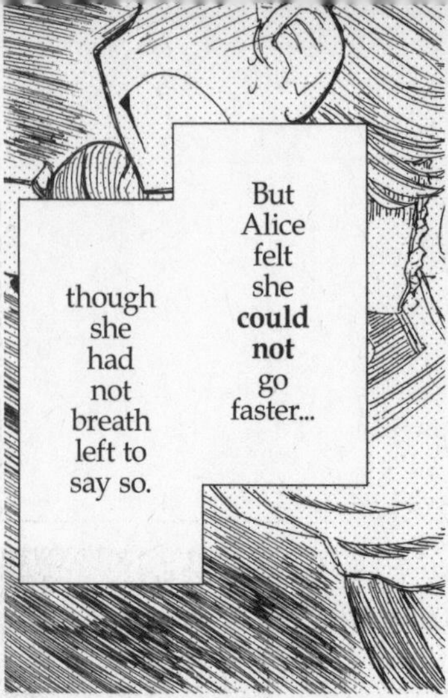
But Alice felt she **could not** go faster...
though she had not breath left to say so.

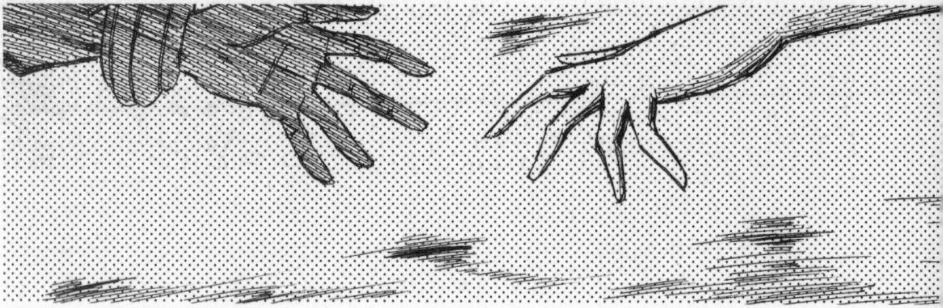

"Now, *here*, you see...

"It takes all the running *you* can do, to keep in the same place. If you want to get somewhere else, you must run at least twice as fast as that!"

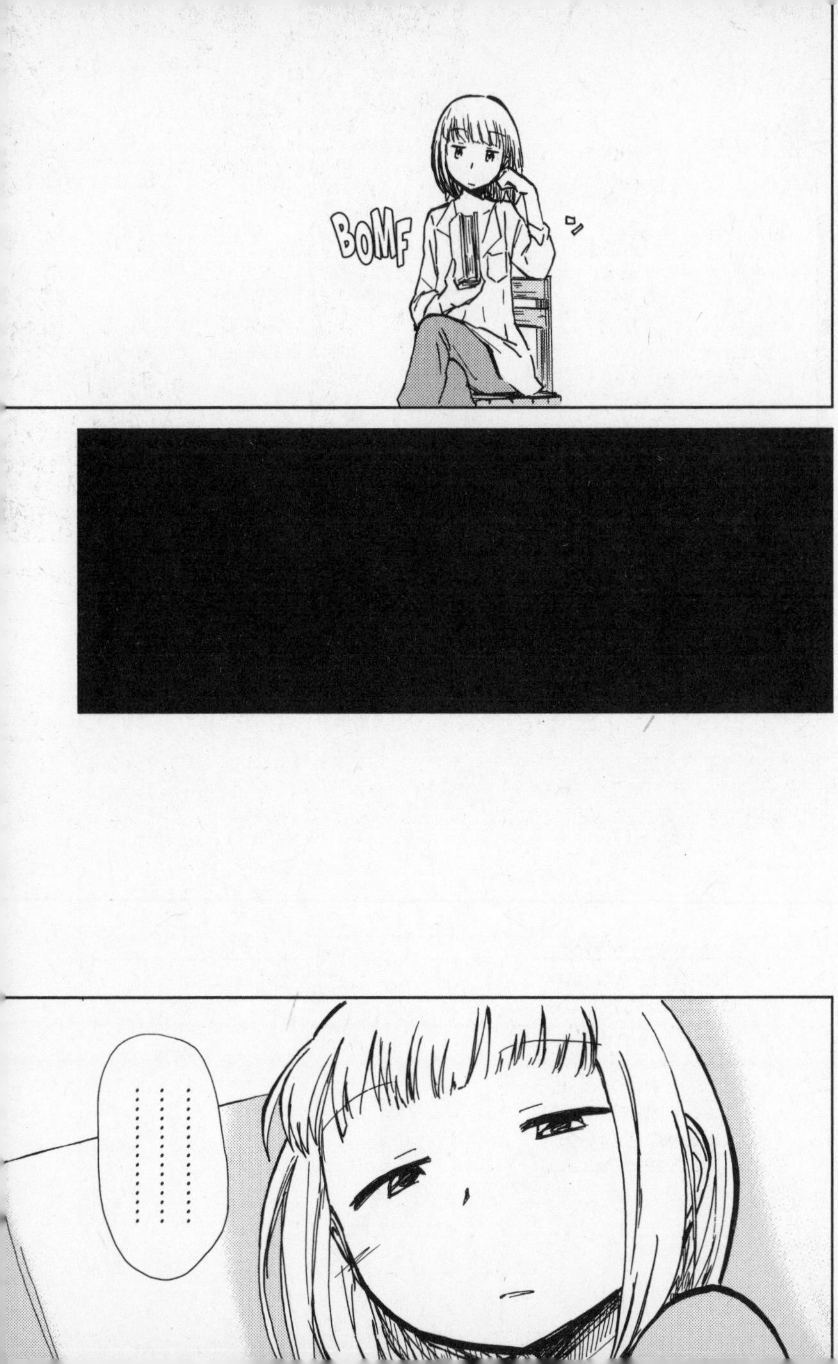
BOMF
......

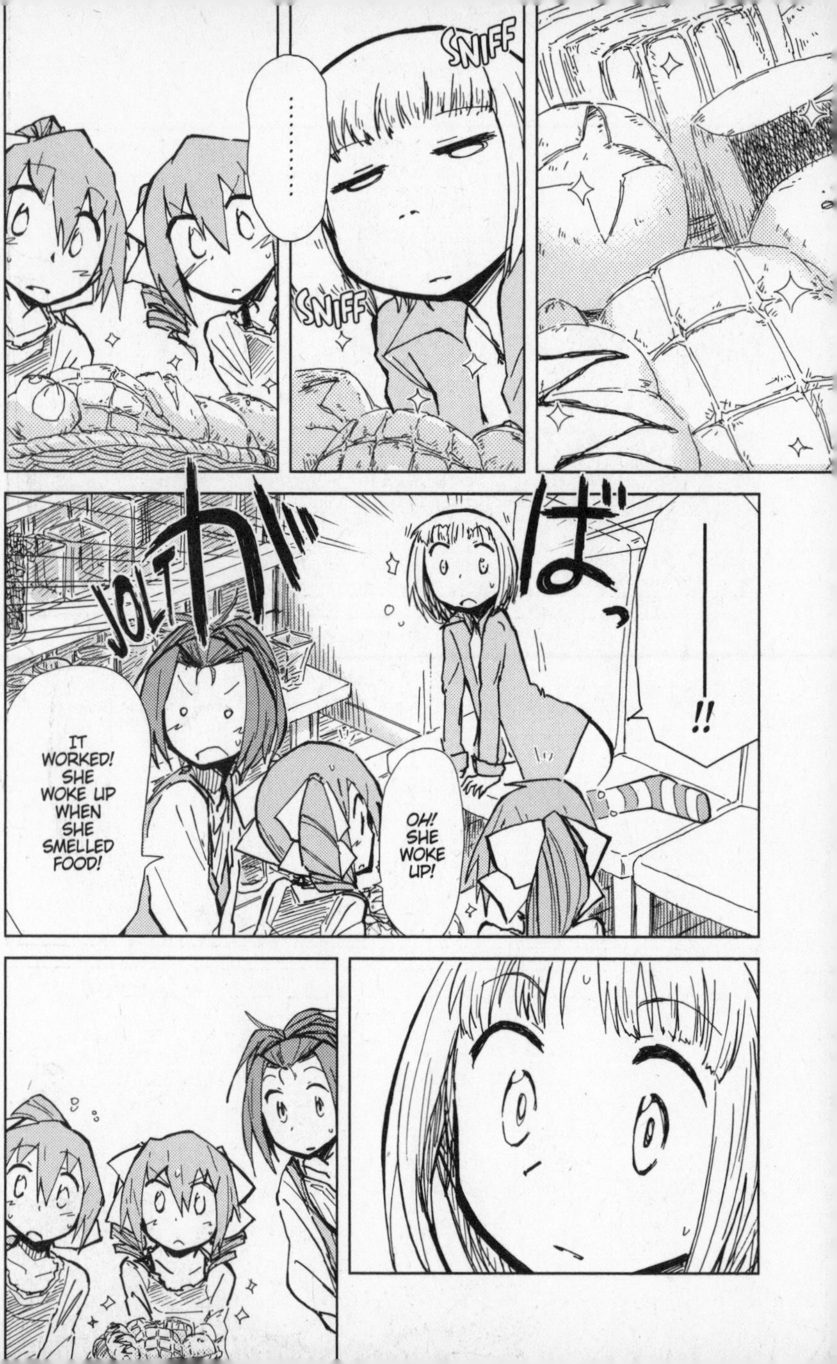
SNIFF
......
SNIFF
!!
ばっ
JOLT
OH! SHE WOKE UP!
IT WORKED! SHE WOKE UP WHEN SHE SMELLED FOOD!

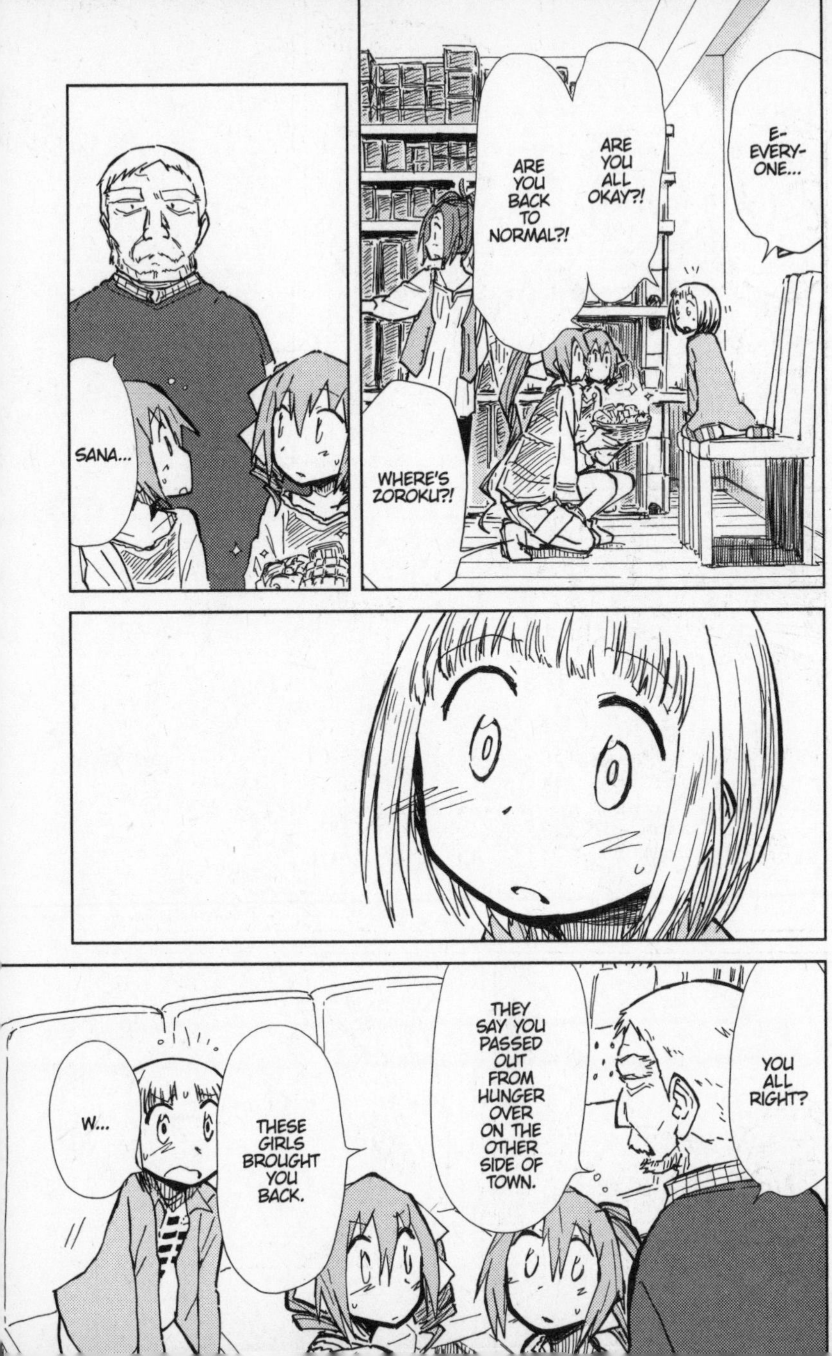
E-EVERY-ONE...
ARE YOU ALL OKAY?!
ARE YOU BACK TO NORMAL?!
WHERE'S ZOROKU?!
SANA...
YOU ALL RIGHT?
THEY SAY YOU PASSED OUT FROM HUNGER OVER ON THE OTHER SIDE OF TOWN.
THESE GIRLS BROUGHT YOU BACK.
W...

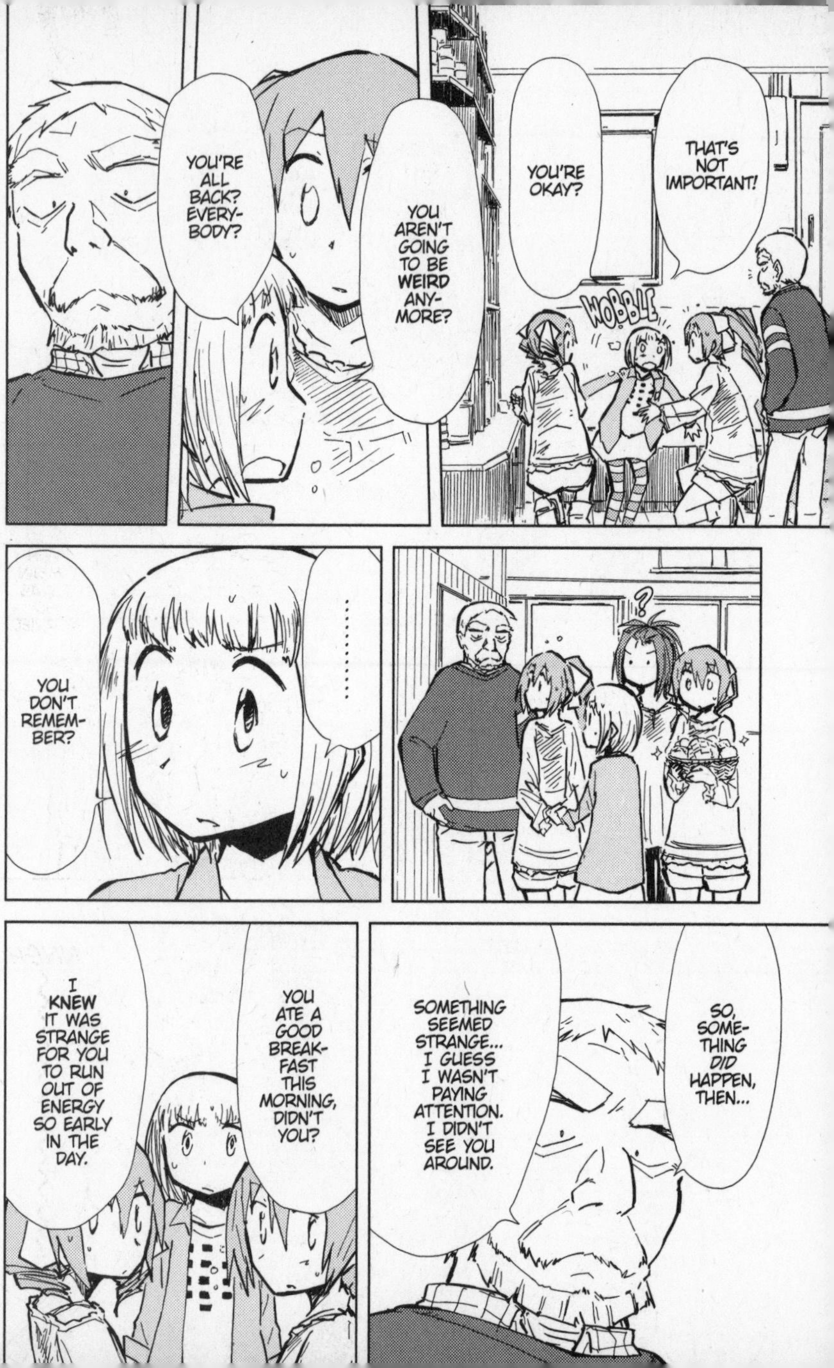
THAT'S NOT IMPORTANT!
YOU'RE OKAY?
WOBBLE
YOU AREN'T GOING TO BE WEIRD ANYMORE?
YOU'RE ALL BACK? EVERYBODY?
?
......
YOU DON'T REMEMBER?
SO, SOMETHING *DID* HAPPEN, THEN...
SOMETHING SEEMED STRANGE... I GUESS I WASN'T PAYING ATTENTION. I DIDN'T SEE YOU AROUND.
YOU ATE A GOOD BREAKFAST THIS MORNING, DIDN'T YOU?
I KNEW IT WAS STRANGE FOR YOU TO RUN OUT OF ENERGY SO EARLY IN THE DAY.

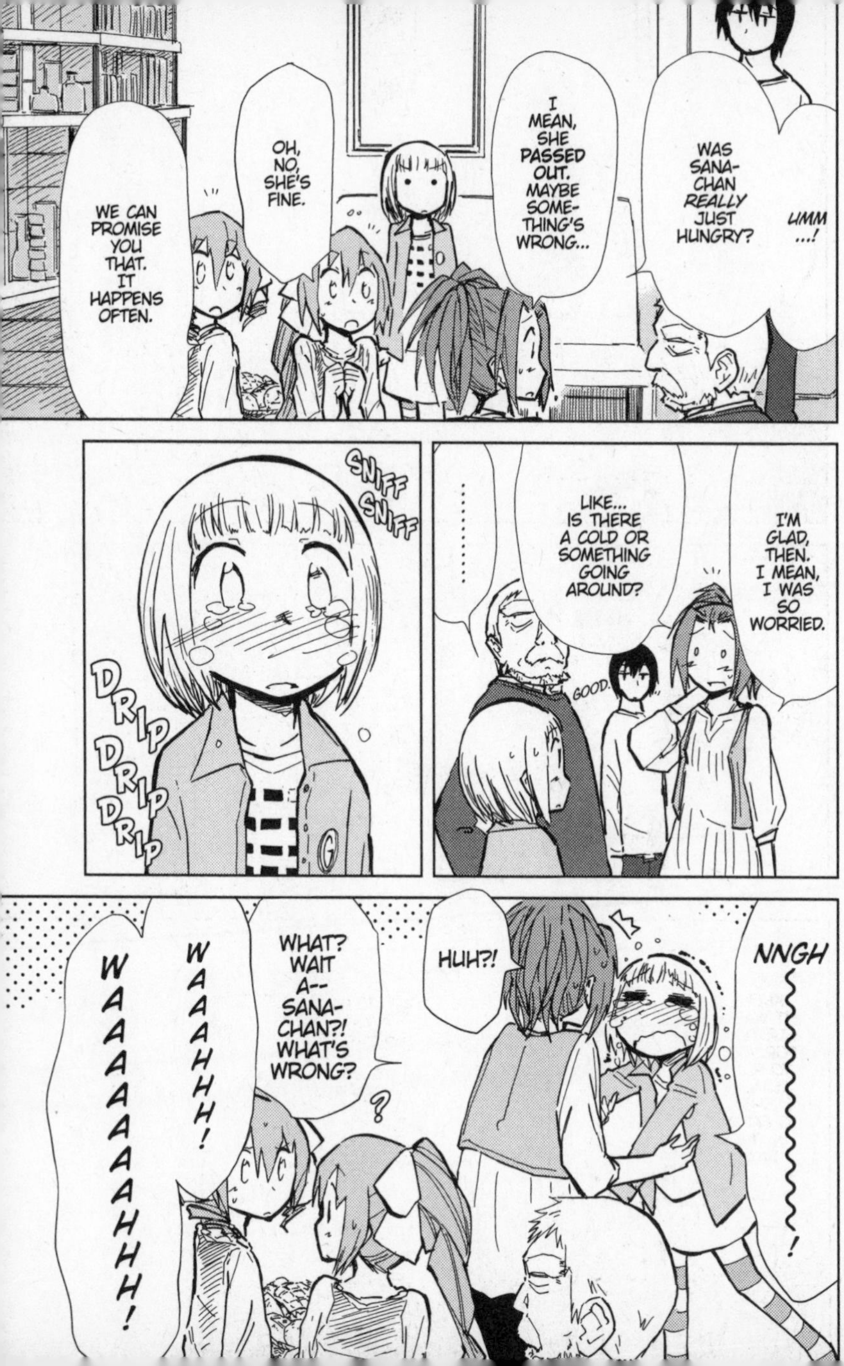
UMM ...!
WAS SANA-CHAN *REALLY* JUST HUNGRY?
I MEAN, SHE PASSED OUT. MAYBE SOMETHING'S WRONG...
OH, NO, SHE'S FINE.
WE CAN PROMISE YOU THAT. IT HAPPENS OFTEN.
I'M GLAD, THEN. I MEAN, I WAS SO WORRIED.
LIKE... IS THERE A COLD OR SOMETHING GOING AROUND?
GOOD.
......
SNIFF SNIFF
DRIP DRIP DRIP
NNGH~!
HUH?!
WHAT? WAIT A-- SANA-CHAN?! WHAT'S WRONG?
WAAAHHH!
WAAAAAAAHHH!

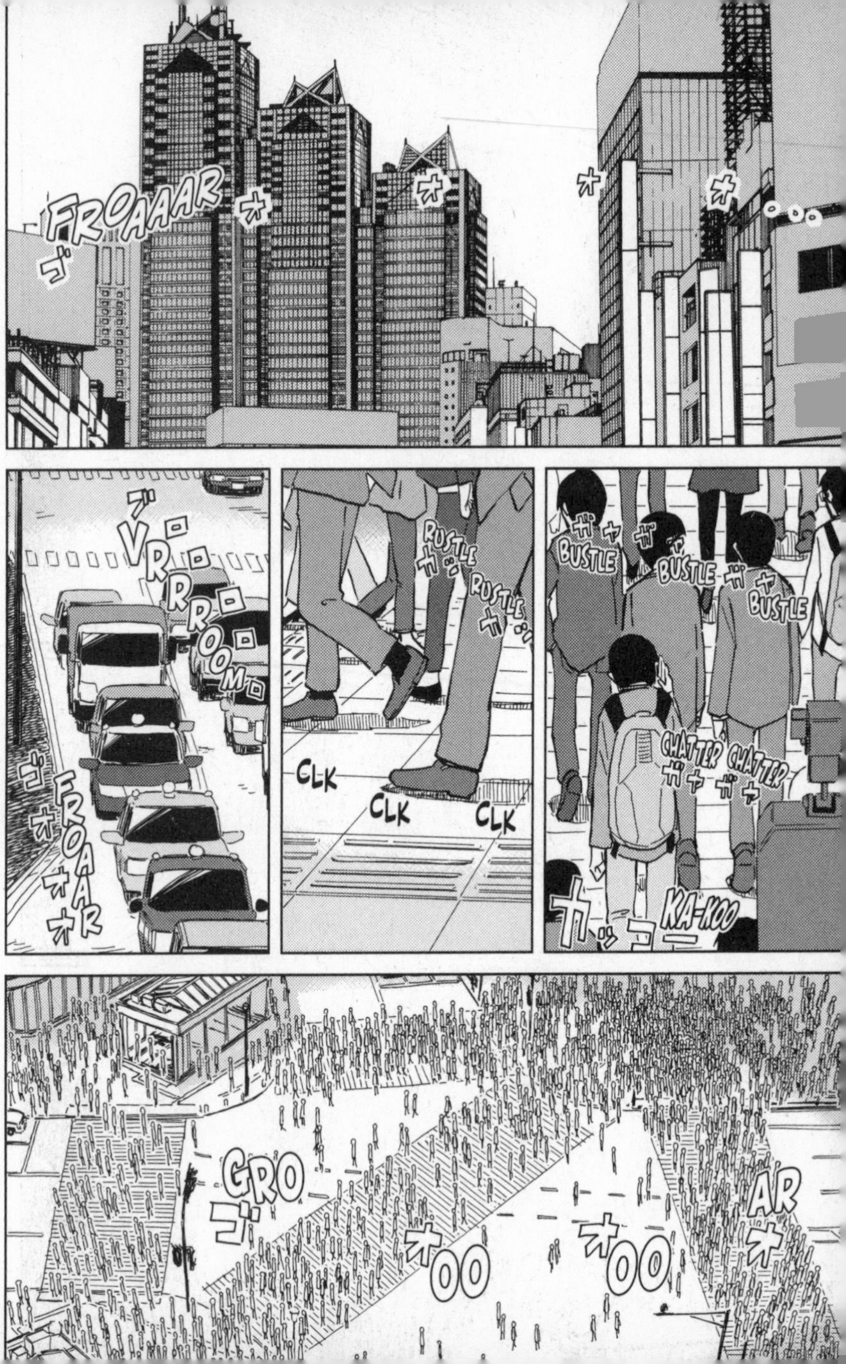

FROAAAR
BUSTLE
BUSTLE
BUSTLE
CHATTER CHATTER
KA-KOO
RUSTLE
RUSTLE
CLK
CLK
CLK
VRRROOM
FROAAAR
AR
OO
OO
GRO

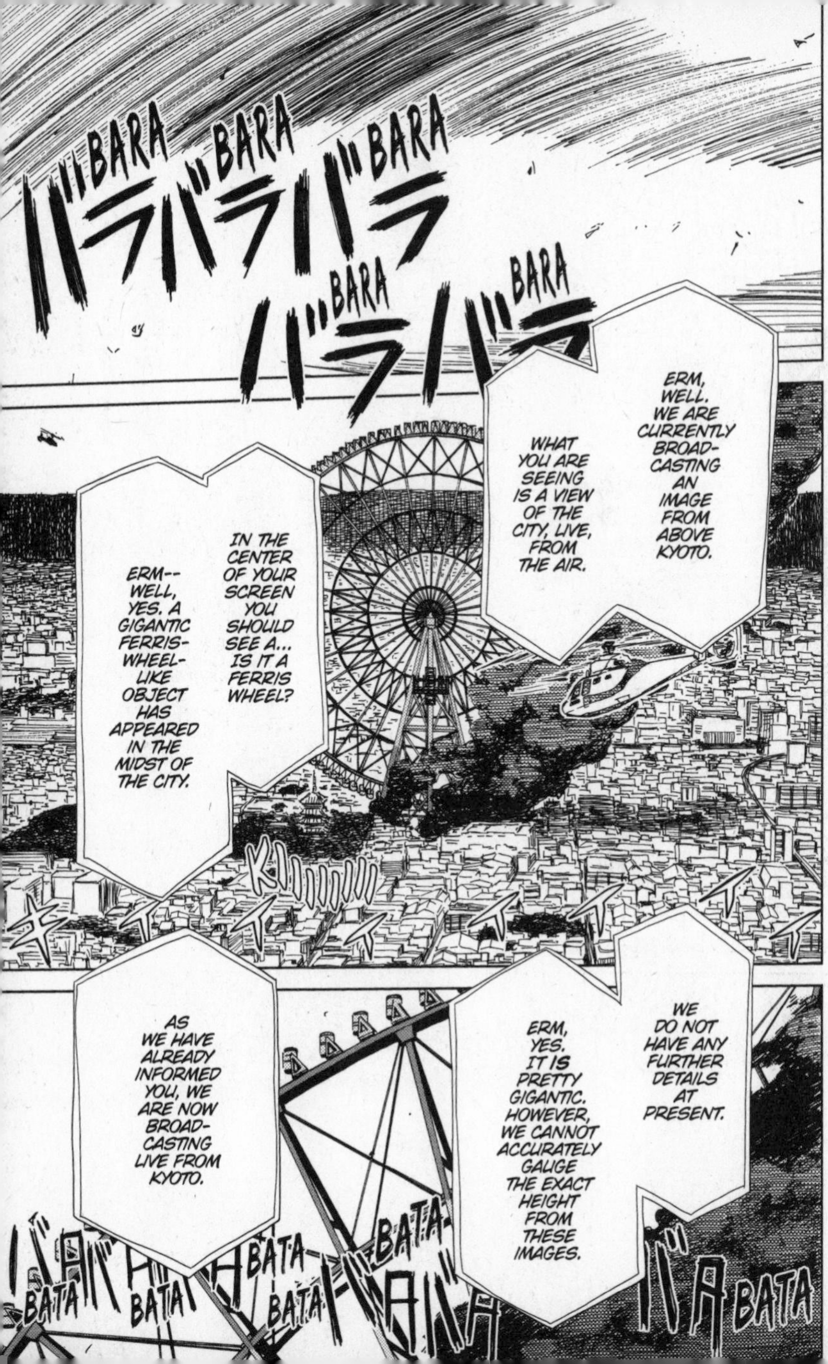
BARA BARA BARA
BARA BARA
ERM, WELL. WE ARE CURRENTLY BROADCASTING AN IMAGE FROM ABOVE KYOTO.
WHAT YOU ARE SEEING IS A VIEW OF THE CITY, LIVE, FROM THE AIR.
IN THE CENTER OF YOUR SCREEN YOU SHOULD SEE A... IS IT A FERRIS WHEEL?
ERM-- WELL, YES. A GIGANTIC FERRIS-WHEEL-LIKE OBJECT HAS APPEARED IN THE MIDST OF THE CITY.
KIIIIIIIII
WE DO NOT HAVE ANY FURTHER DETAILS AT PRESENT.
ERM, YES. IT IS PRETTY GIGANTIC. HOWEVER, WE CANNOT ACCURATELY GAUGE THE EXACT HEIGHT FROM THESE IMAGES.
AS WE HAVE ALREADY INFORMED YOU, WE ARE NOW BROADCASTING LIVE FROM KYOTO.
BATA BATA
BATA BATA
BATA BATA

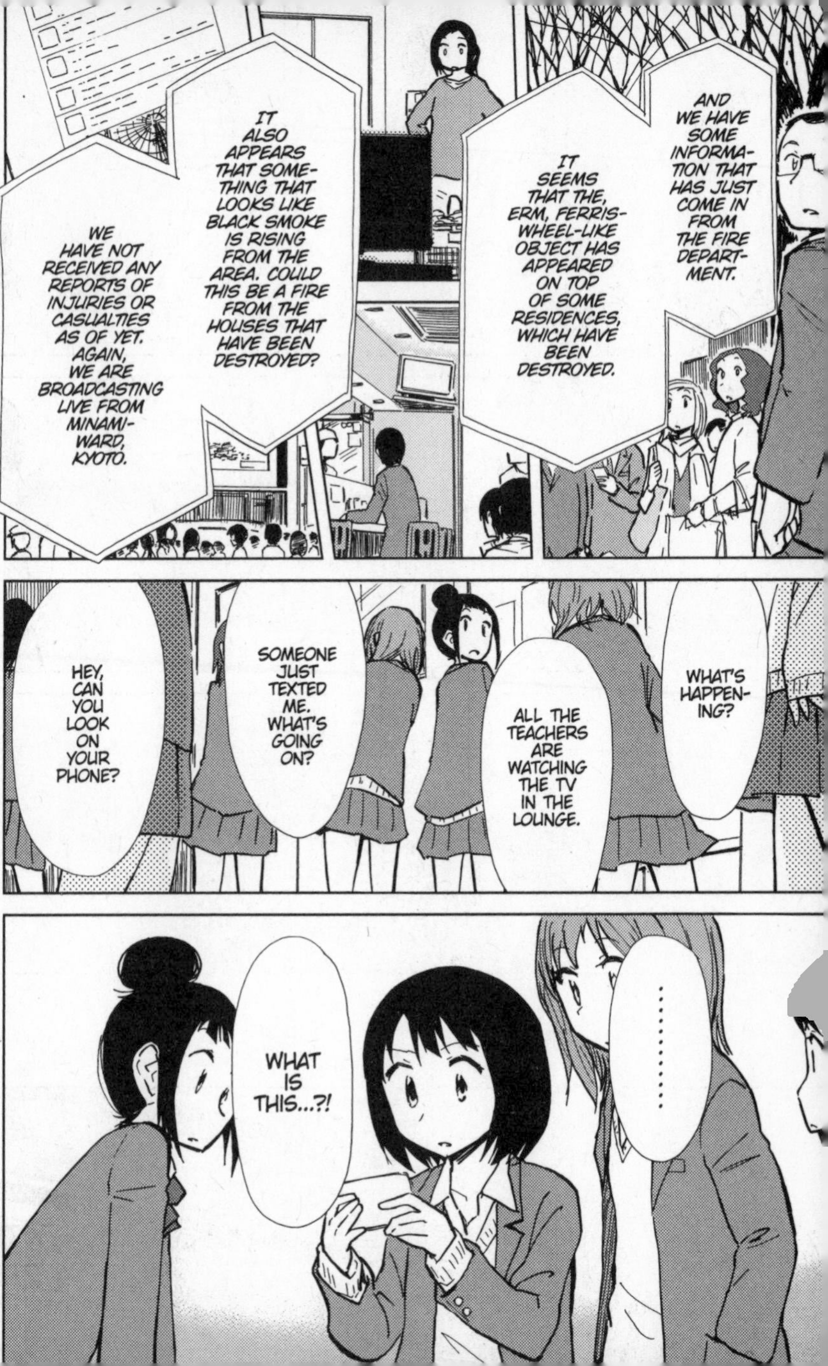
AND WE HAVE SOME INFORMATION THAT HAS JUST COME IN FROM THE FIRE DEPARTMENT.
IT SEEMS THAT THE, ERM, FERRIS-WHEEL-LIKE OBJECT HAS APPEARED ON TOP OF SOME RESIDENCES, WHICH HAVE BEEN DESTROYED.
IT ALSO APPEARS THAT SOMETHING THAT LOOKS LIKE BLACK SMOKE IS RISING FROM THE AREA. COULD THIS BE A FIRE FROM THE HOUSES THAT HAVE BEEN DESTROYED?
WE HAVE NOT RECEIVED ANY REPORTS OF INJURIES OR CASUALTIES AS OF YET. AGAIN, WE ARE BROADCASTING LIVE FROM MINAMI-WARD, KYOTO.
WHAT'S HAPPENING?
ALL THE TEACHERS ARE WATCHING THE TV IN THE LOUNGE.
SOMEONE JUST TEXTED ME. WHAT'S GOING ON?
HEY, CAN YOU LOOK ON YOUR PHONE?
......
WHAT IS THIS...?!

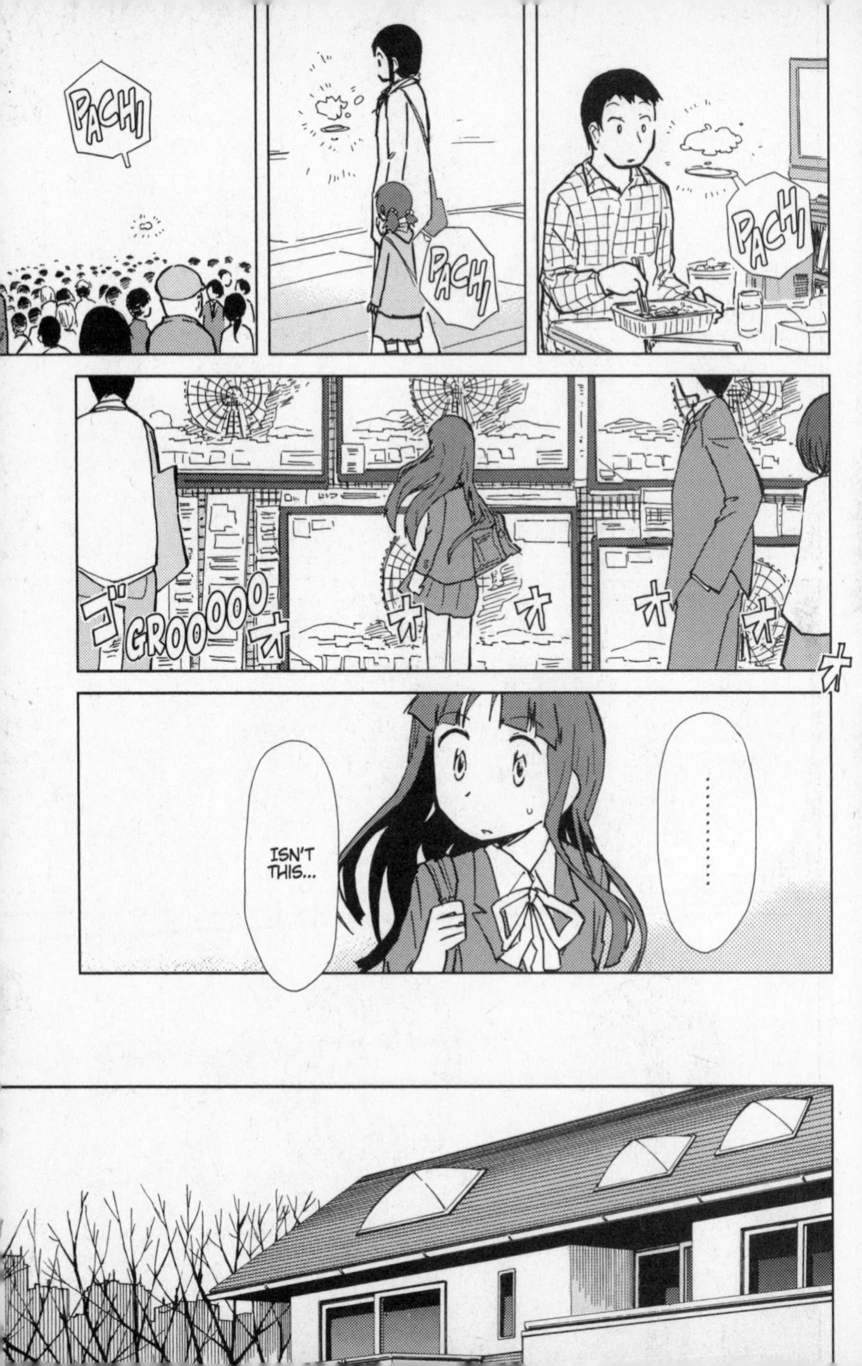
PACHI
PACHI
PACHI
ゴオオオオオオ
GROOOOO
......
ISN'T THIS...

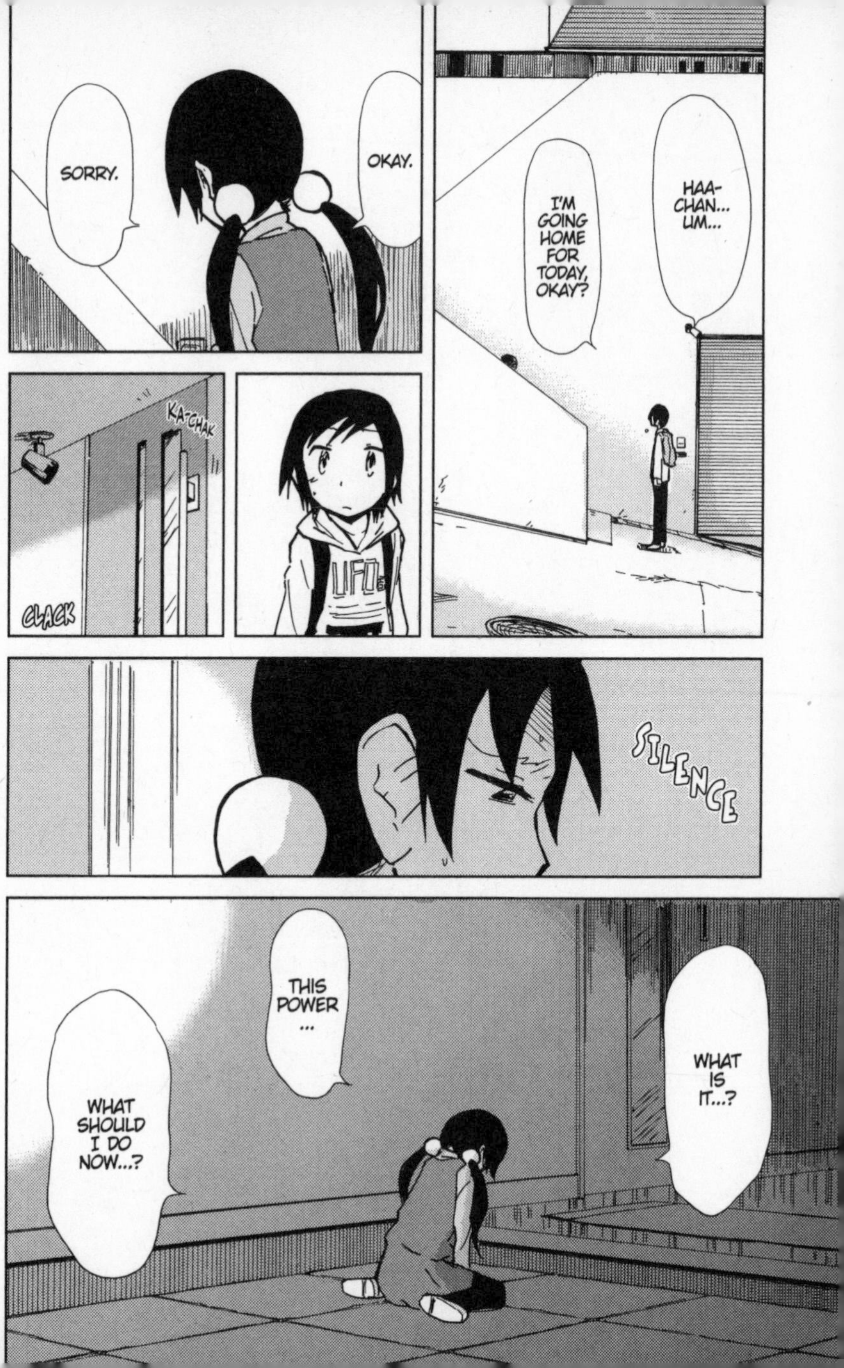
HAA-CHAN... UM...
I'M GOING HOME FOR TODAY, OKAY?
OKAY.
SORRY.
KA-CHAK
CLACK
SILENCE
WHAT IS IT...?
THIS POWER...
WHAT SHOULD I DO NOW...?

Alice & Zoroku

INTERLUDE

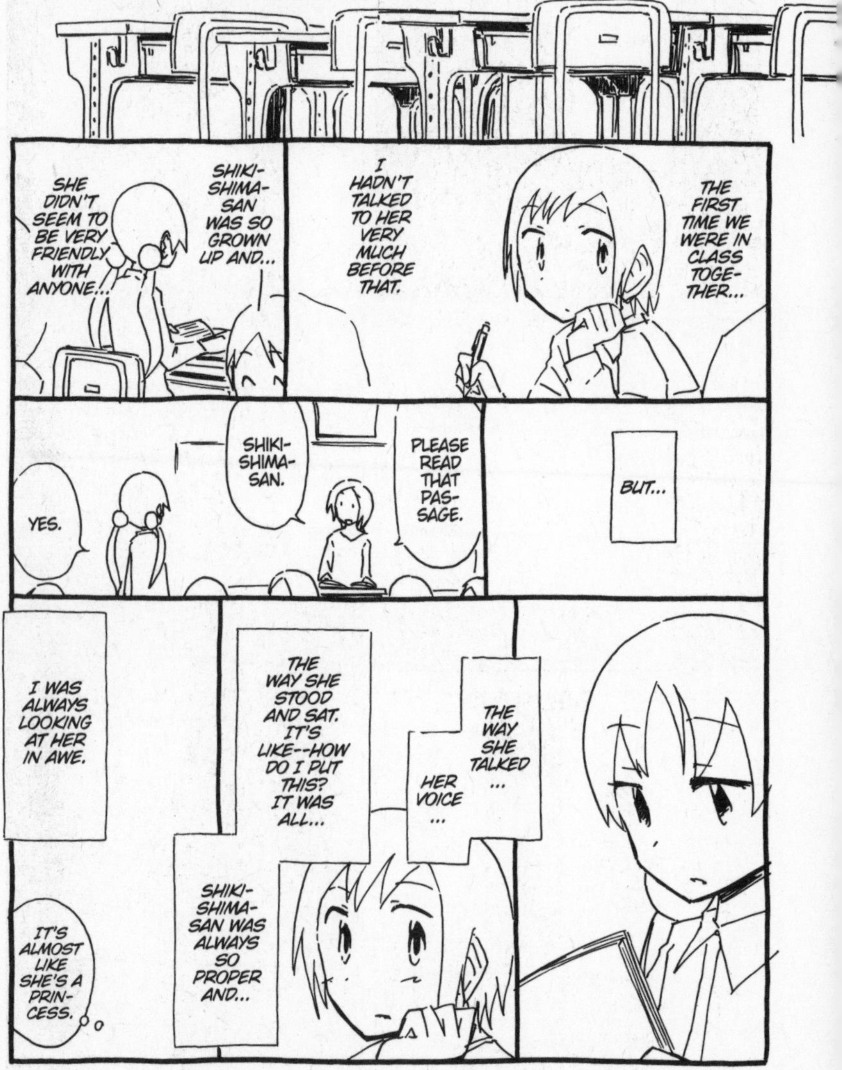
THE FIRST TIME WE WERE IN CLASS TOGETHER...
I HADN'T TALKED TO HER VERY MUCH BEFORE THAT.
SHIKISHIMA-SAN WAS SO GROWN UP AND...
SHE DIDN'T SEEM TO BE VERY FRIENDLY WITH ANYONE...
BUT...
PLEASE READ THAT PASSAGE.
SHIKISHIMA-SAN.
YES.
THE WAY SHE TALKED...
HER VOICE...
THE WAY SHE STOOD AND SAT. IT'S LIKE--HOW DO I PUT THIS? IT WAS ALL...
SHIKISHIMA-SAN WAS ALWAYS SO PROPER AND...
I WAS ALWAYS LOOKING AT HER IN AWE.
IT'S ALMOST LIKE SHE'S A PRINCESS.

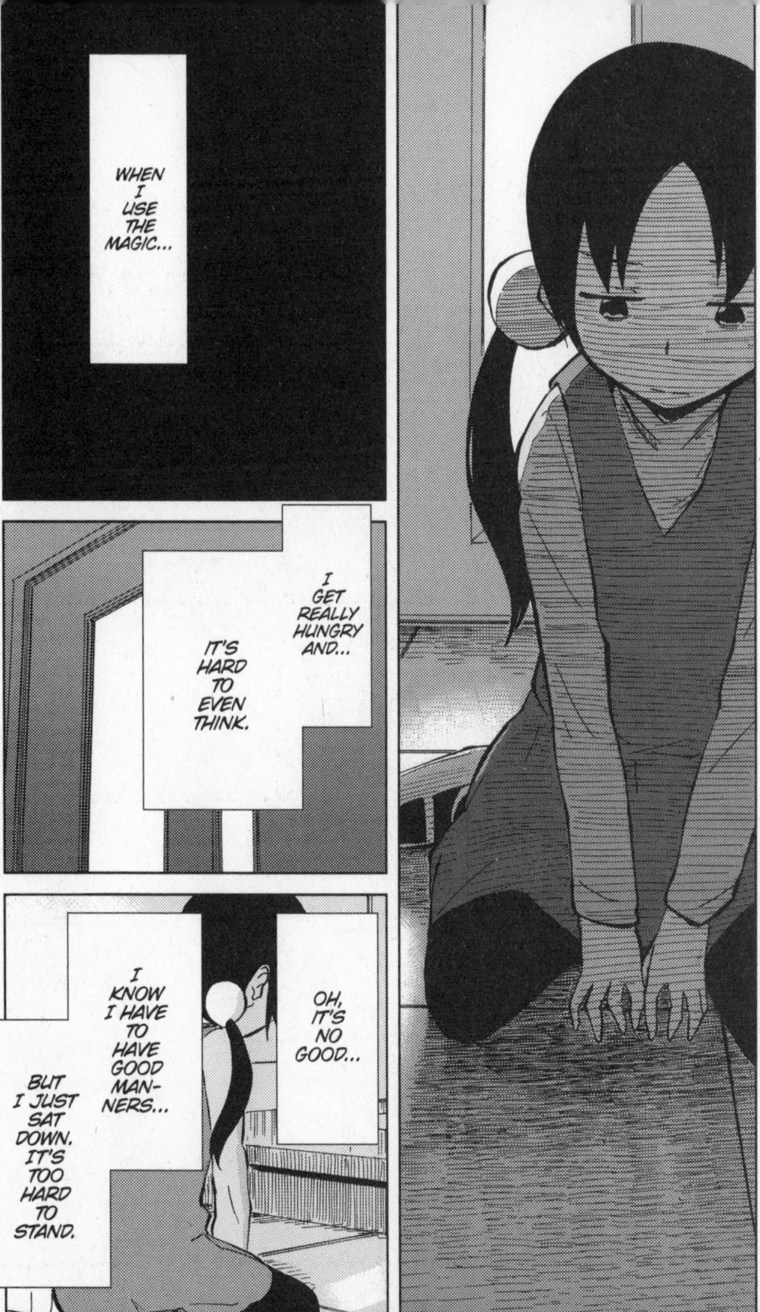
WHEN I USE THE MAGIC...
I GET REALLY HUNGRY AND...
IT'S HARD TO EVEN THINK.
OH, IT'S NO GOOD...
I KNOW I HAVE TO HAVE GOOD MAN-NERS...
BUT I JUST SAT DOWN. IT'S TOO HARD TO STAND.

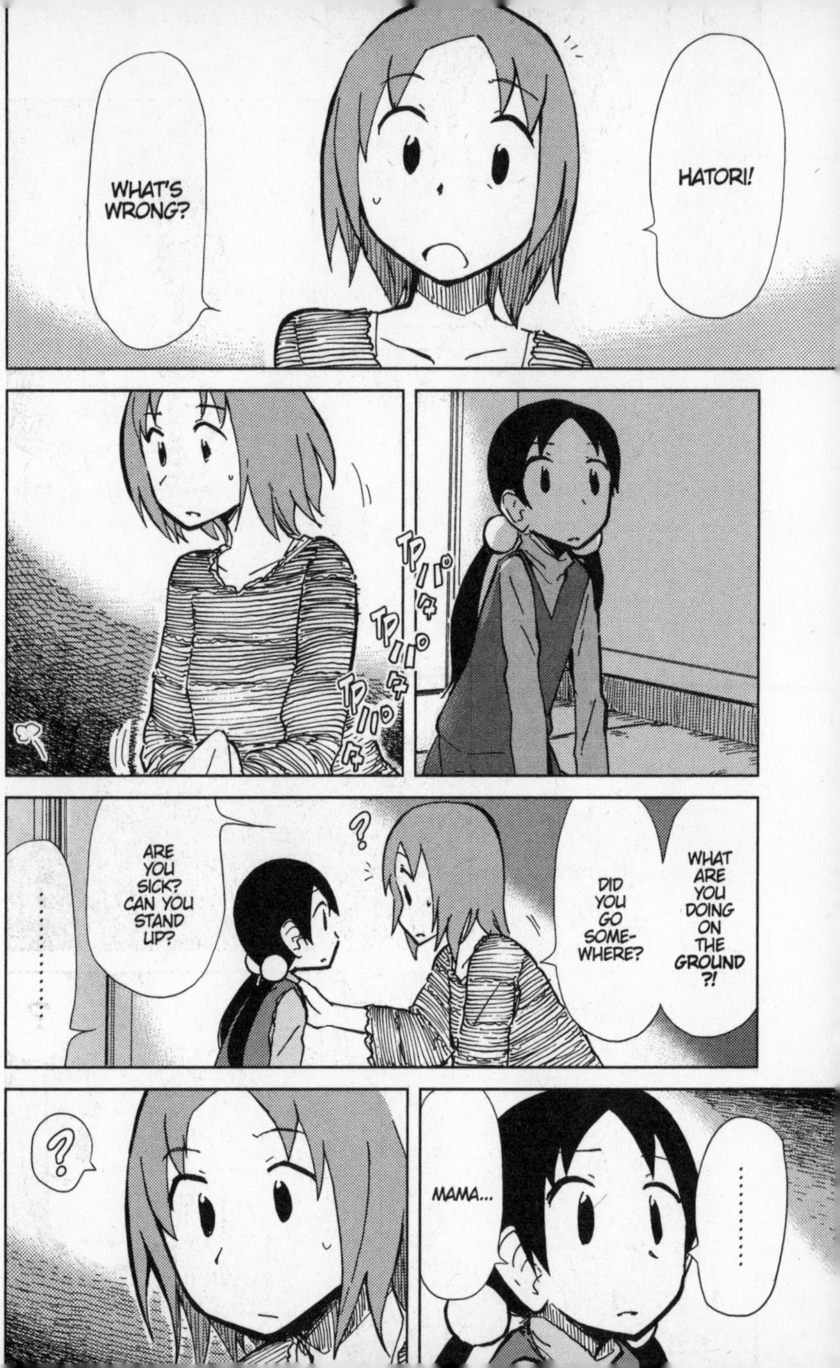
HATORI!
WHAT'S WRONG?
WHAT ARE YOU DOING ON THE GROUND?!
DID YOU GO SOME-WHERE?
?
ARE YOU SICK? CAN YOU STAND UP?
......
......
MAMA...
?

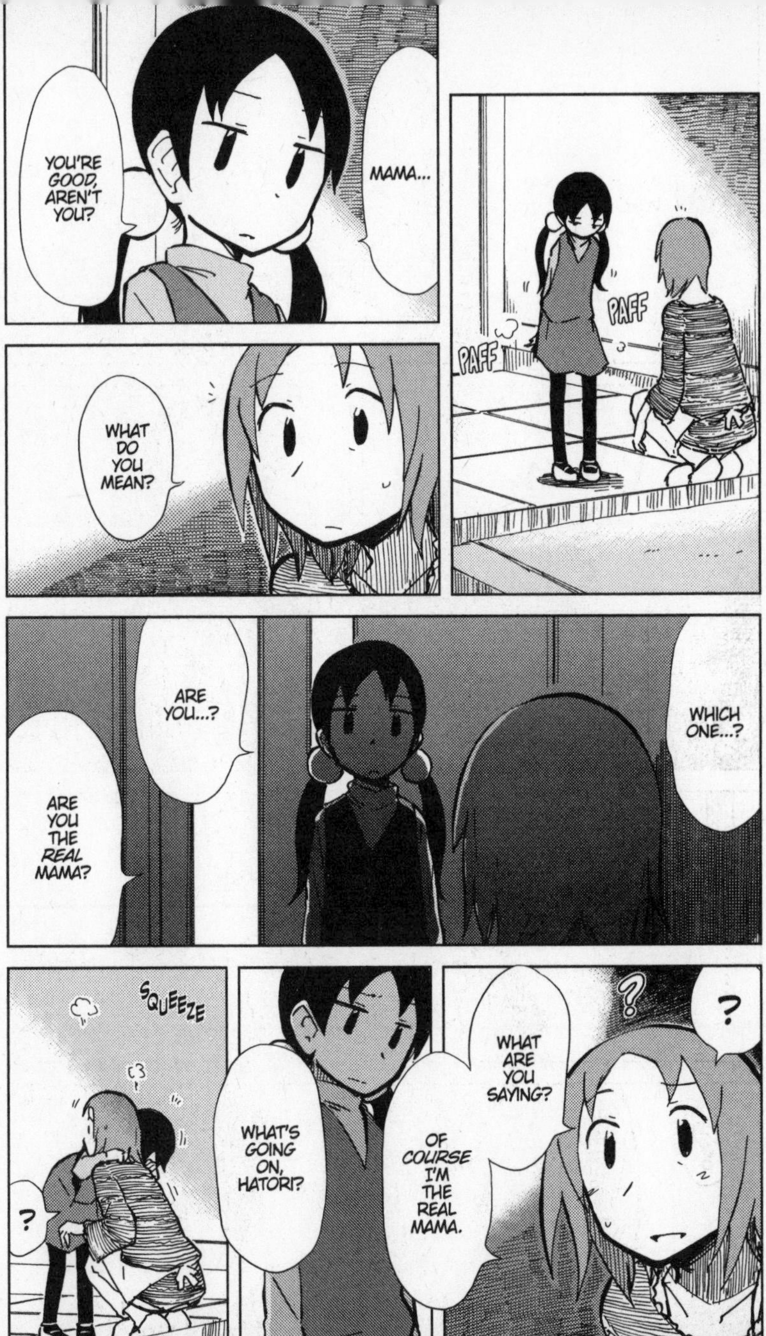
PAFF
PAFF
MAMA...
YOU'RE GOOD, AREN'T YOU?
WHAT DO YOU MEAN?
WHICH ONE...?
ARE YOU...?
ARE YOU THE REAL MAMA?
?
WHAT ARE YOU SAYING?
OF COURSE I'M THE REAL MAMA.
WHAT'S GOING ON, HATORI?
SQUEEZE
?

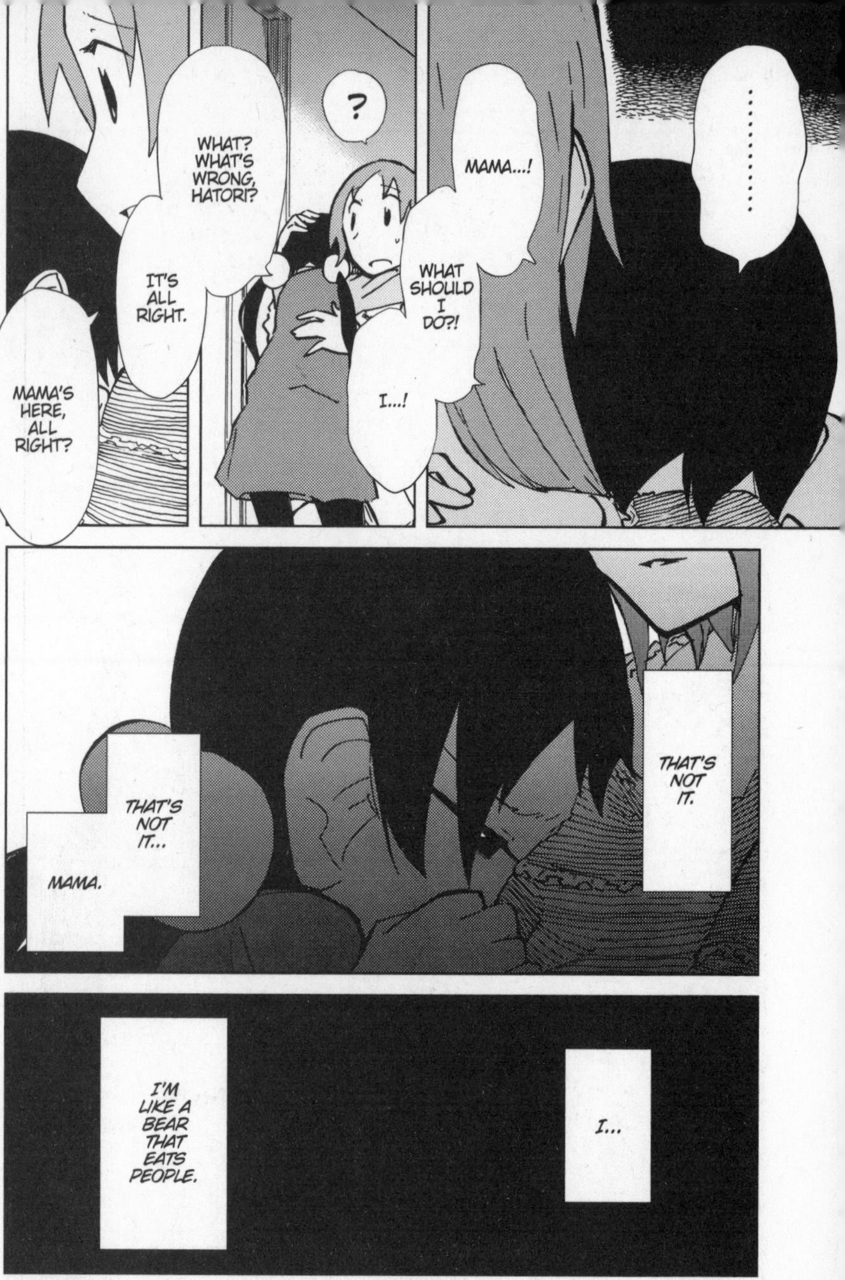
......
MAMA...!
WHAT SHOULD I DO?!
I...!
?
WHAT? WHAT'S WRONG, HATORI?
IT'S ALL RIGHT.
MAMA'S HERE, ALL RIGHT?
THAT'S NOT IT.
THAT'S NOT IT...
MAMA.
I...
I'M LIKE A BEAR THAT EATS PEOPLE.

Chapter 15
The Trial

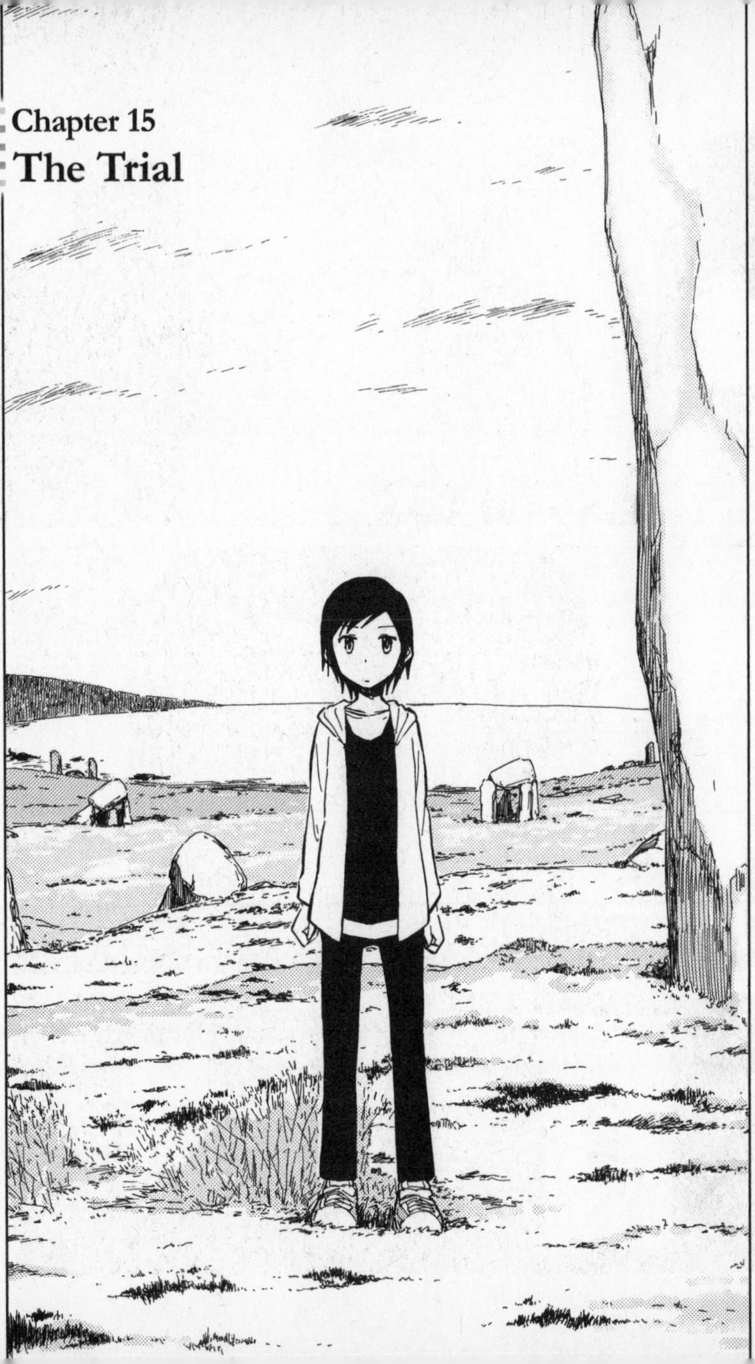

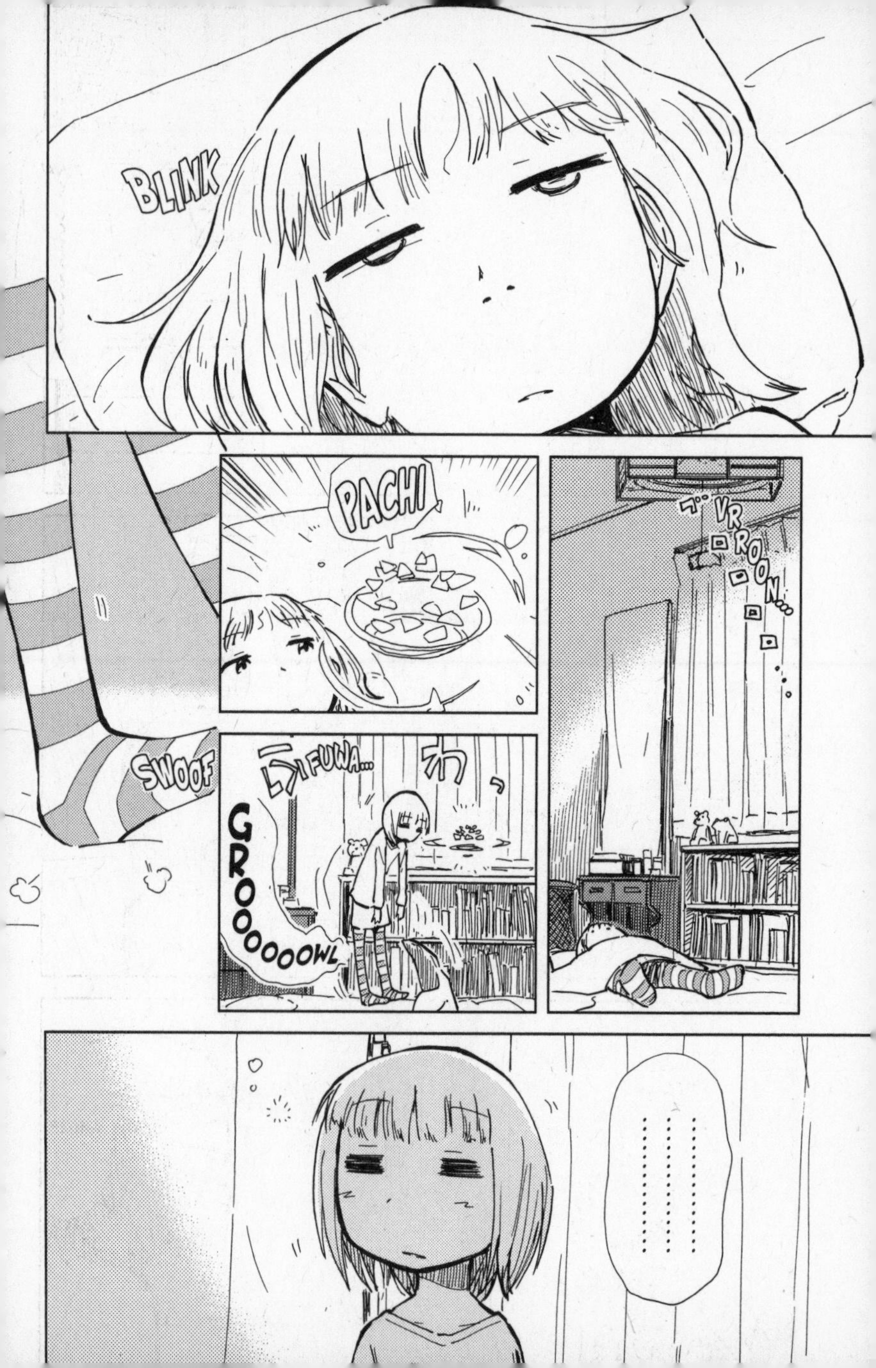
BLINK
VRROOON...
PACHI
FUWA...
わっ
GROOOOOOWL
SWOOF
......

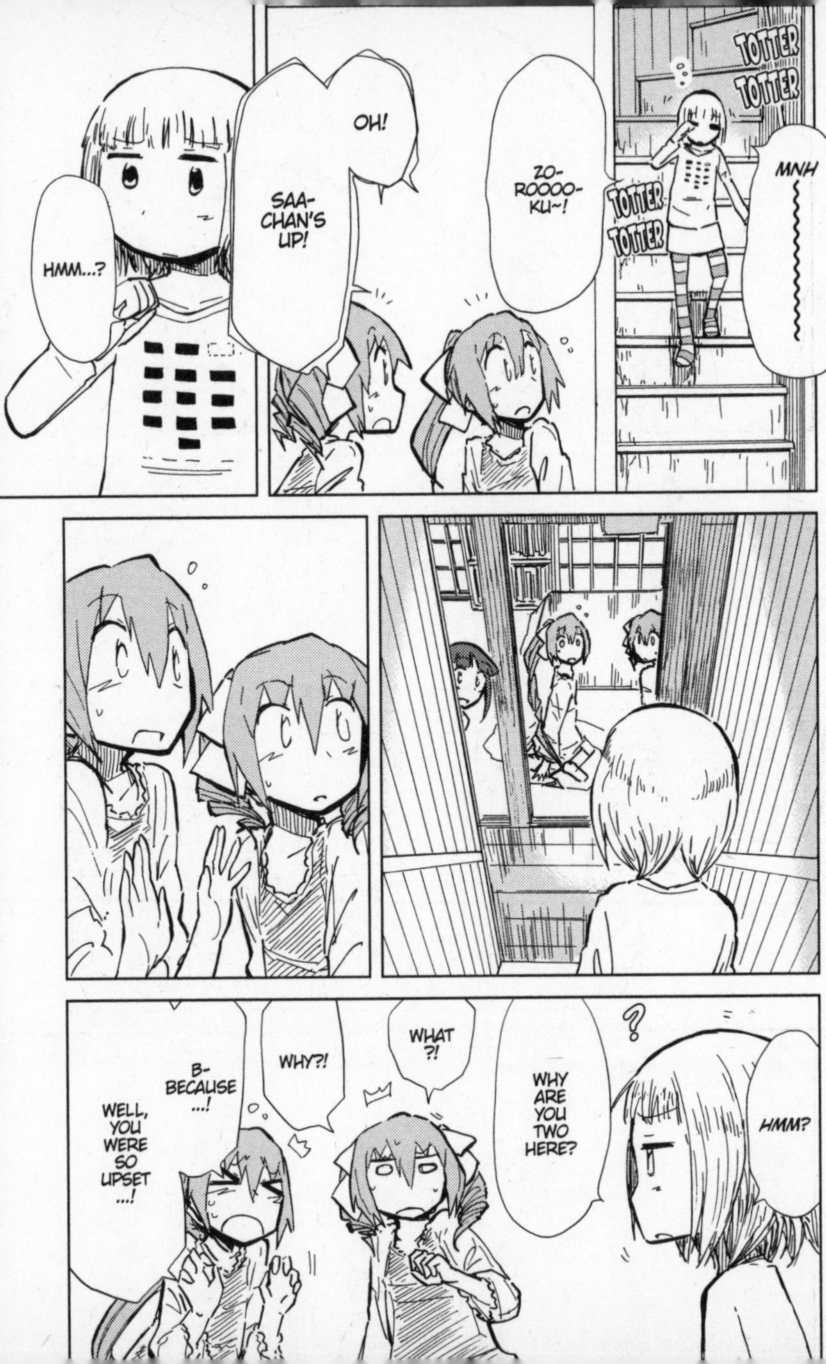
TOTTER TOTTER
MNH~
TOTTER TOTTER
ZO-ROOOOKU~!
OH!
SAA-CHAN'S UP!
HMM...?
HMM?
WHY ARE YOU TWO HERE?
WHAT?!
WHY?!
B-BECAUSE...!
WELL, YOU WERE SO UPSET...!

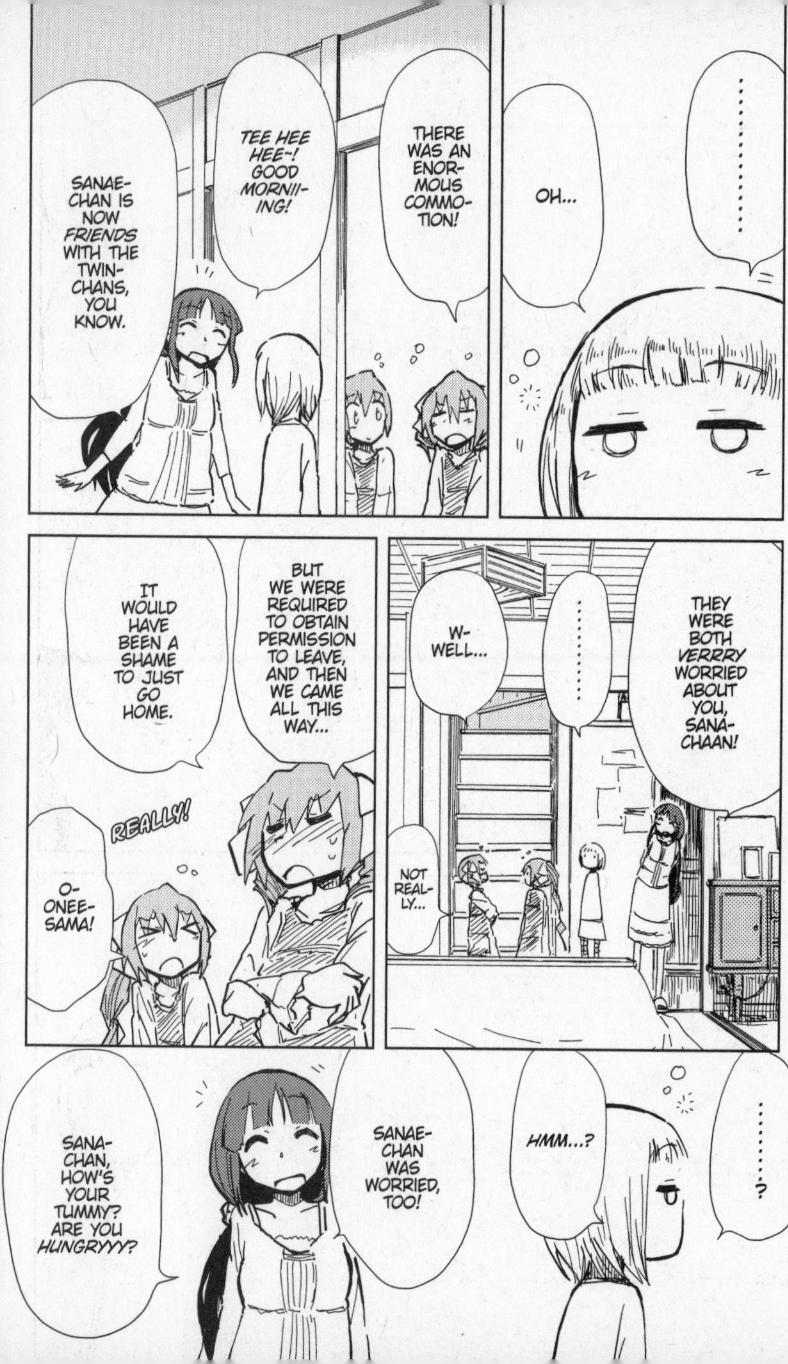
......
OH...
THERE WAS AN ENORMOUS COMMOTION!
TEE HEE HEE~! GOOD MORNIIING!
SANAE-CHAN IS NOW FRIENDS WITH THE TWIN-CHANS, YOU KNOW.
THEY WERE BOTH VERRRY WORRIED ABOUT YOU, SANA-CHAAN!
......
W-WELL...
NOT REALLY...
BUT WE WERE REQUIRED TO OBTAIN PERMISSION TO LEAVE, AND THEN WE CAME ALL THIS WAY...
IT WOULD HAVE BEEN A SHAME TO JUST GO HOME.
REALLY!
O-ONEE-SAMA!
......?
HMM...?
SANAE-CHAN WAS WORRIED, TOO!
SANA-CHAN, HOW'S YOUR TUMMY? ARE YOU HUNGRYYY?

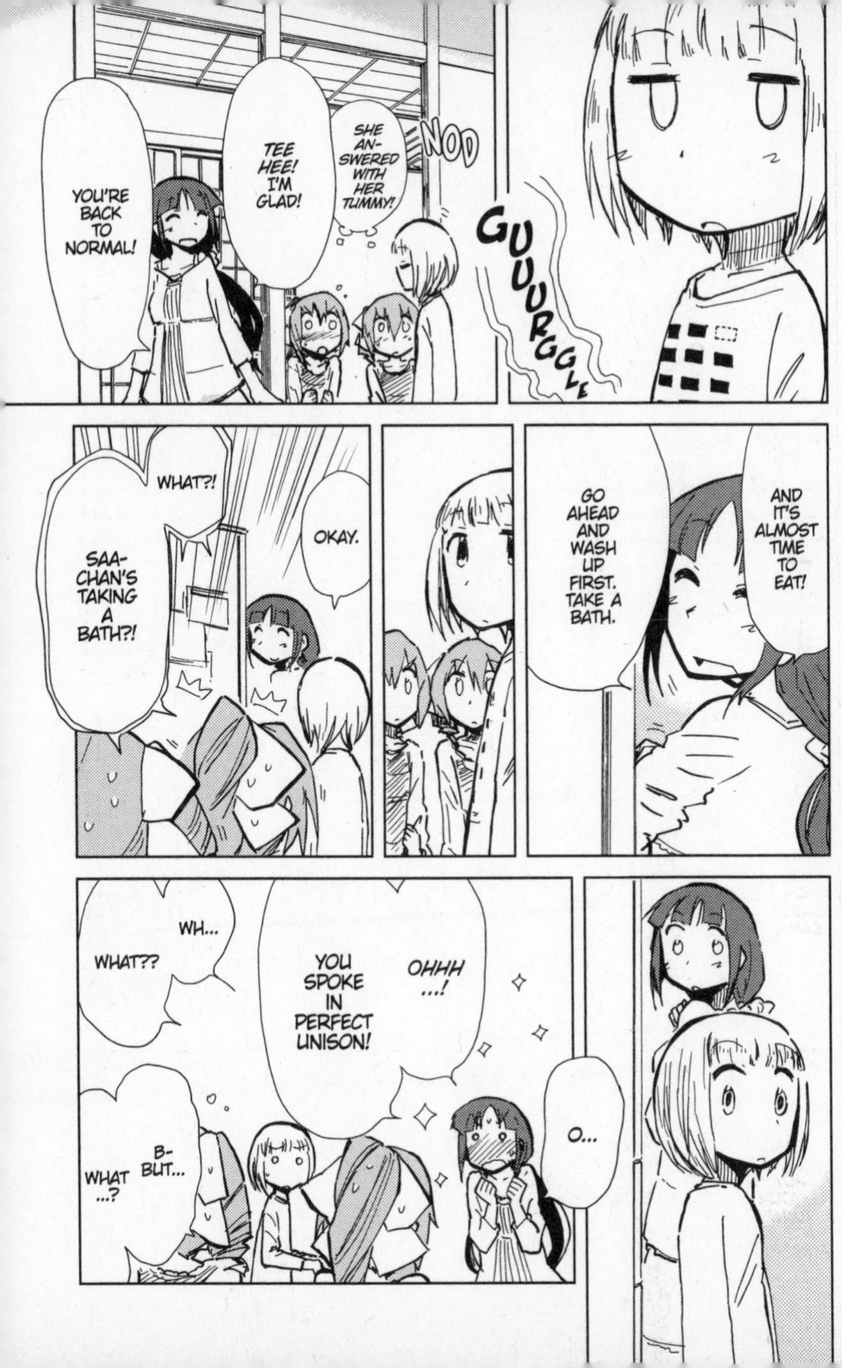
GUUURGGLE
NOD
SHE ANSWERED WITH HER TUMMY!
TEE HEE! I'M GLAD!
YOU'RE BACK TO NORMAL!
AND IT'S ALMOST TIME TO EAT!
GO AHEAD AND WASH UP FIRST. TAKE A BATH.
OKAY.
WHAT?!
SAA-CHAN'S TAKING A BATH?!
O...
OHHH ...!
YOU SPOKE IN PERFECT UNISON!
WH...
WHAT??
B-BUT...
WHAT ...?

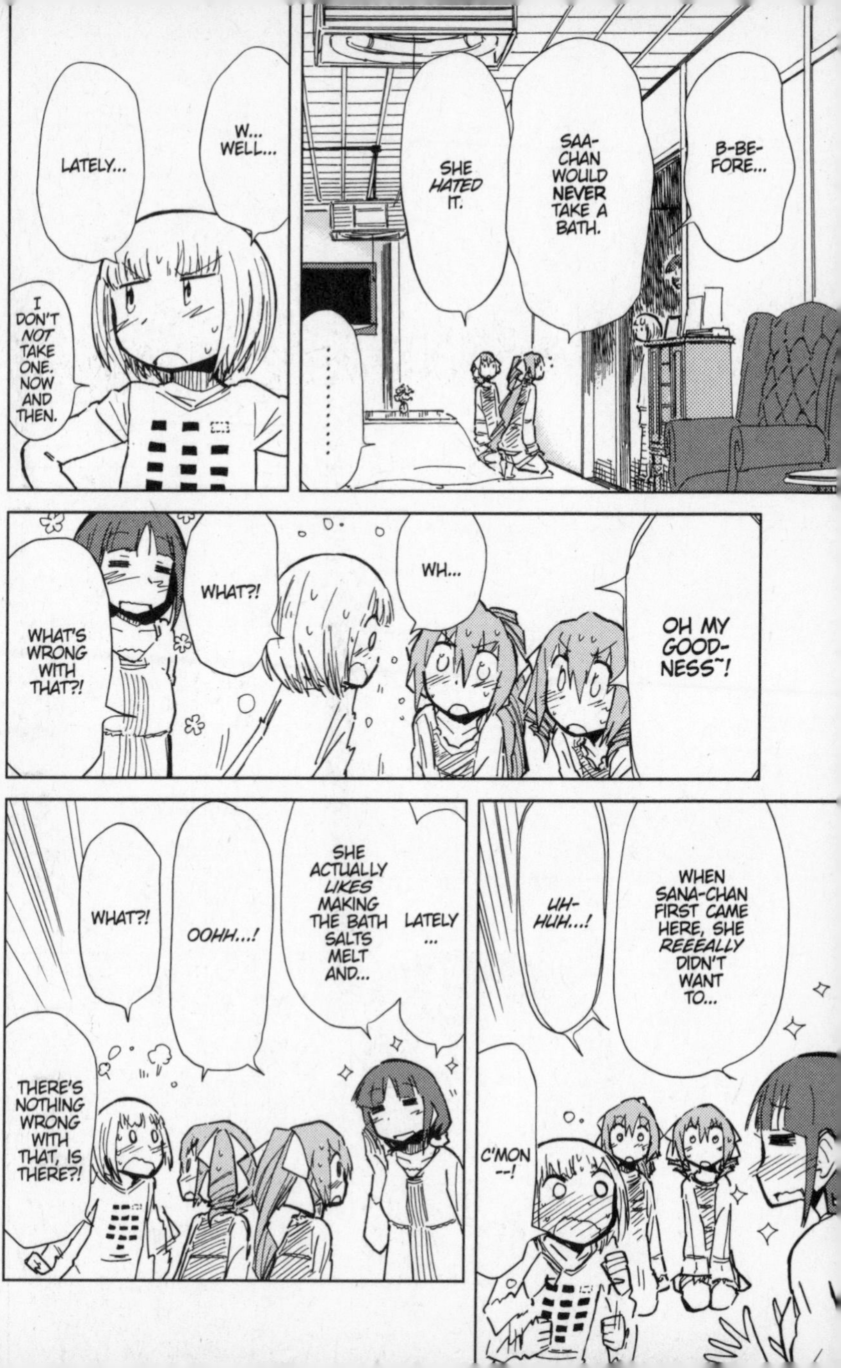
B-BEFORE...
SAA-CHAN WOULD NEVER TAKE A BATH.
SHE *HATED* IT.
W... WELL...
LATELY...
I DON'T *NOT* TAKE ONE. NOW AND THEN.
OH MY GOODNESS~!
WH...
WHAT?!
WHAT'S WRONG WITH THAT?!
WHEN SANA-CHAN FIRST CAME HERE, SHE *REEEALLY* DIDN'T WANT TO...
UH-HUH...!
C'MON--!
LATELY...
SHE ACTUALLY *LIKES* MAKING THE BATH SALTS MELT AND...
OOHH...!
WHAT?!
THERE'S NOTHING WRONG WITH THAT, IS THERE?!

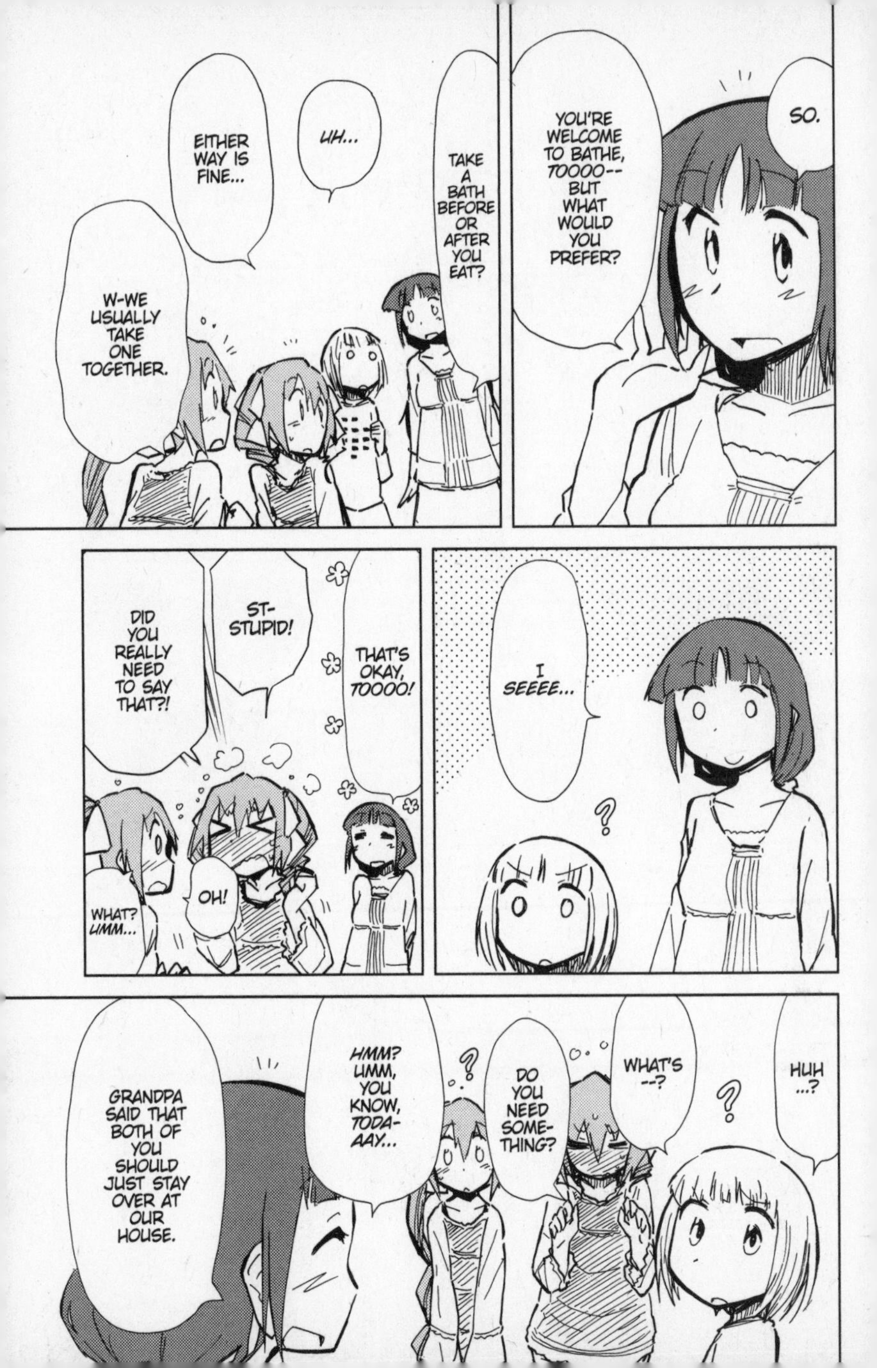
SO.
YOU'RE WELCOME TO BATHE, TOOOO-- BUT WHAT WOULD YOU PREFER?
TAKE A BATH BEFORE OR AFTER YOU EAT?
UH...
EITHER WAY IS FINE...
W-WE USUALLY TAKE ONE TOGETHER.
I SEEEE...
THAT'S OKAY, TOOOO!
ST- STUPID!
DID YOU REALLY NEED TO SAY THAT?!
OH!
WHAT? UMM...
HUH ...?
WHAT'S --?
DO YOU NEED SOME- THING?
HMM? UMM, YOU KNOW, TODA- AAY...
GRANDPA SAID THAT BOTH OF YOU SHOULD JUST STAY OVER AT OUR HOUSE.

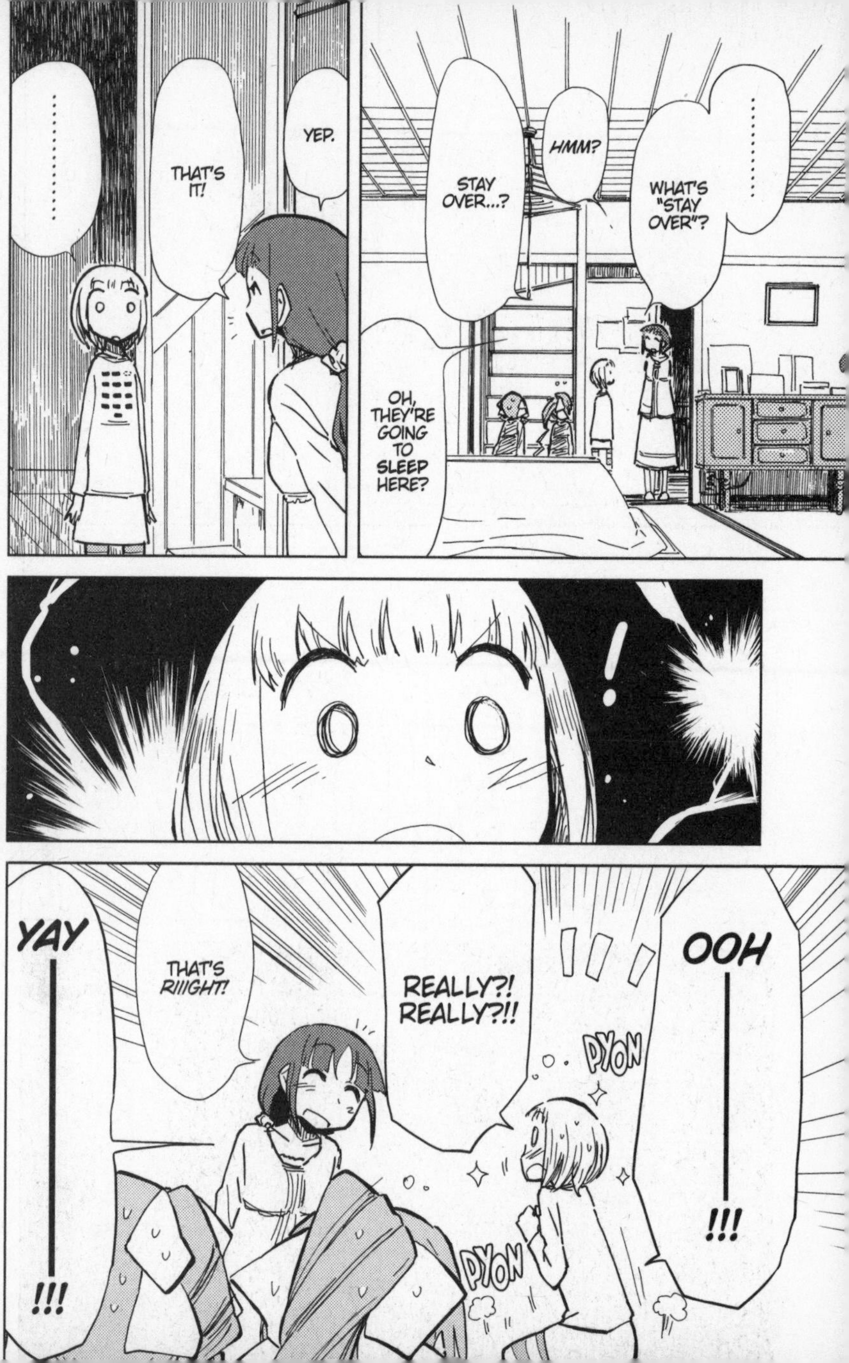
......
WHAT'S "STAY OVER"?
HMM?
STAY OVER...?
OH, THEY'RE GOING TO SLEEP HERE?
YEP.
THAT'S IT!
......
!
OOH———!!!
!!!
PYON
REALLY?! REALLY?!!
THAT'S RIIIGHT!
PYON
YAY———!!!

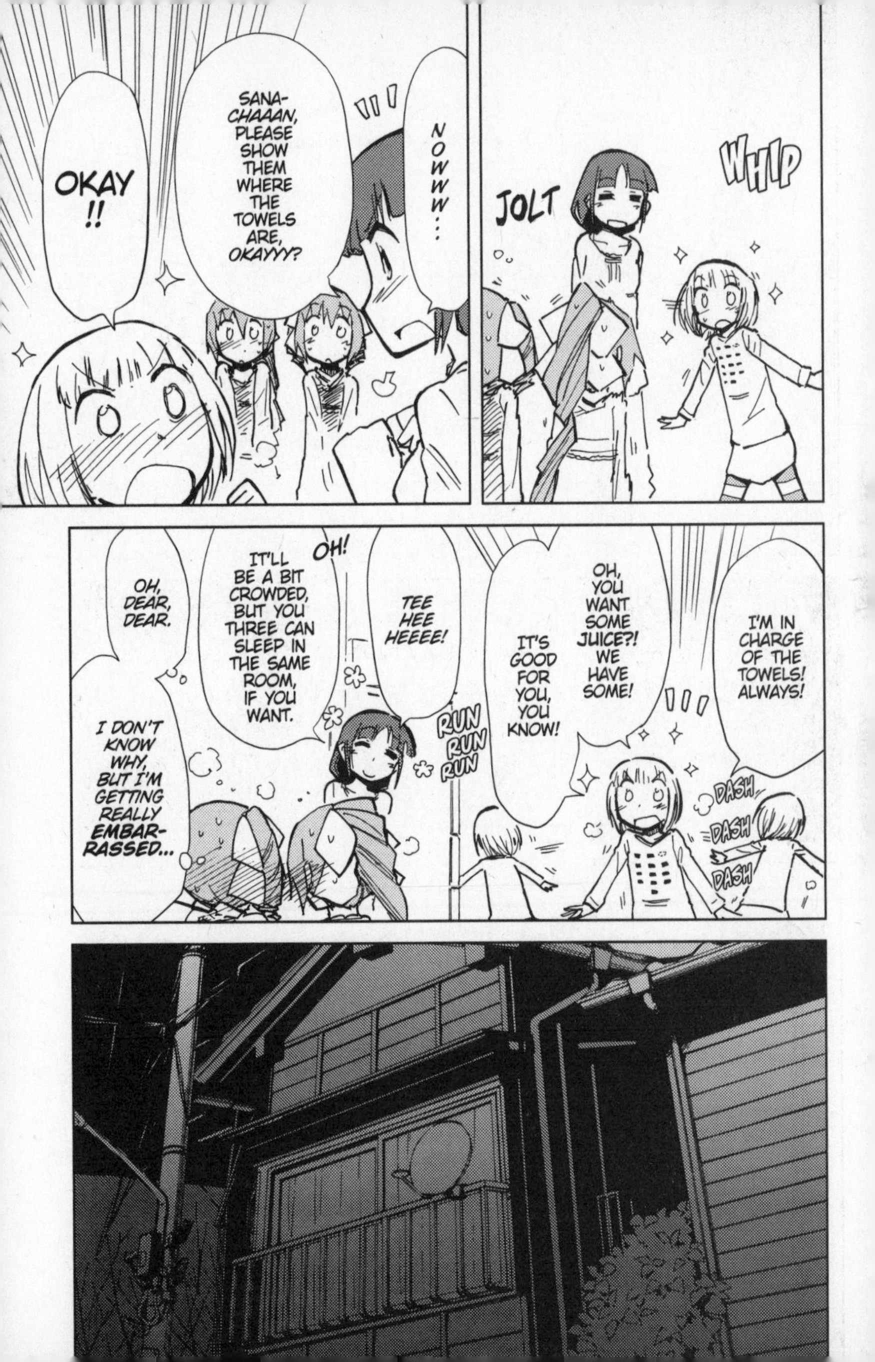
WHIP
JOLT
NOWWW...
SANA-CHAAAN, PLEASE SHOW THEM WHERE THE TOWELS ARE, OKAYYY?
OKAY!!
I'M IN CHARGE OF THE TOWELS! ALWAYS!
DASH
DASH
DASH
OH, YOU WANT SOME JUICE?! WE HAVE SOME!
IT'S GOOD FOR YOU, YOU KNOW!
RUN RUN RUN
TEE HEE HEEEE!
OH!
IT'LL BE A BIT CROWDED, BUT YOU THREE CAN SLEEP IN THE SAME ROOM, IF YOU WANT.
OH, DEAR, DEAR.
I DON'T KNOW WHY, BUT I'M GETTING REALLY EMBARRASSED...

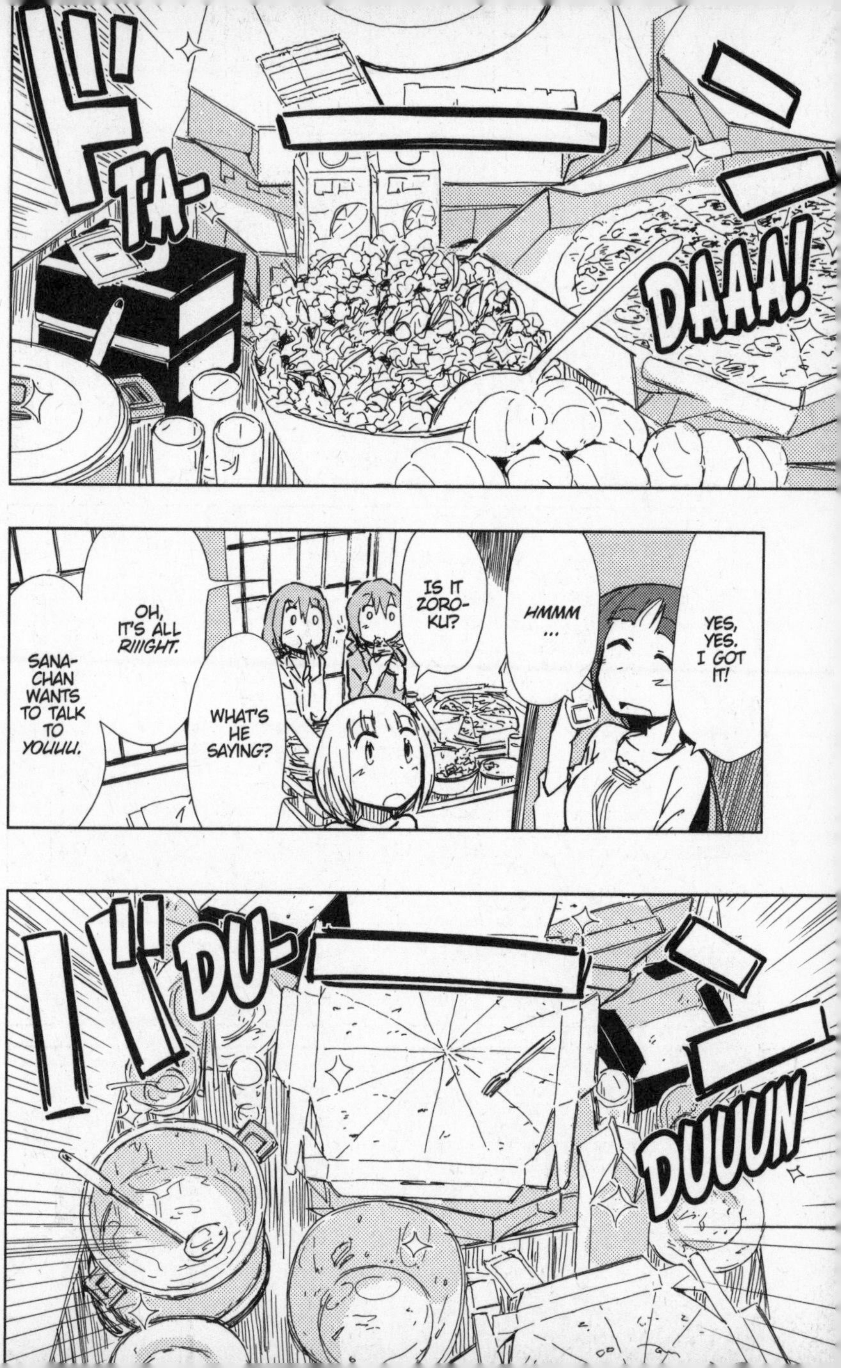
TA-
DAAA!
YES, YES. I GOT IT!
HMMM ...
IS IT ZOROKU?
WHAT'S HE SAYING?
OH, IT'S ALL RIIIGHT.
SANA-CHAN WANTS TO TALK TO YOUUU.
DU-
DUUUN

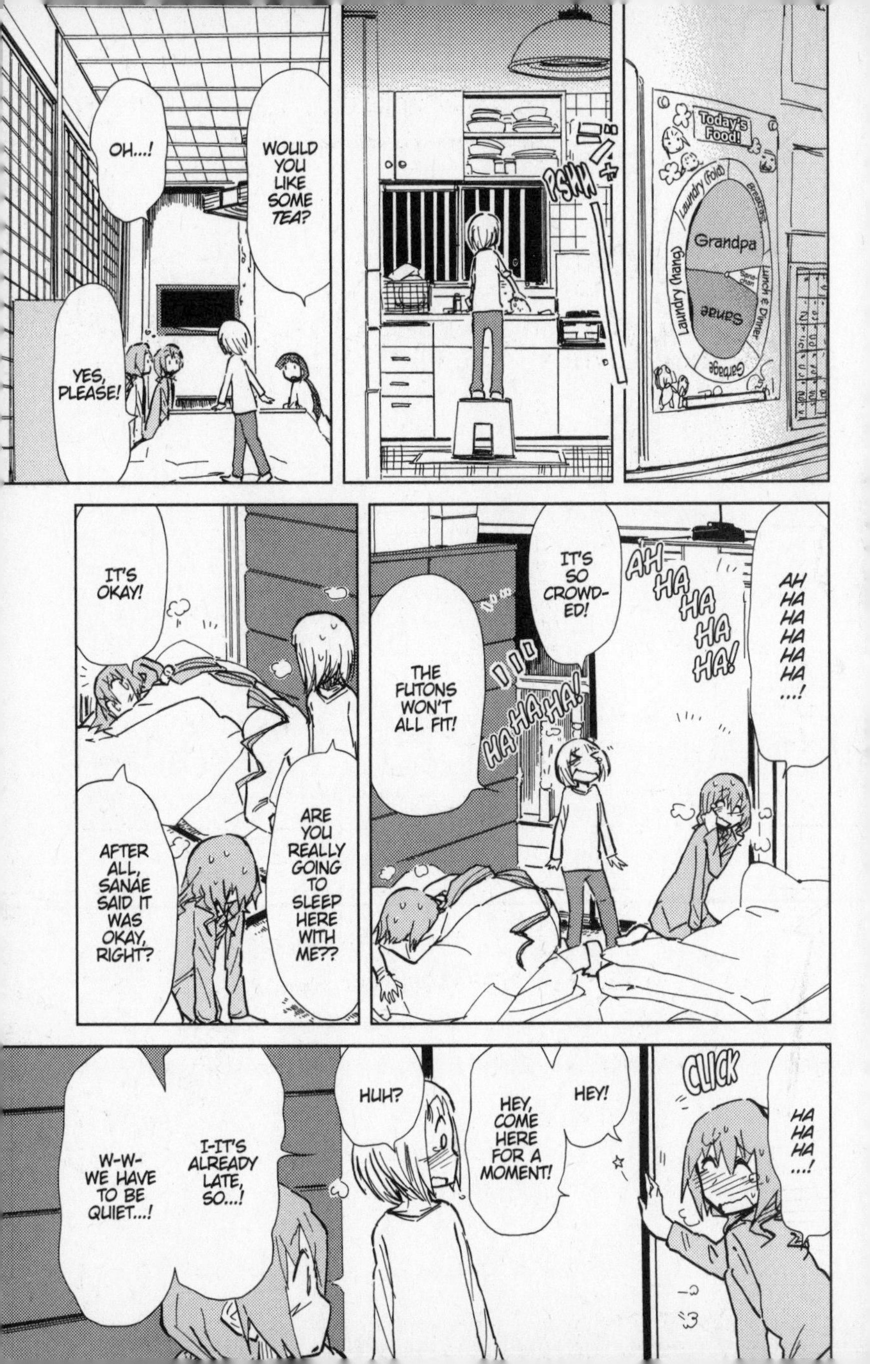
Today's Food!
Laundry (Fold)
Breakfast
Grandpa
Lunch & Dinner
Sana-chan
Sanae
Garbage
Laundry (Nana)
PSHH
WOULD YOU LIKE SOME TEA?
OH...!
YES, PLEASE!
AH HA HA HA HA HA HA...!
AH HA HA HA HA!
IT'S SO CROWDED!
THE FUTONS WON'T ALL FIT!
HA HA HA!
ARE YOU REALLY GOING TO SLEEP HERE WITH ME??
IT'S OKAY!
AFTER ALL, SANAE SAID IT WAS OKAY, RIGHT?
CLICK
HA HA HA...!
HEY!
HEY, COME HERE FOR A MOMENT!
HUH?
I-IT'S ALREADY LATE, SO...!
W-W-WE HAVE TO BE QUIET...!

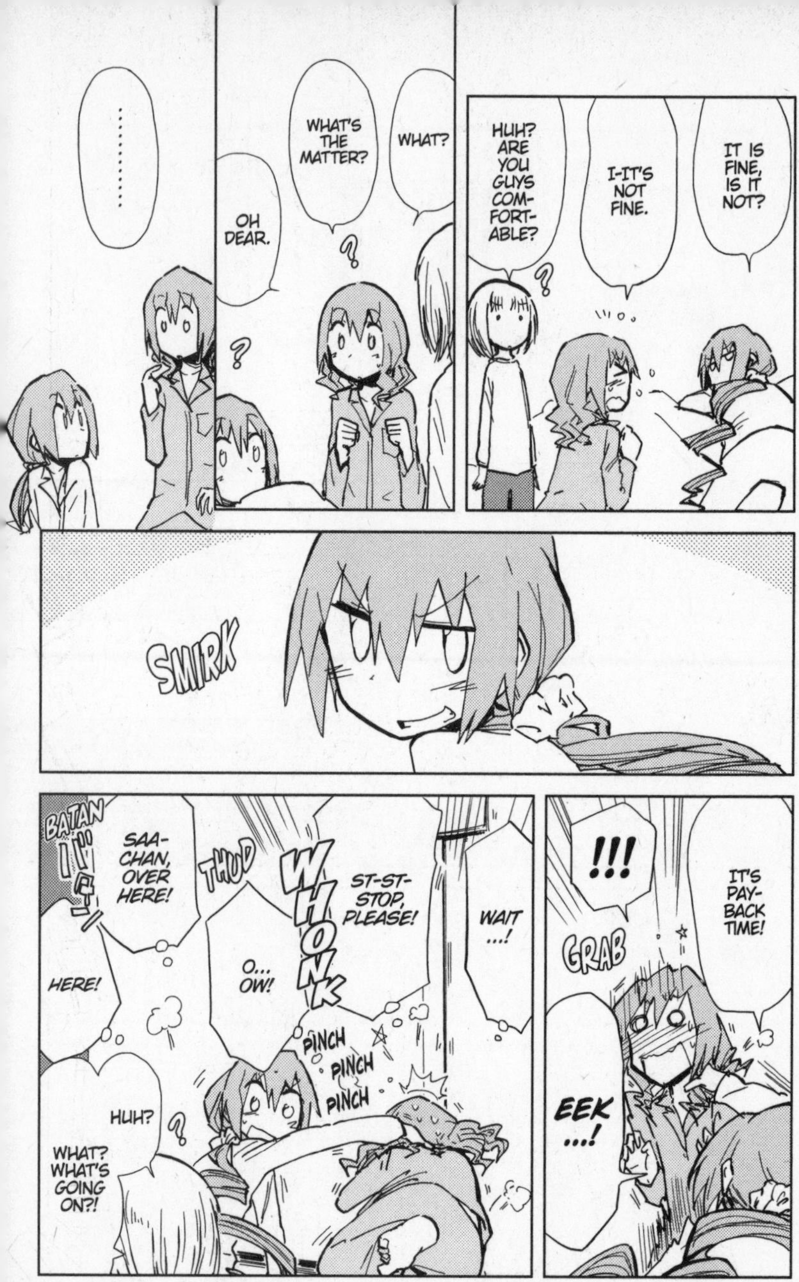
IT IS FINE, IS IT NOT?
I-IT'S NOT FINE.
HUH? ARE YOU GUYS COM-FORT-ABLE?
WHAT?
WHAT'S THE MATTER?
OH DEAR.
......
SMIRK
IT'S PAY-BACK TIME!
!!!
GRAB
EEK ...!
WAIT ...!
ST-ST-STOP, PLEASE!
WHONK
THUD
SAA-CHAN, OVER HERE!
BATAN
O... OW!
PINCH
PINCH
PINCH
HERE!
HUH?
WHAT? WHAT'S GOING ON?!

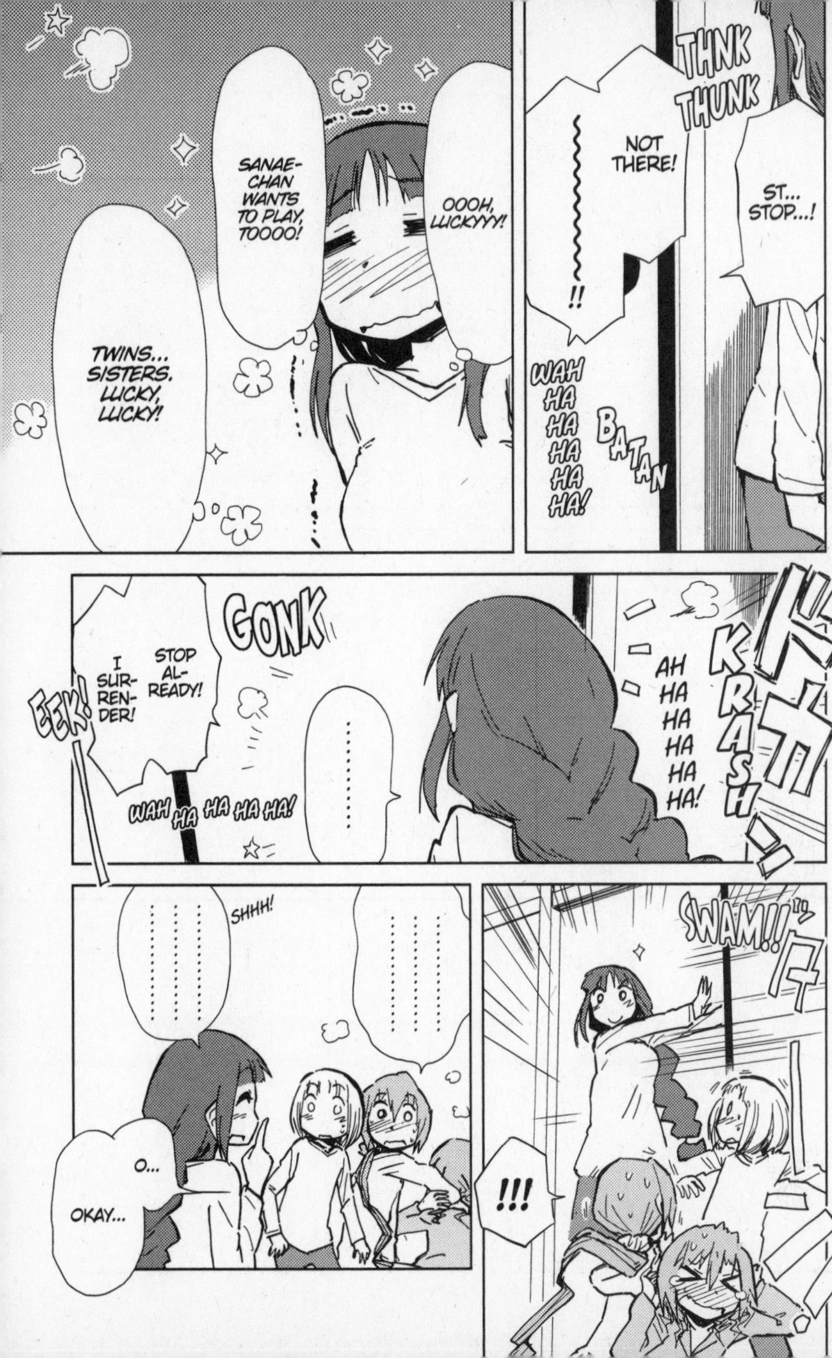
THNK
THUNK
ST... STOP...!
NOT THERE!
!!
WAH HA HA HA HA HA!
BATAN
OOOH, LUCKYYY!
SANAE-CHAN WANTS TO PLAY, TOOOO!
TWINS... SISTERS. LUCKY, LUCKY!
KRASH
AH HA HA HA HA HA HA!
......
GONK
STOP AL-READY!
I SUR-REN-DER!
EEK!
WAH HA HA HA HA!
SWAM!!
!!!
......
SHHH!
......
O...
OKAY...

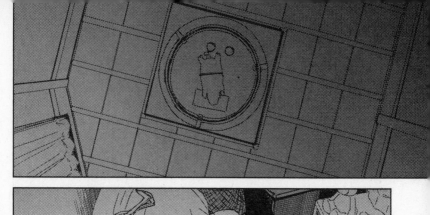

....

HE'S
STILL
NOT
HOME...

ZOROKU
...

....

ARE
YOU
AWAKE?

SAA-
CHAN?

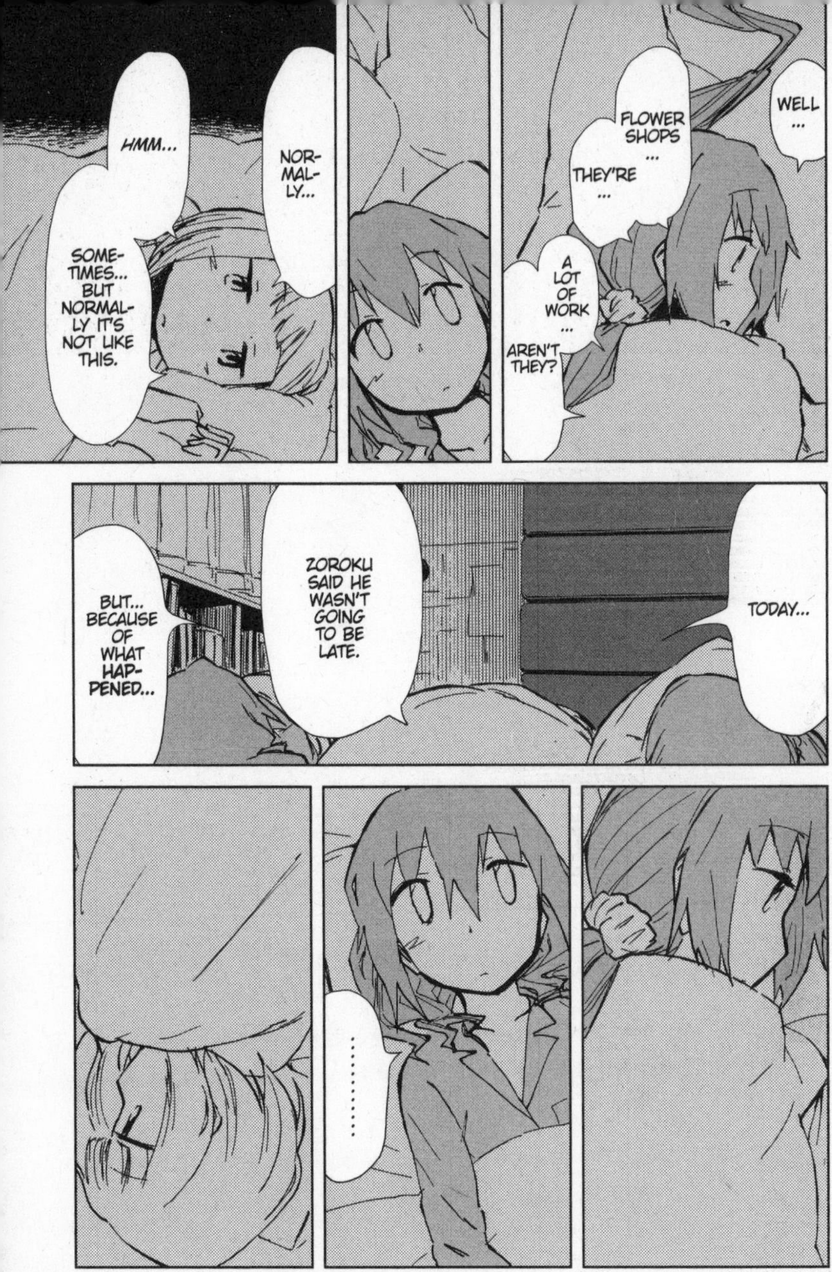

WELL ...
FLOWER SHOPS ... THEY'RE ...
A LOT OF WORK ... AREN'T THEY?
NORMALLY...
HMM...
SOMETIMES... BUT NORMALLY IT'S NOT LIKE THIS.
TODAY...
ZOROKU SAID HE WASN'T GOING TO BE LATE.
BUT... BECAUSE OF WHAT HAPPENED...
....

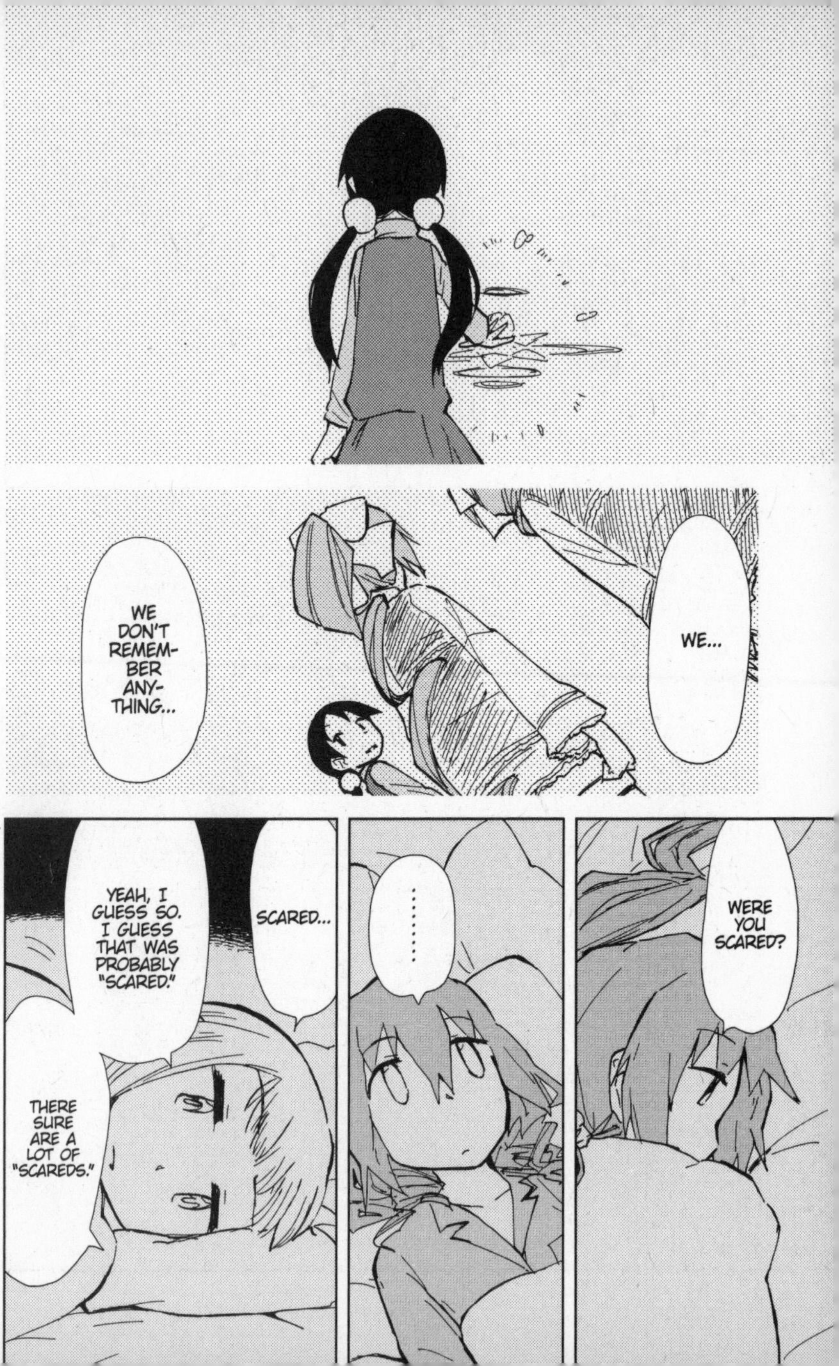
WE...
WE DON'T REMEMBER ANYTHING...
WERE YOU SCARED?
......
SCARED...
YEAH, I GUESS SO. I GUESS THAT WAS PROBABLY "SCARED."
THERE SURE ARE A LOT OF "SCAREDS."

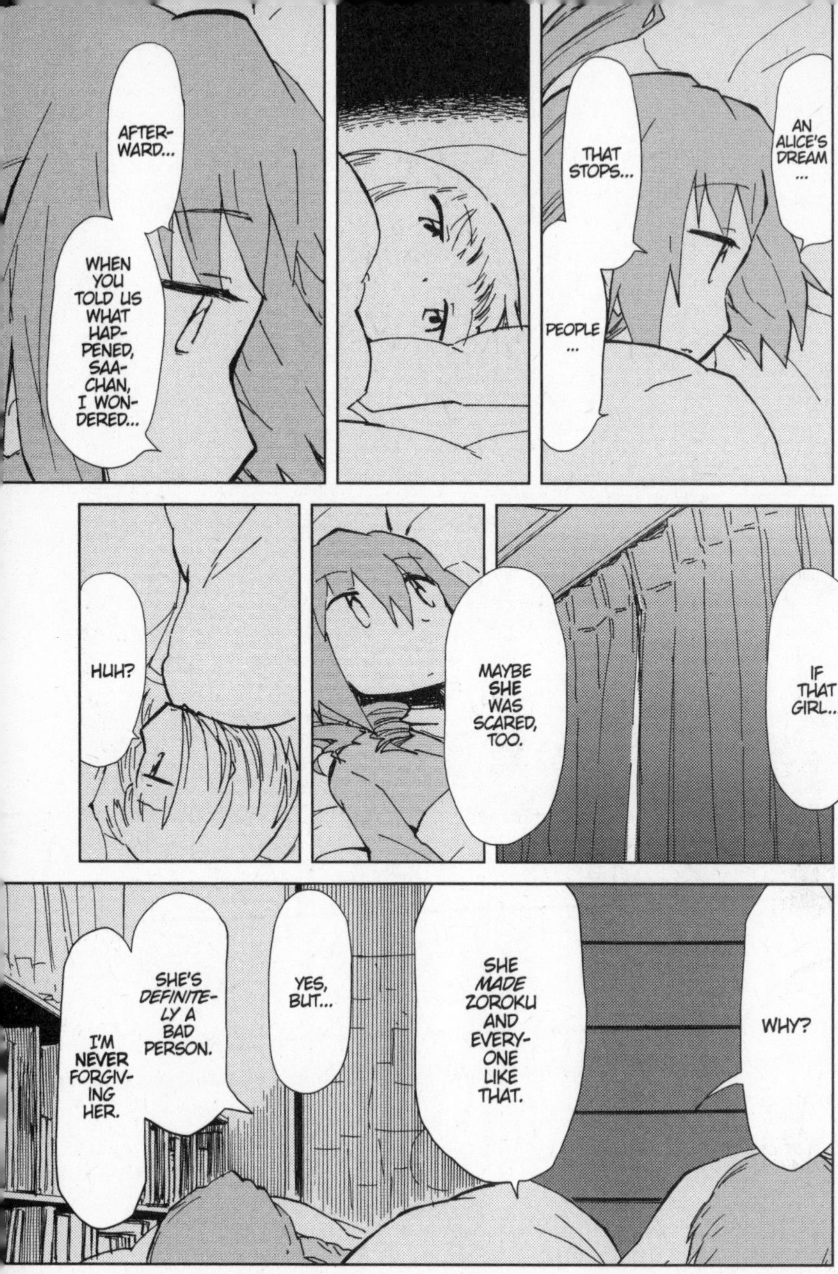
AN ALICE'S DREAM...
THAT STOPS...
PEOPLE...
AFTERWARD...
WHEN YOU TOLD US WHAT HAPPENED, SAA-CHAN, I WONDERED...
IF THAT GIRL...
MAYBE SHE WAS SCARED, TOO.
HUH?
WHY?
SHE *MADE* ZOROKU AND EVERYONE LIKE THAT.
YES, BUT...
SHE'S *DEFINITELY* A BAD PERSON.
I'M NEVER FORGIVING HER.

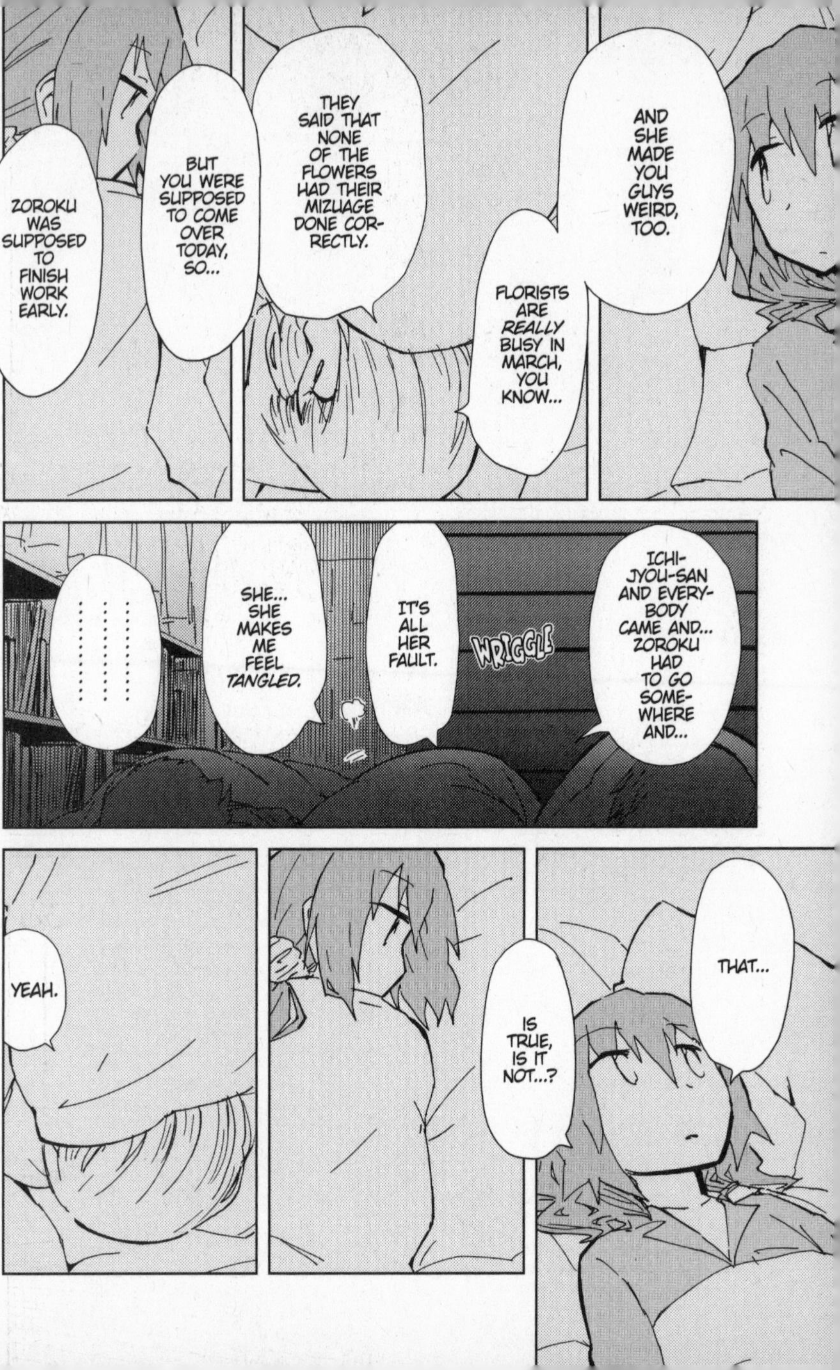
AND SHE MADE YOU GUYS WEIRD, TOO.
FLORISTS ARE *REALLY* BUSY IN MARCH, YOU KNOW...
THEY SAID THAT NONE OF THE FLOWERS HAD THEIR MIZUAGE DONE CORRECTLY.
BUT YOU WERE SUPPOSED TO COME OVER TODAY, SO...
ZOROKU WAS SUPPOSED TO FINISH WORK EARLY.
ICHIJYOU-SAN AND EVERYBODY CAME AND... ZOROKU HAD TO GO SOMEWHERE AND...
WRIGGLE
IT'S ALL HER FAULT.
SHE... SHE MAKES ME FEEL *TANGLED.*
......
THAT...
IS TRUE, IS IT NOT...?
YEAH.

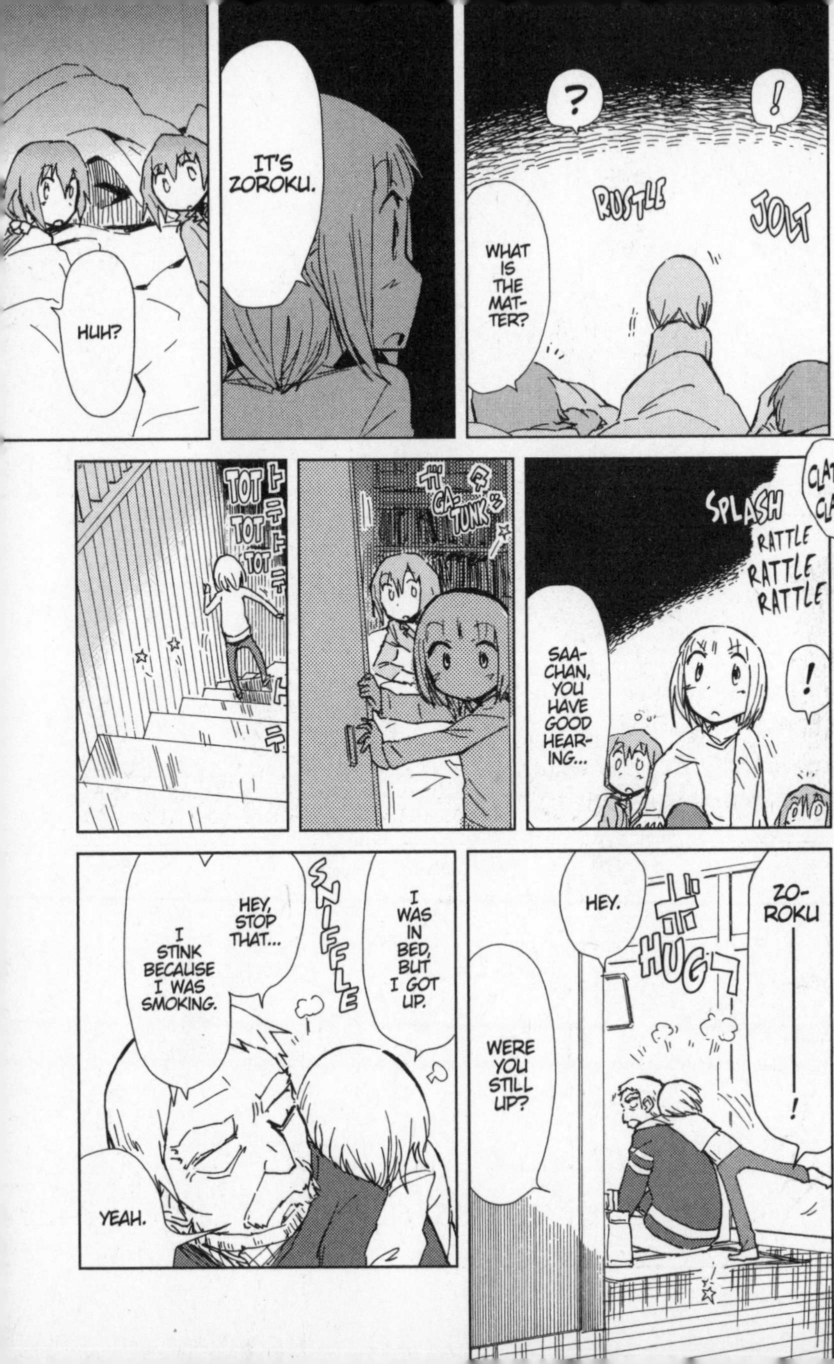
?
!
RUSTLE
JOLT
WHAT IS THE MAT-TER?
IT'S ZOROKU.
HUH?
CLATTER CLATTER
SPLASH
RATTLE RATTLE RATTLE
!
SAA-CHAN, YOU HAVE GOOD HEAR-ING...
GA-TUNK
TOT TOT TOT
ZO-ROKU—!
HUG
HEY.
WERE YOU STILL UP?
I WAS IN BED, BUT I GOT UP.
SNIFFLE
HEY, STOP THAT...
I STINK BECAUSE I WAS SMOKING.
YEAH.

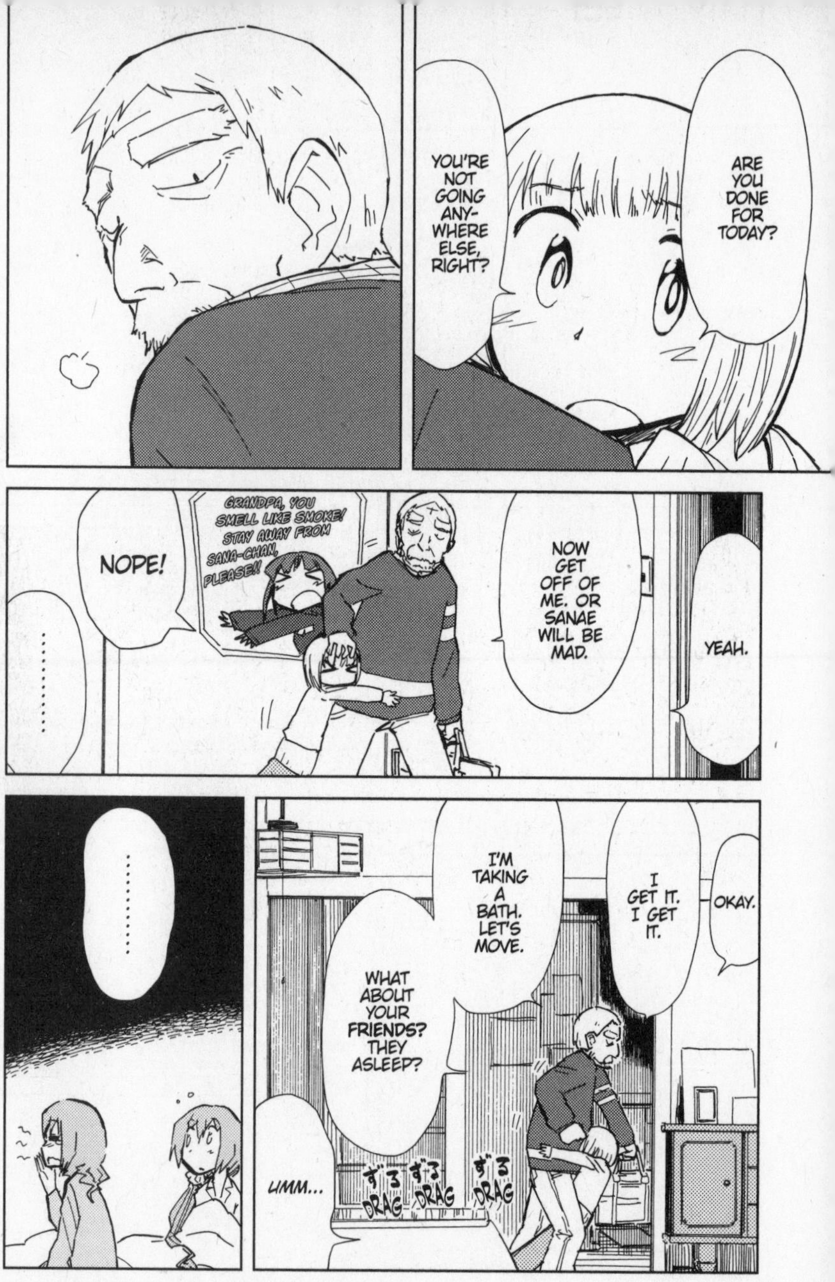
ARE YOU DONE FOR TODAY?
YOU'RE NOT GOING ANY-WHERE ELSE, RIGHT?
YEAH.
NOW GET OFF OF ME. OR SANAE WILL BE MAD.
GRANDPA, YOU SMELL LIKE SMOKE! STAY AWAY FROM SANA-CHAN, PLEASE!!
NOPE!
......
OKAY.
I GET IT. I GET IT.
I'M TAKING A BATH. LET'S MOVE.
WHAT ABOUT YOUR FRIENDS? THEY ASLEEP?
ずる DRAG
ずる DRAG
ずる DRAG
UMM...
......

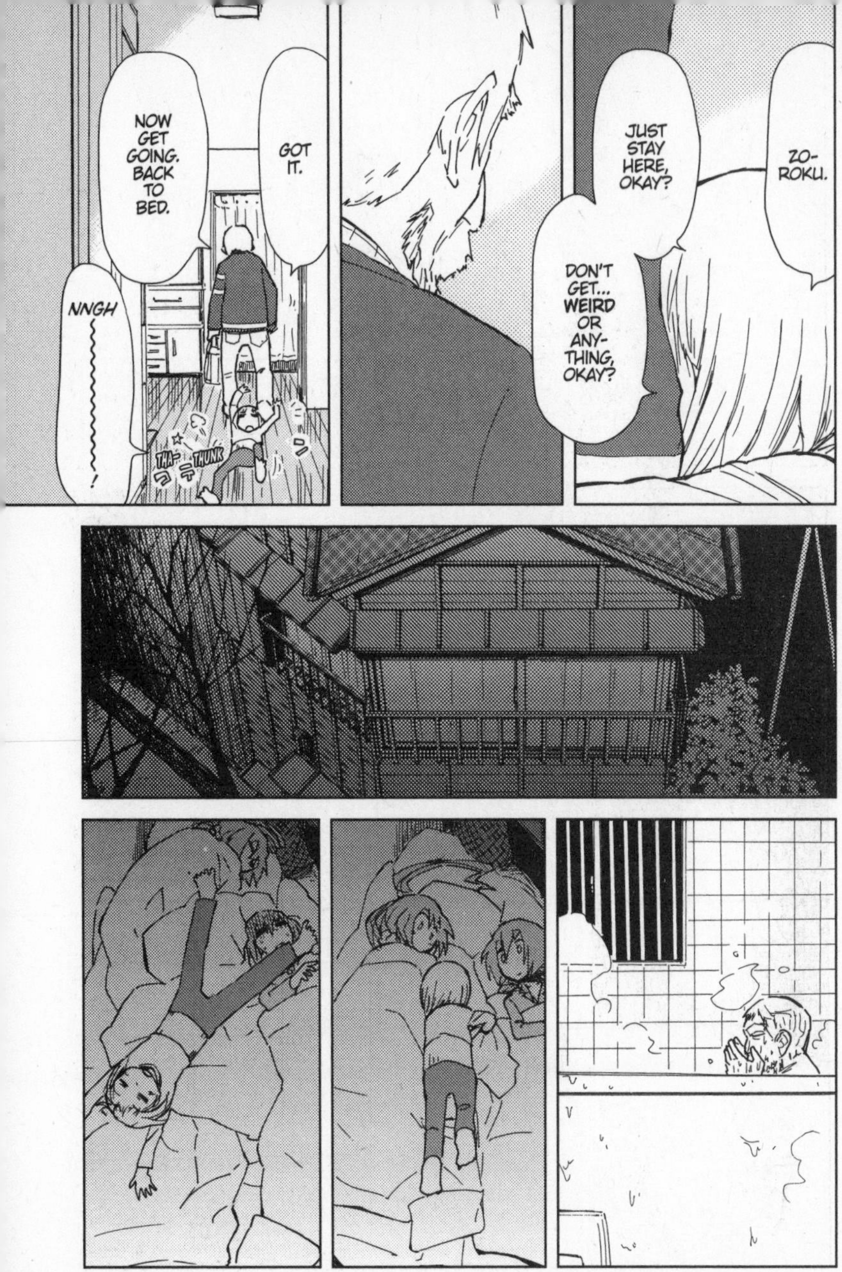
ZO-ROKU.
JUST STAY HERE, OKAY?
DON'T GET... WEIRD OR ANYTHING, OKAY?
GOT IT.
NOW GET GOING. BACK TO BED.
NNGH !
THA-THUNK

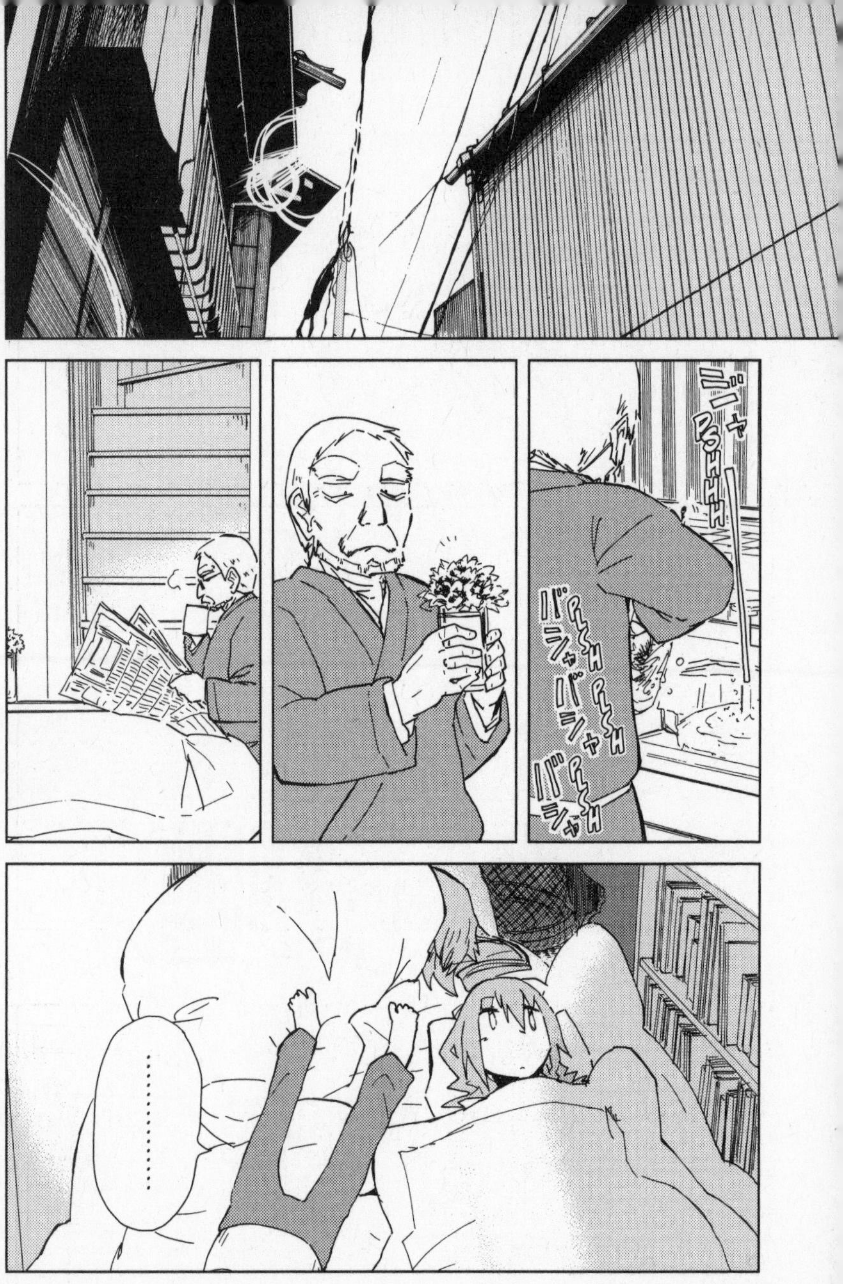
ジャ
PSHHH
バシャ
PLSH
バシャ
PLSH
バシャ
PLSH
……

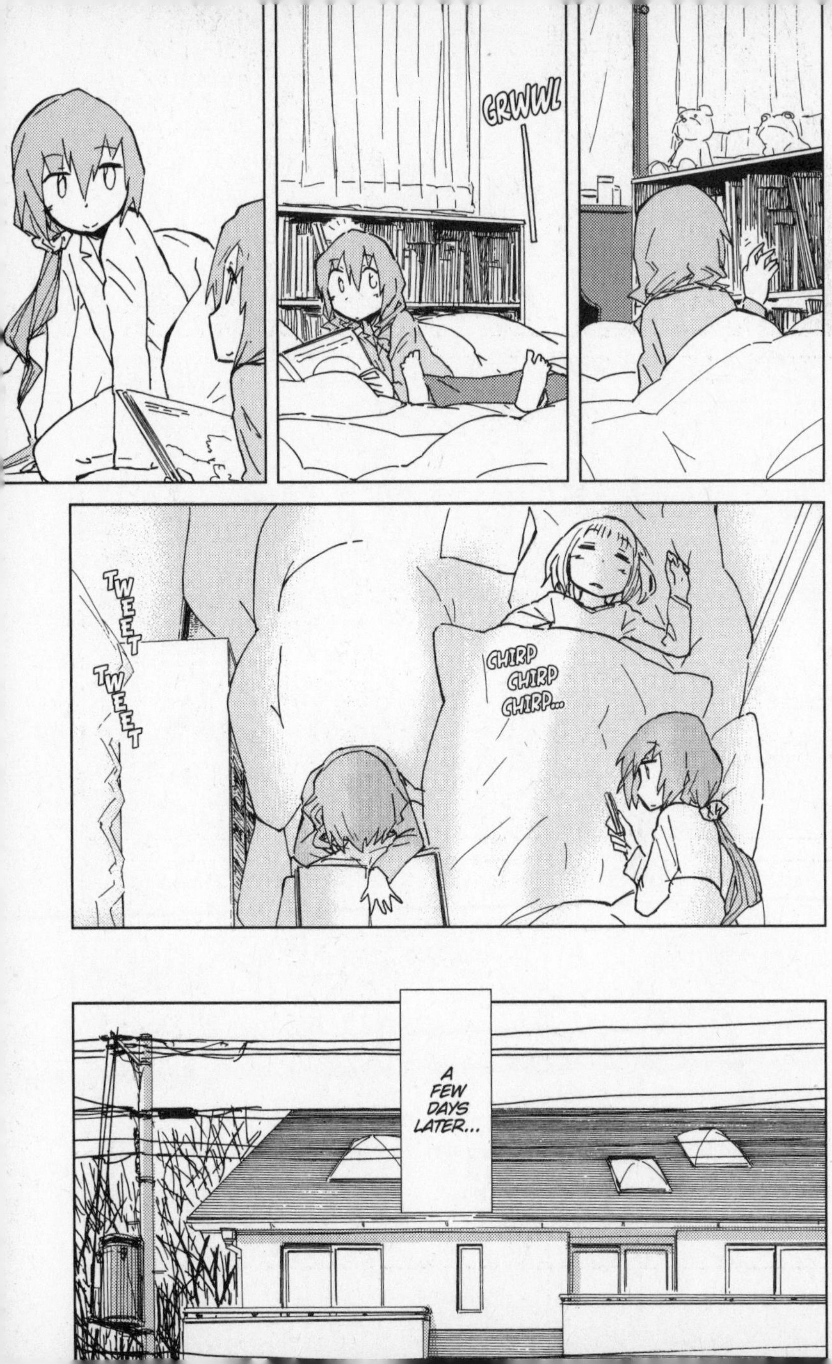
GRWWL
CHIRP CHIRP CHIRP...
TWEET TWEET
A FEW DAYS LATER...

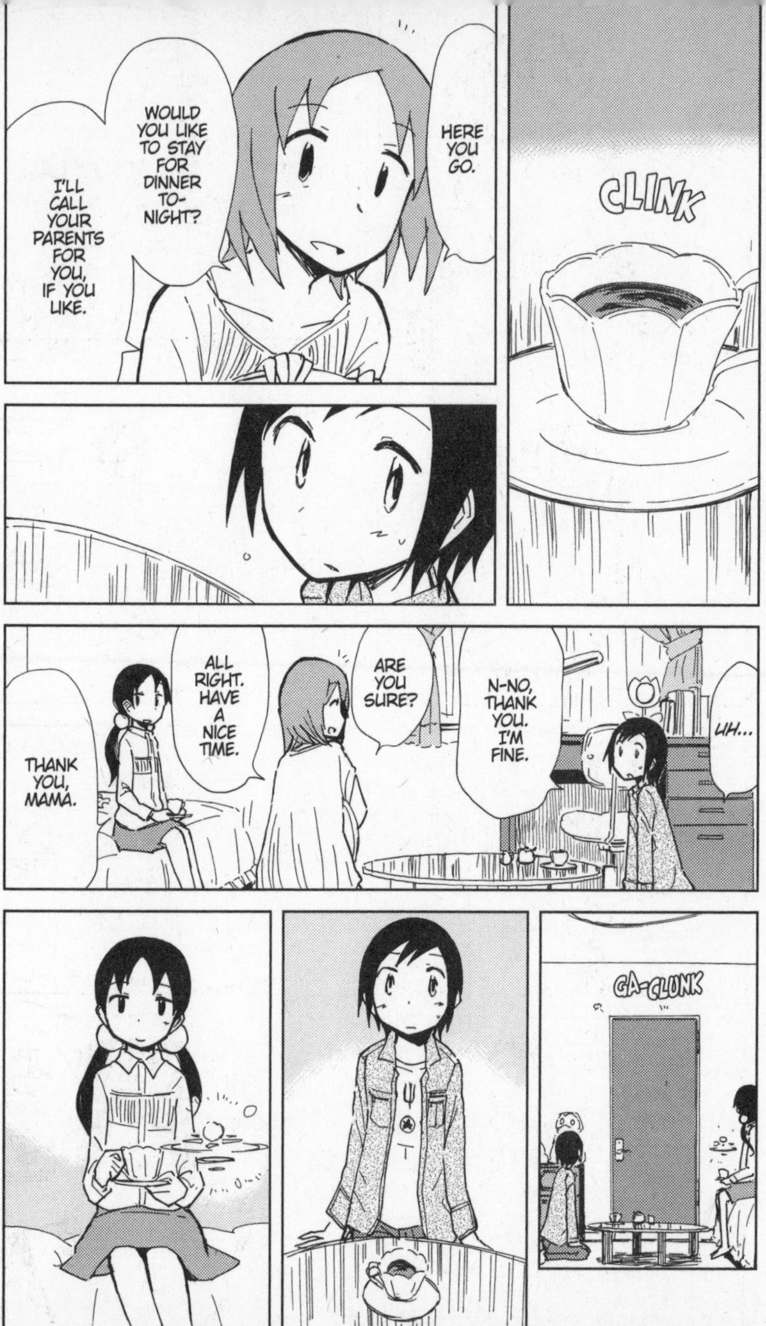
CLINK
HERE YOU GO.
WOULD YOU LIKE TO STAY FOR DINNER TO-NIGHT?
I'LL CALL YOUR PARENTS FOR YOU, IF YOU LIKE.
UH...
N-NO, THANK YOU. I'M FINE.
ARE YOU SURE?
ALL RIGHT. HAVE A NICE TIME.
THANK YOU, MAMA.
GA-CLUNK

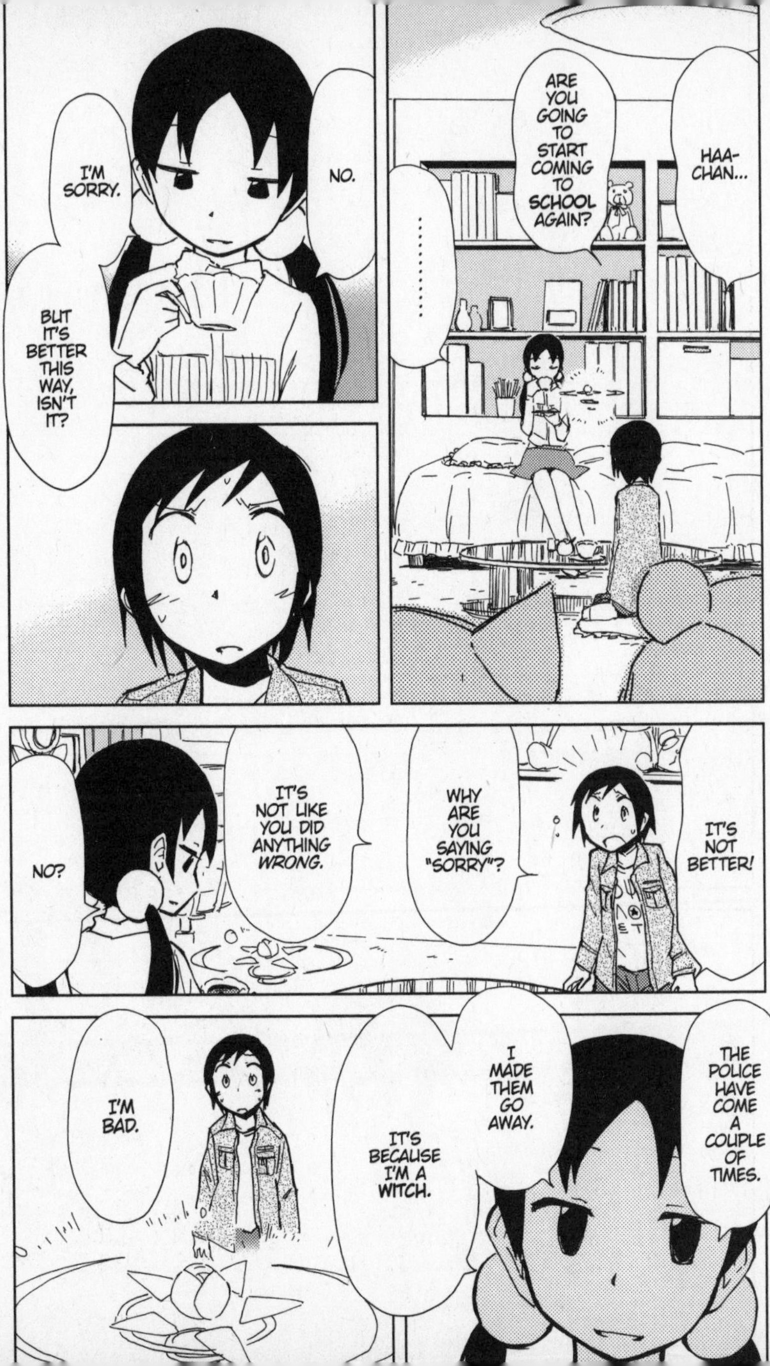
HAA-CHAN...
ARE YOU GOING TO START COMING TO SCHOOL AGAIN?
......
NO.
I'M SORRY.
BUT IT'S BETTER THIS WAY, ISN'T IT?
IT'S NOT BETTER!
WHY ARE YOU SAYING "SORRY"?
IT'S NOT LIKE YOU DID ANYTHING *WRONG*.
NO?
THE POLICE HAVE COME A COUPLE OF TIMES.
I MADE THEM GO AWAY.
IT'S BECAUSE I'M A WITCH.
I'M BAD.

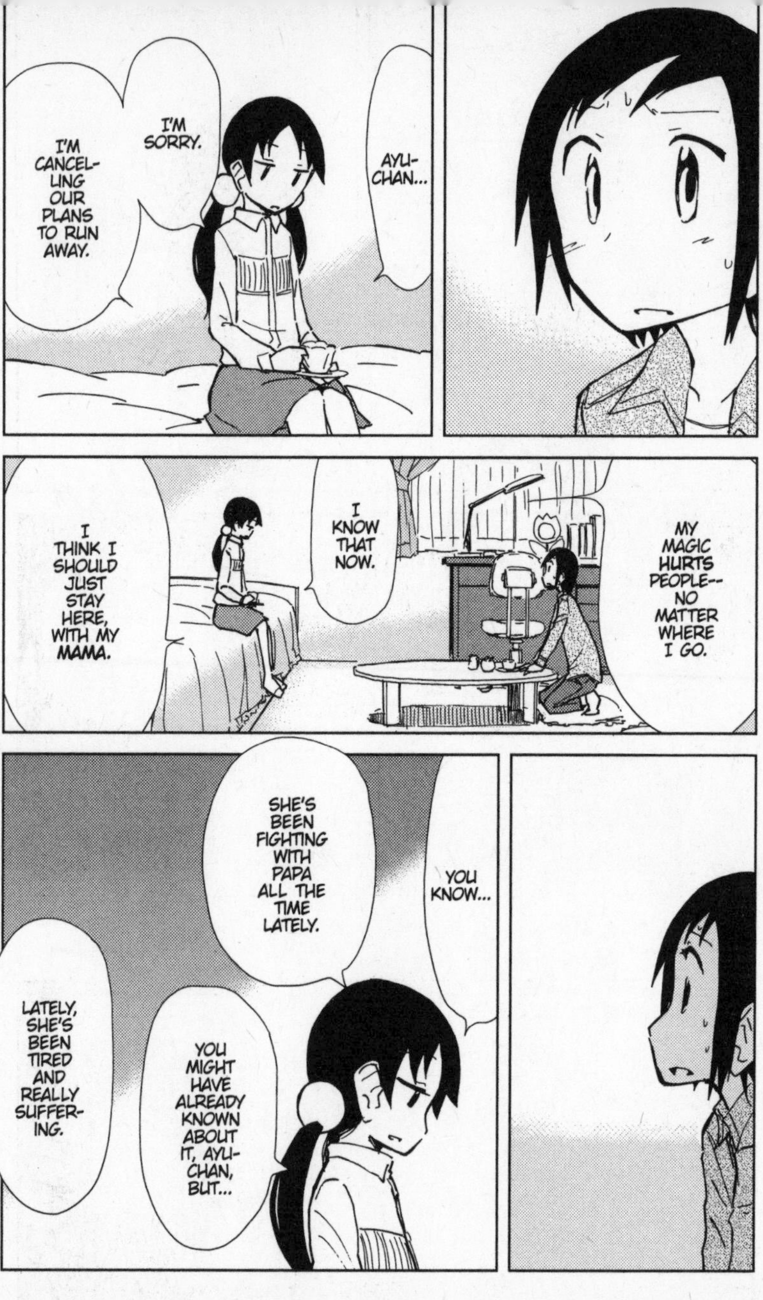
AYU-CHAN...
I'M SORRY.
I'M CANCELLING OUR PLANS TO RUN AWAY.
MY MAGIC HURTS PEOPLE-- NO MATTER WHERE I GO.
I KNOW THAT NOW.
I THINK I SHOULD JUST STAY HERE, WITH MY MAMA.
YOU KNOW...
SHE'S BEEN FIGHTING WITH PAPA ALL THE TIME LATELY.
YOU MIGHT HAVE ALREADY KNOWN ABOUT IT, AYU-CHAN, BUT...
LATELY, SHE'S BEEN TIRED AND REALLY SUFFERING.

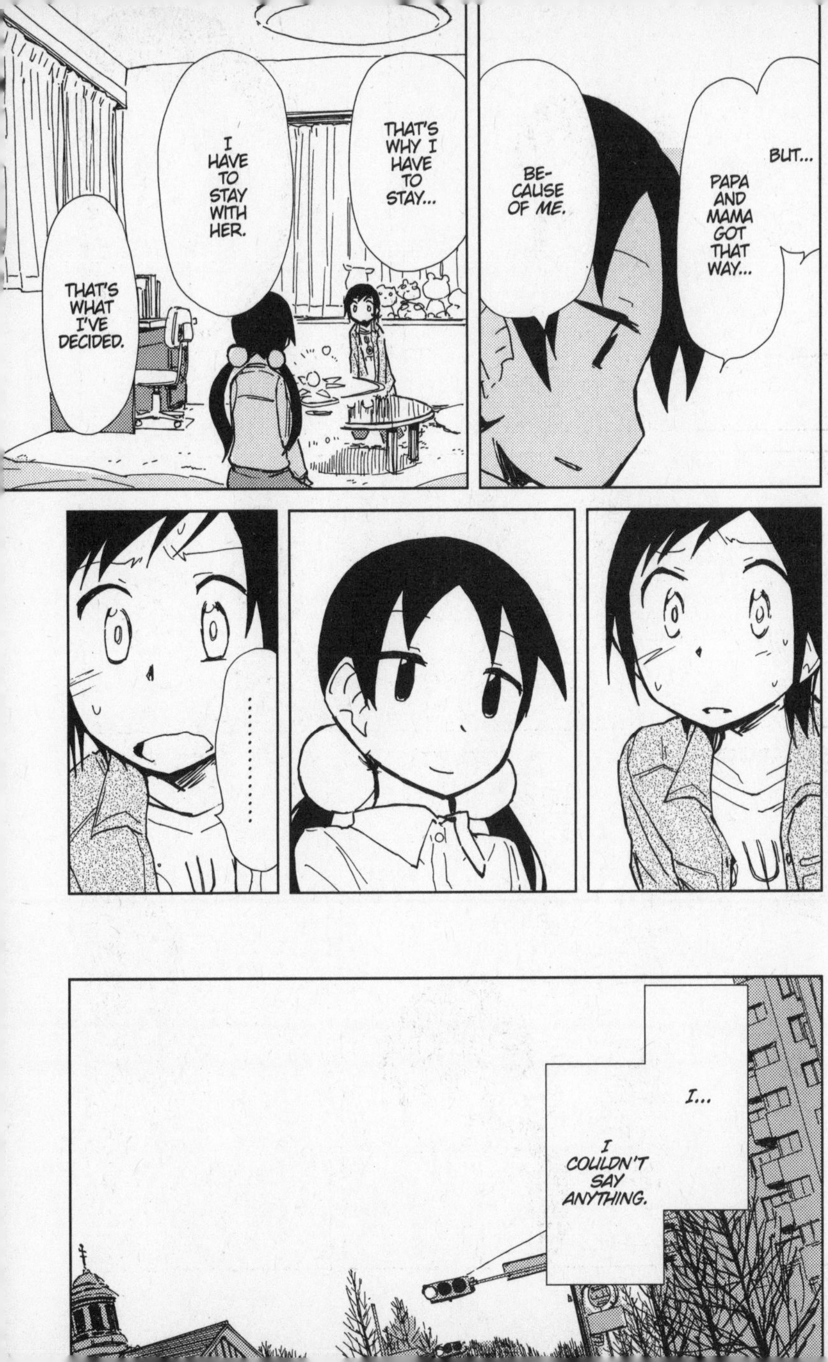
BUT...
PAPA AND MAMA GOT THAT WAY...
BE-CAUSE OF ME.
THAT'S WHY I HAVE TO STAY...
I HAVE TO STAY WITH HER.
THAT'S WHAT I'VE DECIDED.
......
I...
I COULDN'T SAY ANYTHING.

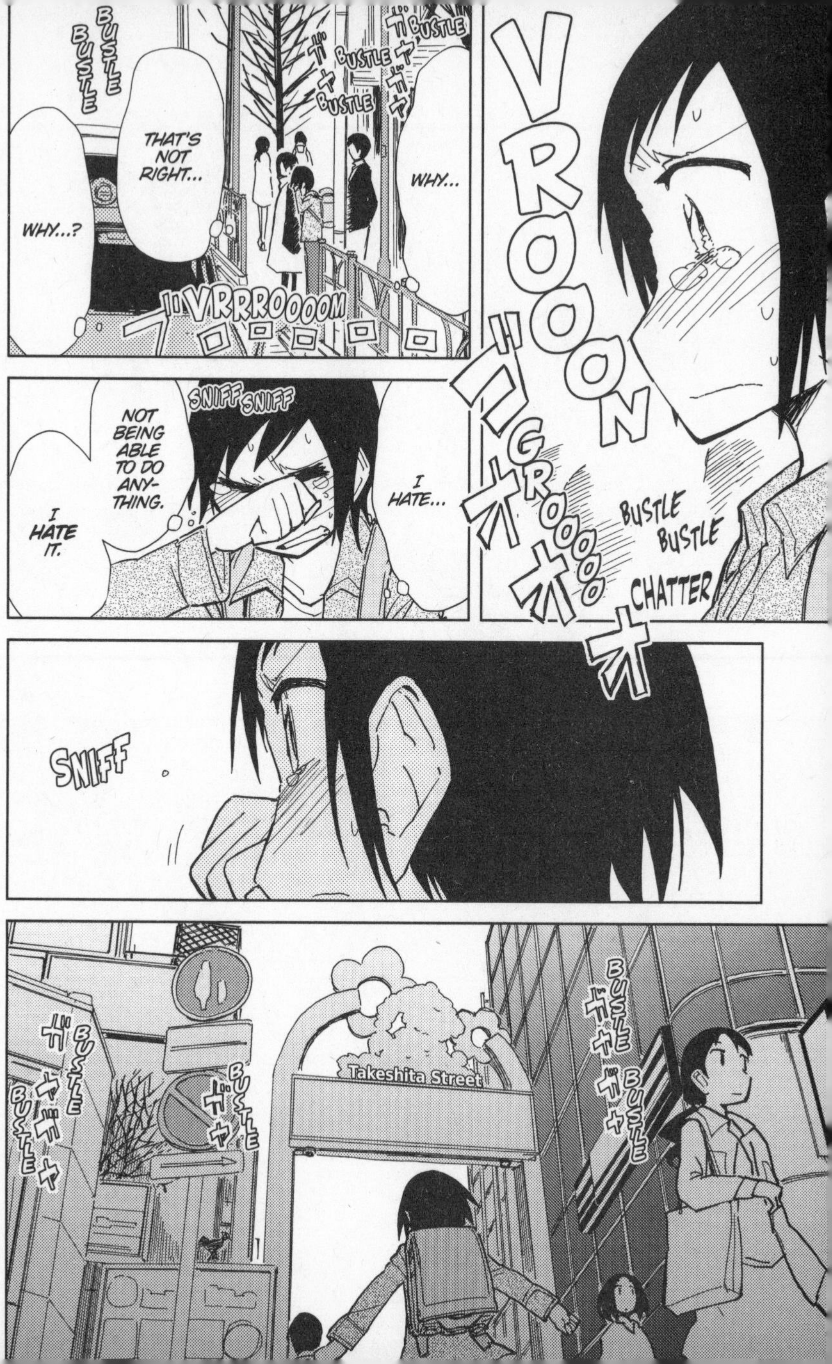
VROOOON
GROOOOOO
BUSTLE BUSTLE
CHATTER
BUSTLE BUSTLE
BUSTLE BUSTLE
WHY...
THAT'S NOT RIGHT...
BUSTLE BUSTLE
WHY...?
VRRROOOOM
I HATE...
SNIFF SNIFF
NOT BEING ABLE TO DO ANY-THING.
I HATE IT.
SNIFF
BUSTLE BUSTLE
Takeshita Street
BUSTLE BUSTLE
BUSTLE BUSTLE

Alice & Zoroku

INTERLUDE

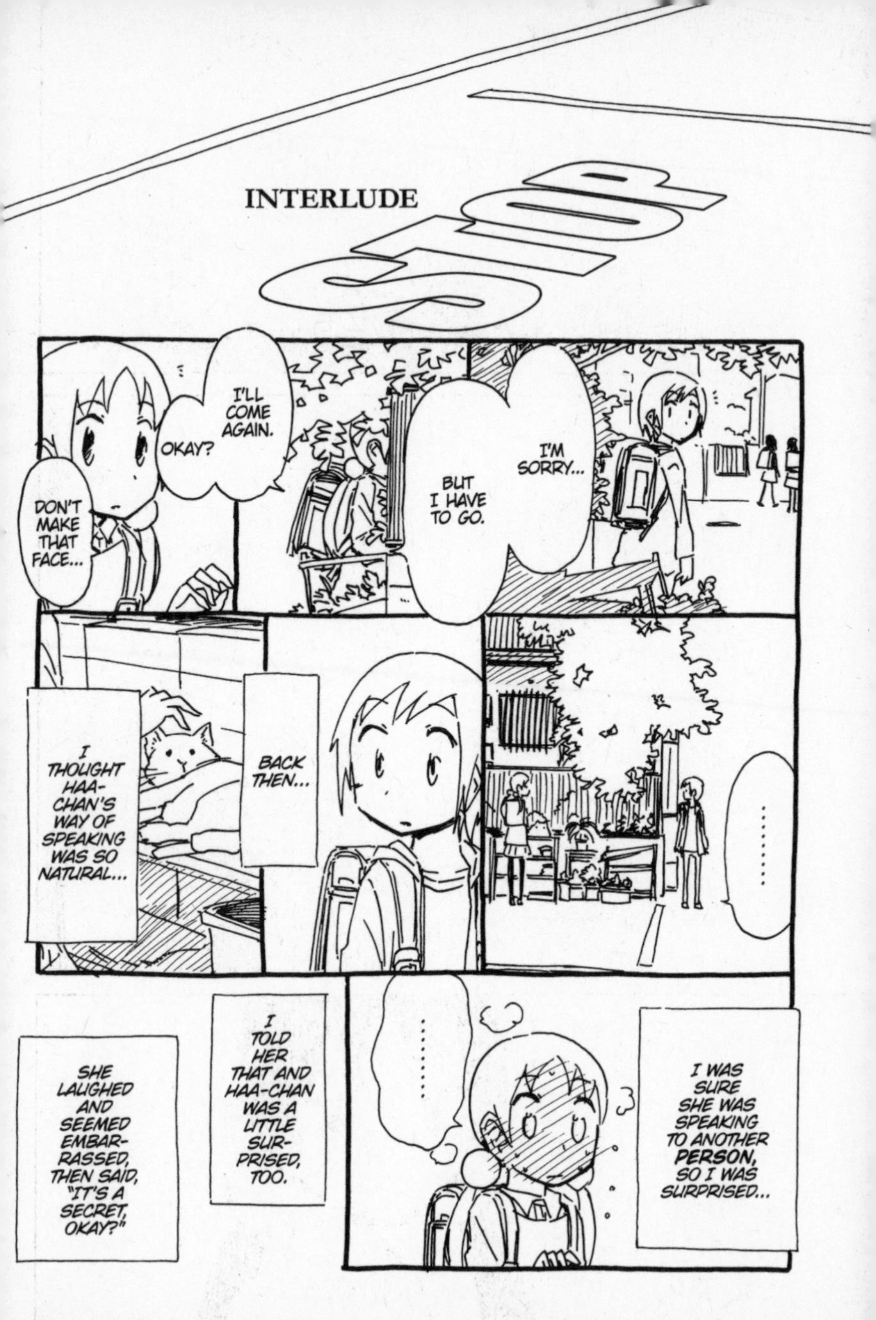

STOP
I'M SORRY...
BUT I HAVE TO GO.
I'LL COME AGAIN.
OKAY?
DON'T MAKE THAT FACE...
......
BACK THEN...
I THOUGHT HAA-CHAN'S WAY OF SPEAKING WAS SO NATURAL...
I WAS SURE SHE WAS SPEAKING TO ANOTHER **PERSON**, SO I WAS SURPRISED...
......
I TOLD HER THAT AND HAA-CHAN WAS A LITTLE SURPRISED, TOO.
SHE LAUGHED AND SEEMED EMBARRASSED, THEN SAID, "IT'S A SECRET, OKAY?"

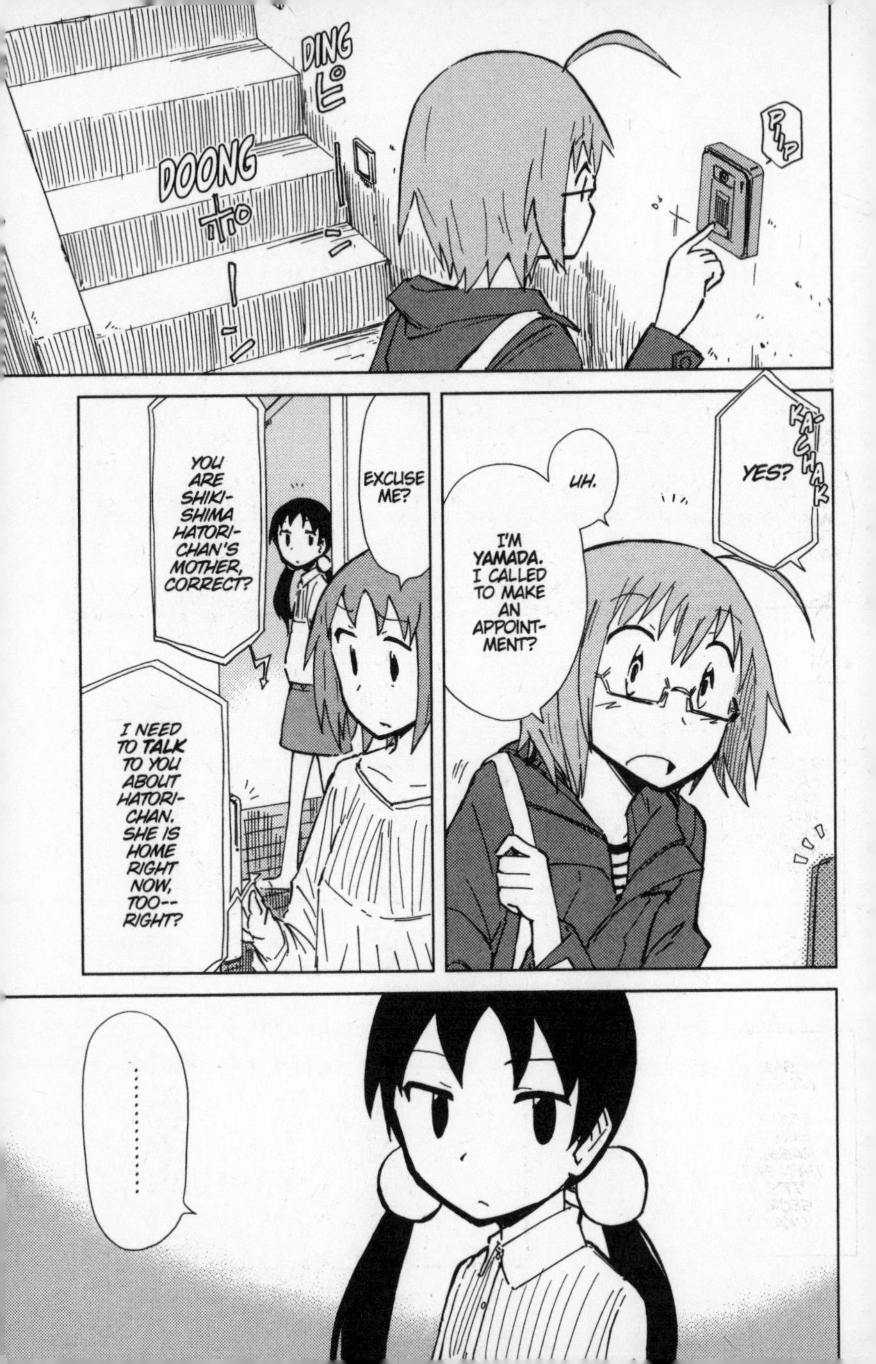
PIP
DING ピ
DOONG ポ
KA'CHAK
YES?
UH.
I'M YAMADA. I CALLED TO MAKE AN APPOINTMENT?
EXCUSE ME?
YOU ARE SHIKISHIMA HATORI-CHAN'S MOTHER, CORRECT?
I NEED TO TALK TO YOU ABOUT HATORI-CHAN. SHE IS HOME RIGHT NOW, TOO--RIGHT?
......

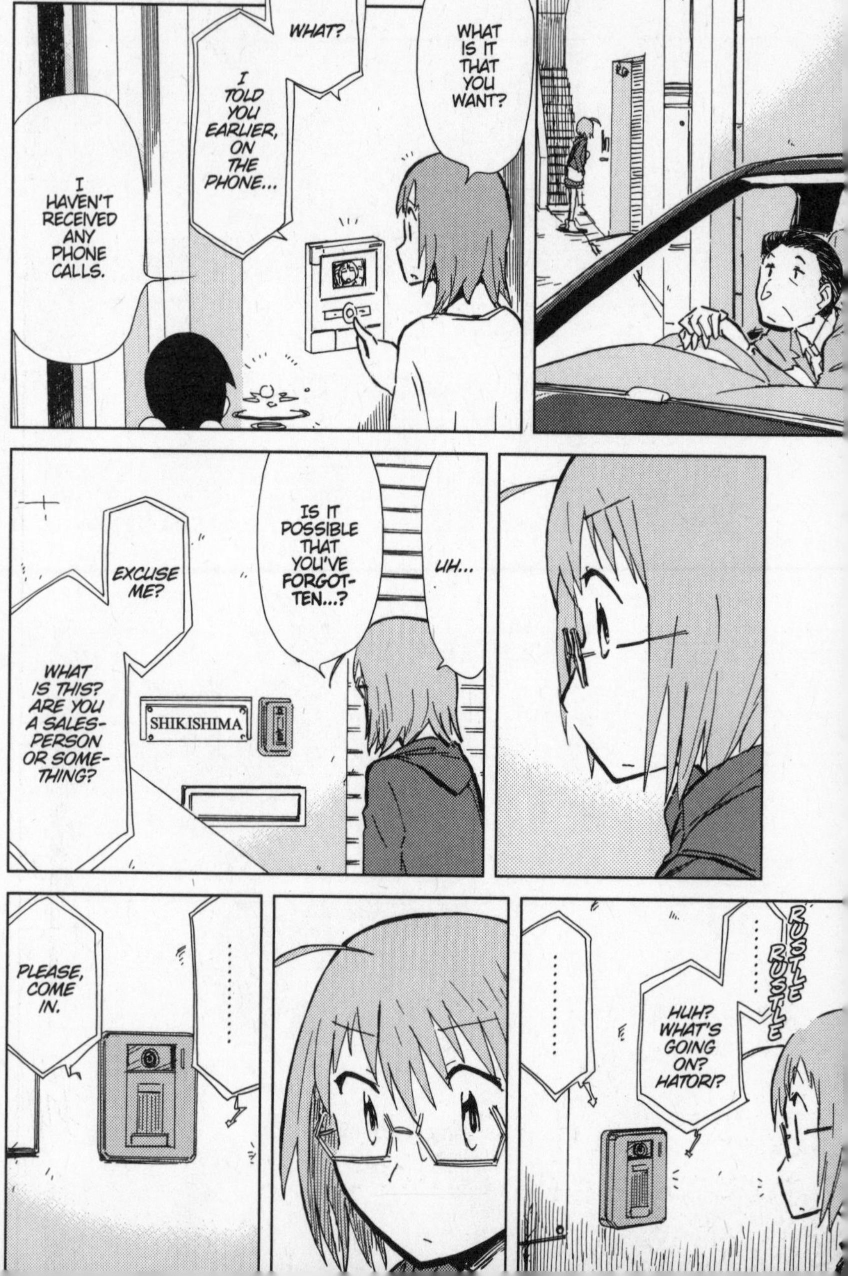
WHAT IS IT THAT YOU WANT?
WHAT? I TOLD YOU EARLIER, ON THE PHONE...
I HAVEN'T RECEIVED ANY PHONE CALLS.
UH...
IS IT POSSIBLE THAT YOU'VE FORGOT-TEN...?
EXCUSE ME?
SHIKISHIMA
WHAT IS THIS? ARE YOU A SALES-PERSON OR SOME-THING?
RUSTLE RUSTLE
......
HUH? WHAT'S GOING ON? HATORI?
......
......
PLEASE, COME IN.

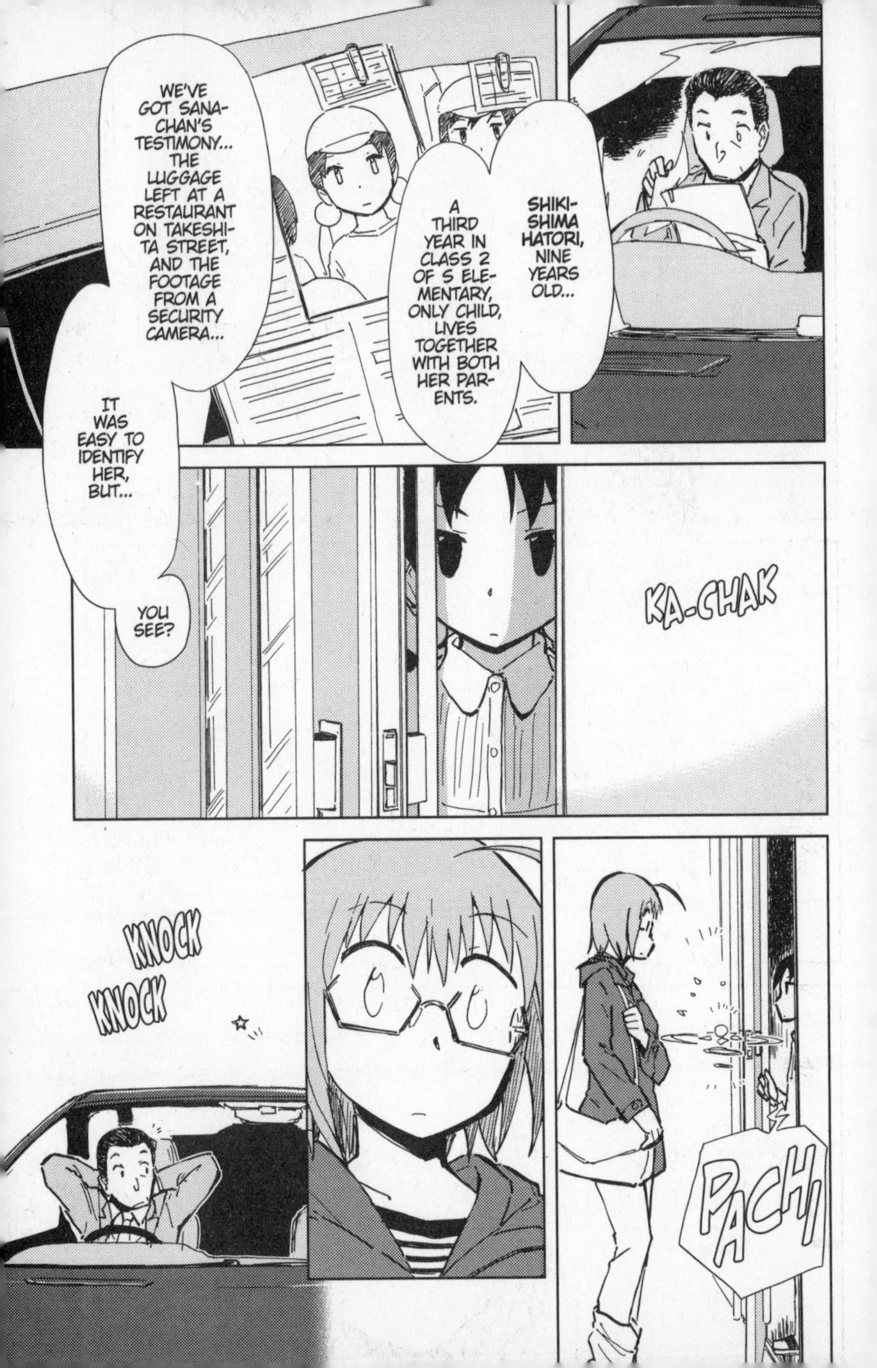
SHIKISHIMA HATORI, NINE YEARS OLD...
A THIRD YEAR IN CLASS 2 OF S ELEMENTARY, ONLY CHILD, LIVES TOGETHER WITH BOTH HER PARENTS.
WE'VE GOT SANA-CHAN'S TESTIMONY... THE LUGGAGE LEFT AT A RESTAURANT ON TAKESHITA STREET, AND THE FOOTAGE FROM A SECURITY CAMERA...
IT WAS EASY TO IDENTIFY HER, BUT...
YOU SEE?
KA-CHAK
PACHI
KNOCK
KNOCK

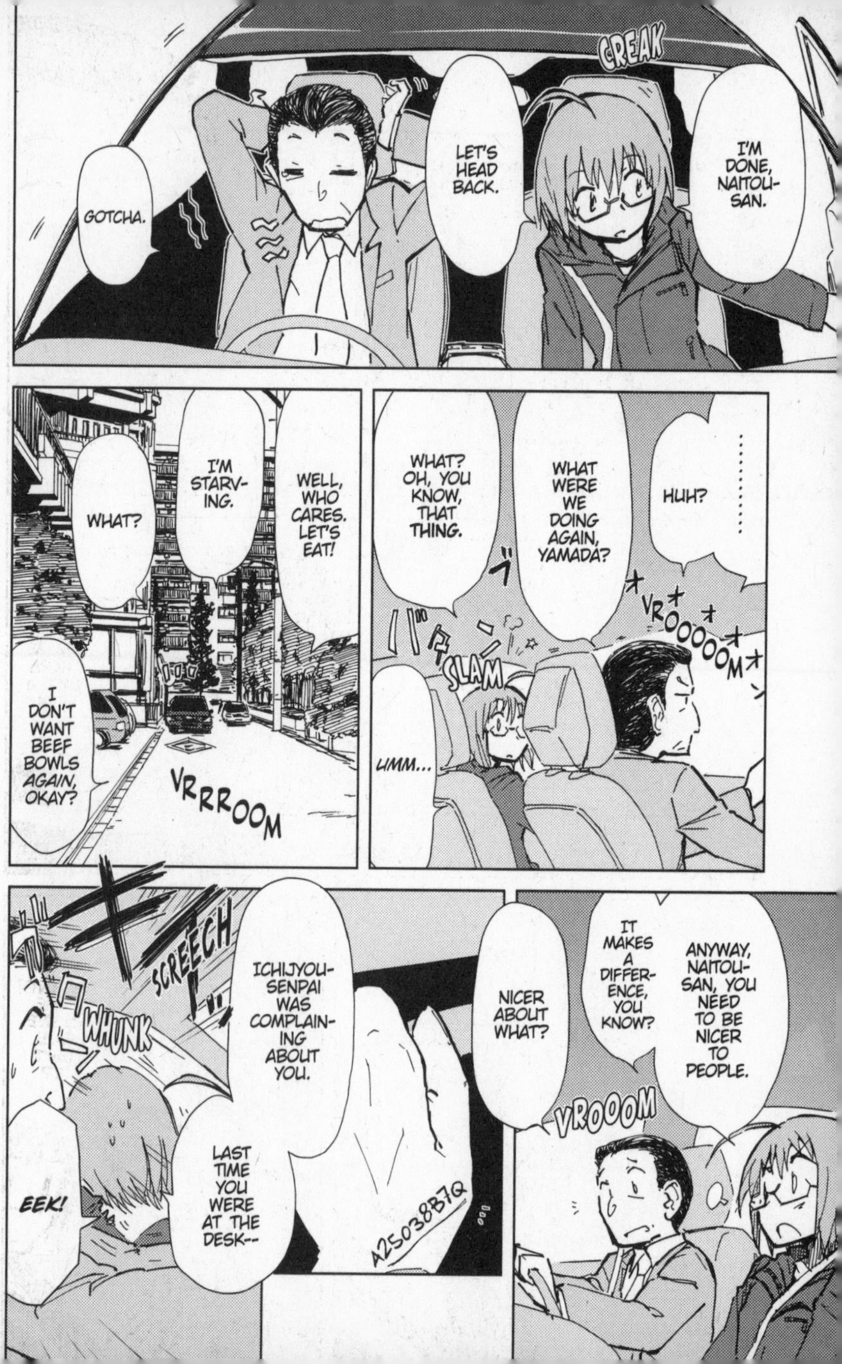
CREAK
I'M DONE, NAITOU-SAN.
LET'S HEAD BACK.
GOTCHA.
......
HUH?
WHAT WERE WE DOING AGAIN, YAMADA?
WHAT? OH, YOU KNOW, THAT THING.
VROOOOOM
SLAM
UMM...
WELL, WHO CARES. LET'S EAT!
I'M STARV-ING.
WHAT?
I DON'T WANT BEEF BOWLS AGAIN, OKAY?
VRRROOM
ANYWAY, NAITOU-SAN, YOU NEED TO BE NICER TO PEOPLE.
IT MAKES A DIFFER-ENCE, YOU KNOW?
NICER ABOUT WHAT?
VROOOM
ICHIJYOU-SENPAI WAS COMPLAIN-ING ABOUT YOU.
SCREECH
LAST TIME YOU WERE AT THE DESK--
A25038B7Q
WHUNK
EEK!

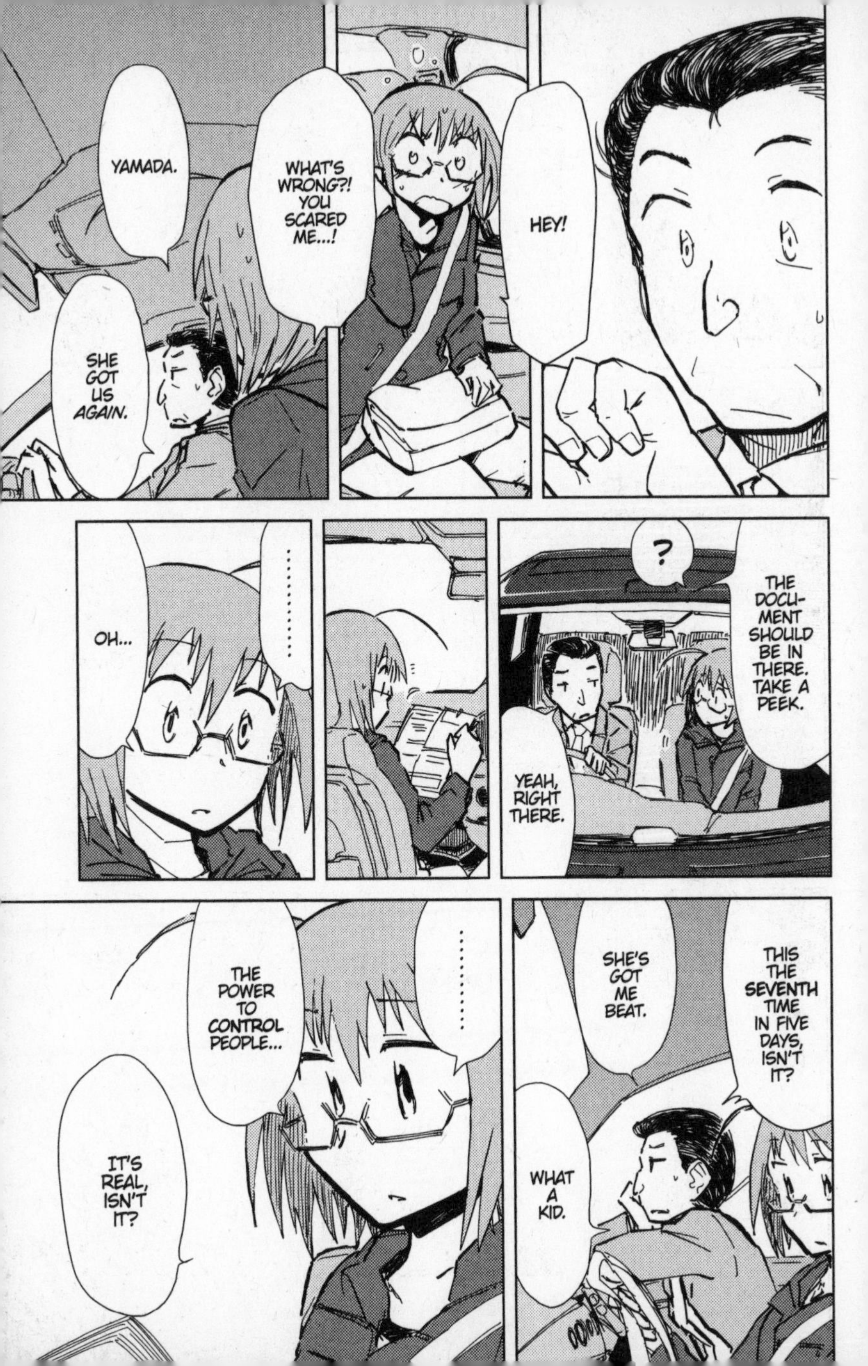
HEY!
WHAT'S WRONG?! YOU SCARED ME...!
YAMADA.
SHE GOT US AGAIN.
THE DOCU-MENT SHOULD BE IN THERE. TAKE A PEEK.
?
YEAH, RIGHT THERE.
....
OH...
THIS THE SEVENTH TIME IN FIVE DAYS, ISN'T IT?
SHE'S GOT ME BEAT.
WHAT A KID.
....
THE POWER TO CONTROL PEOPLE...
IT'S REAL, ISN'T IT?

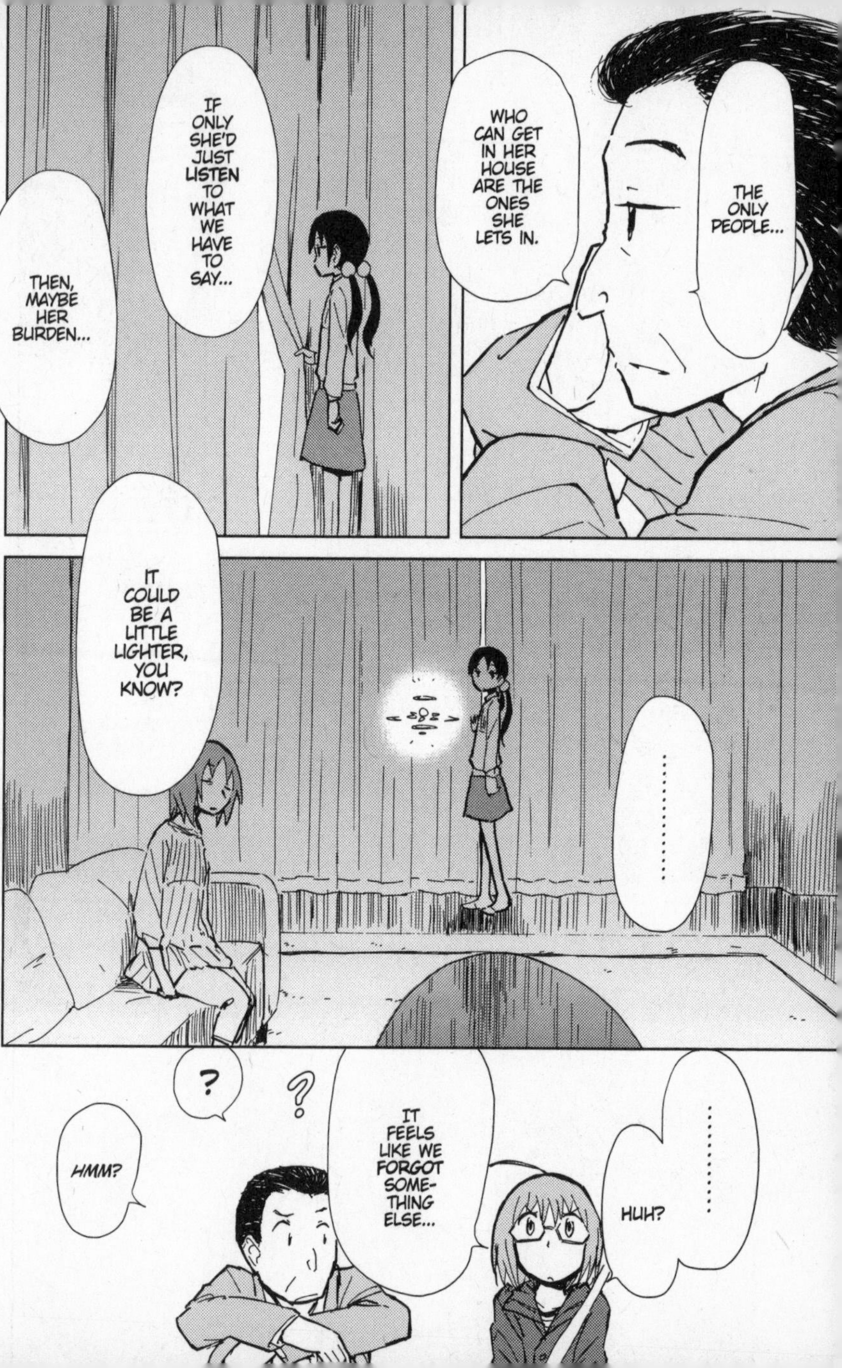
THE ONLY PEOPLE...
WHO CAN GET IN HER HOUSE ARE THE ONES SHE LETS IN.
IF ONLY SHE'D JUST LISTEN TO WHAT WE HAVE TO SAY...
THEN, MAYBE HER BURDEN...
IT COULD BE A LITTLE LIGHTER, YOU KNOW?
......
......
HUH?
IT FEELS LIKE WE FORGOT SOME-THING ELSE...
?
?
HMM?

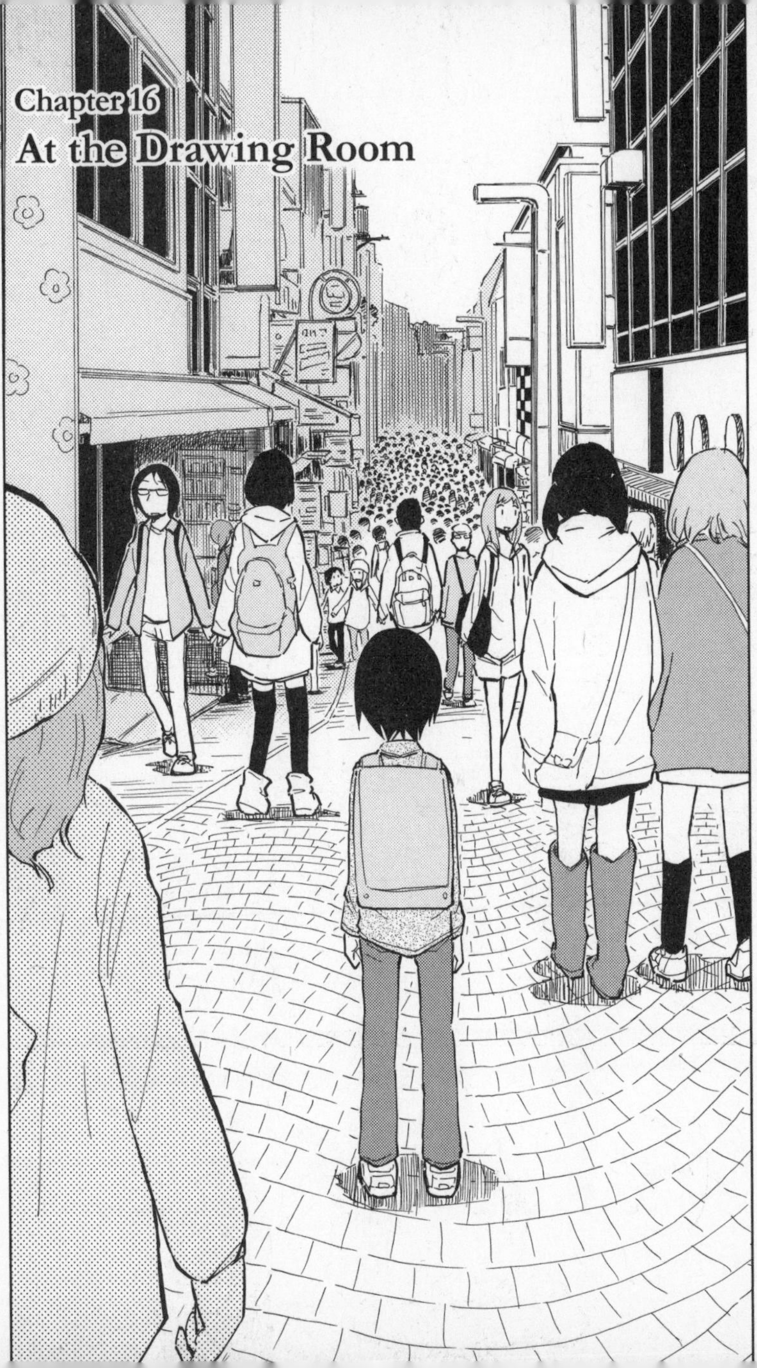
Chapter 16
At the Drawing Room

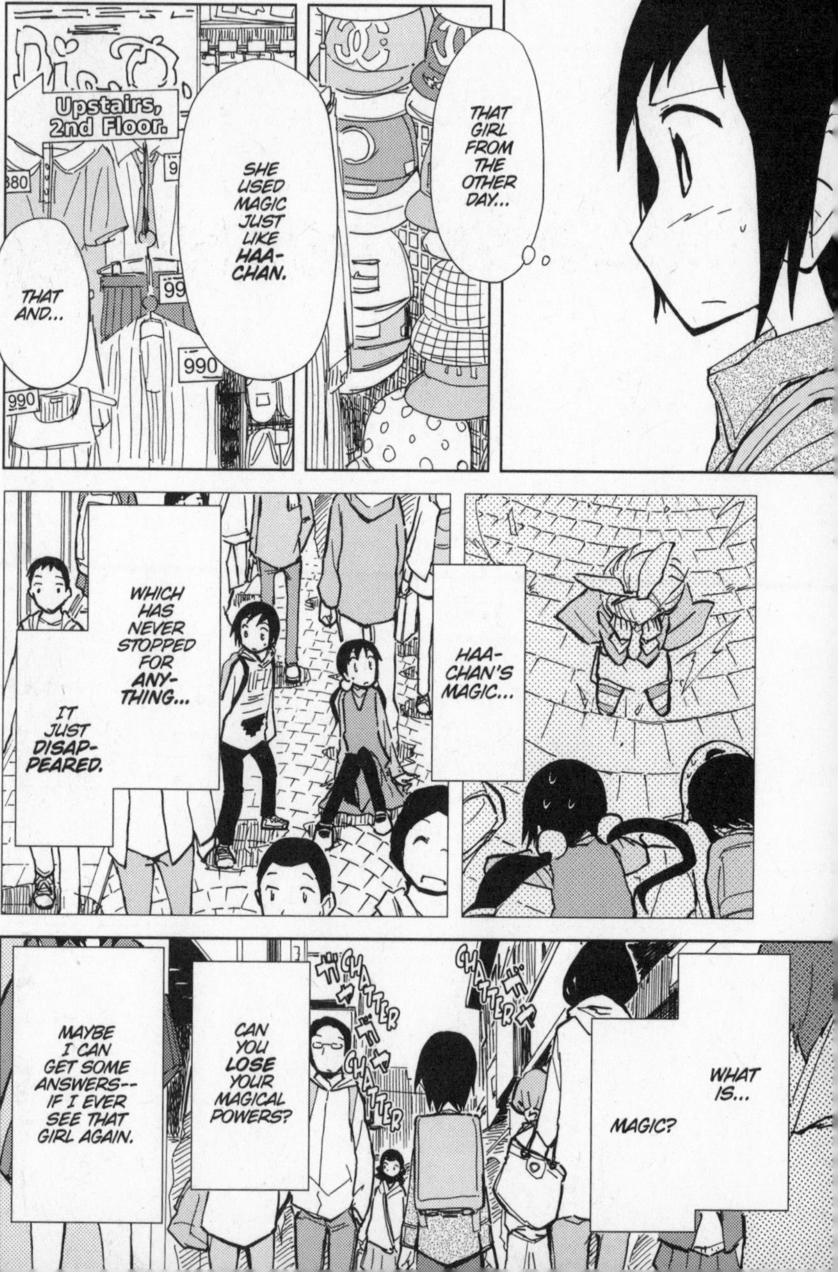
THAT GIRL FROM THE OTHER DAY...
SHE USED MAGIC JUST LIKE HAA-CHAN.
Upstairs, 2nd Floor.
THAT AND...
HAA-CHAN'S MAGIC...
WHICH HAS NEVER STOPPED FOR ANYTHING...
IT JUST DISAPPEARED.
WHAT IS...
MAGIC?
CHATTER
CHATTER
CHATTER
CHATTER
CAN YOU LOSE YOUR MAGICAL POWERS?
MAYBE I CAN GET SOME ANSWERS-- IF I EVER SEE THAT GIRL AGAIN.

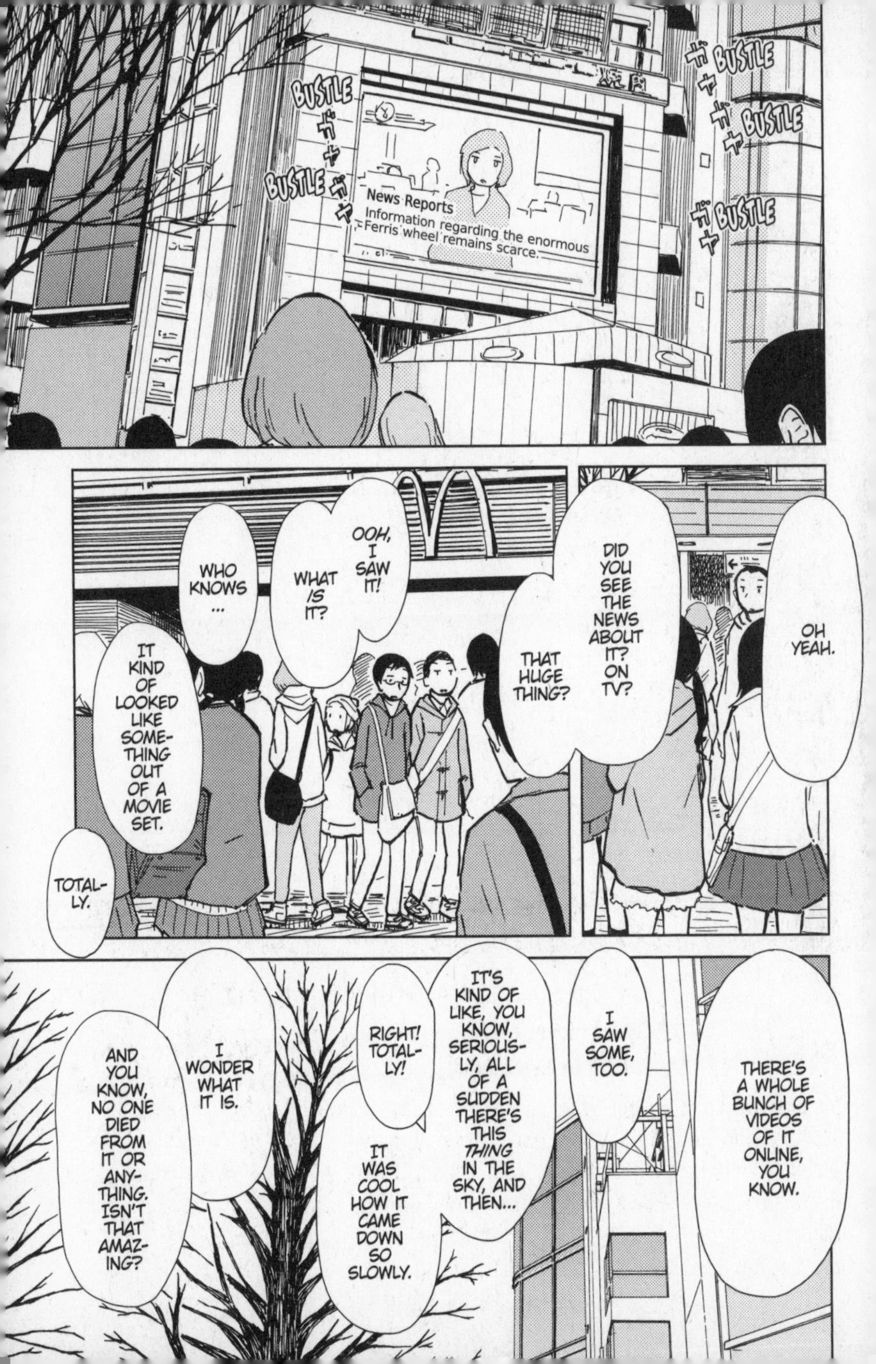

BUSTLE
BUSTLE
BUSTLE
News Reports
Information regarding the enormous Ferris wheel remains scarce.
BUSTLE
BUSTLE
OH YEAH.
DID YOU SEE THE NEWS ABOUT IT? ON TV?
THAT HUGE THING?
OOH, I SAW IT!
WHAT *IS* IT?
WHO KNOWS...
IT KIND OF LOOKED LIKE SOME-THING OUT OF A MOVIE SET.
TOTAL-LY.
THERE'S A WHOLE BUNCH OF VIDEOS OF IT ONLINE, YOU KNOW.
I SAW SOME, TOO.
IT'S KIND OF LIKE, YOU KNOW, SERIOUS-LY, ALL OF A SUDDEN THERE'S THIS *THING* IN THE SKY, AND THEN...
RIGHT! TOTAL-LY!
IT WAS COOL HOW IT CAME DOWN SO SLOWLY.
I WONDER WHAT IT IS.
AND YOU KNOW, NO ONE DIED FROM IT OR ANY-THING. ISN'T THAT AMAZ-ING?

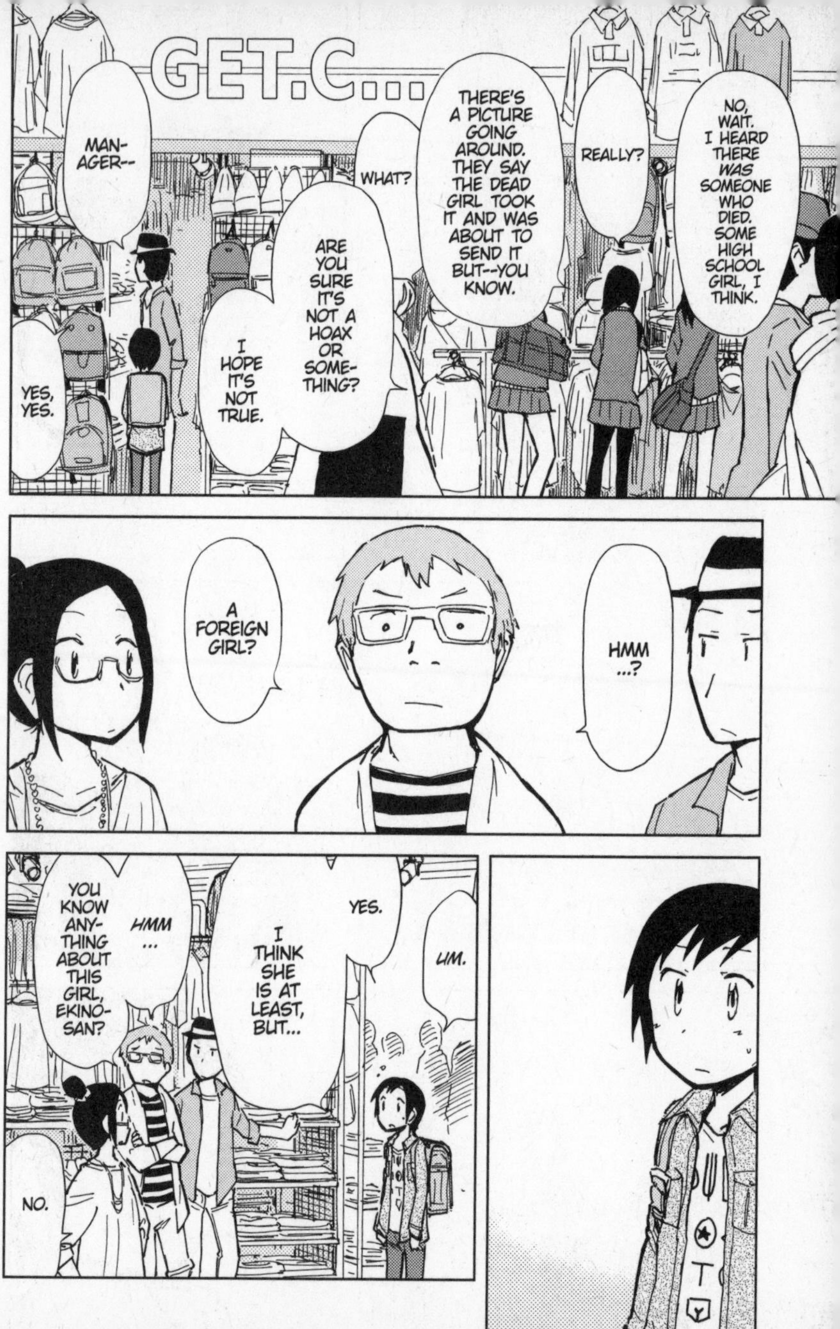
GET.C...
NO, WAIT. I HEARD THERE WAS SOMEONE WHO DIED. SOME HIGH SCHOOL GIRL, I THINK.
REALLY?
THERE'S A PICTURE GOING AROUND. THEY SAY THE DEAD GIRL TOOK IT AND WAS ABOUT TO SEND IT BUT--YOU KNOW.
WHAT?
ARE YOU SURE IT'S NOT A HOAX OR SOME-THING?
MAN-AGER--
I HOPE IT'S NOT TRUE.
YES, YES.
HMM ...?
A FOREIGN GIRL?
UM.
YES.
I THINK SHE IS AT LEAST, BUT...
HMM ...
YOU KNOW ANY-THING ABOUT THIS GIRL, EKINO-SAN?
NO.

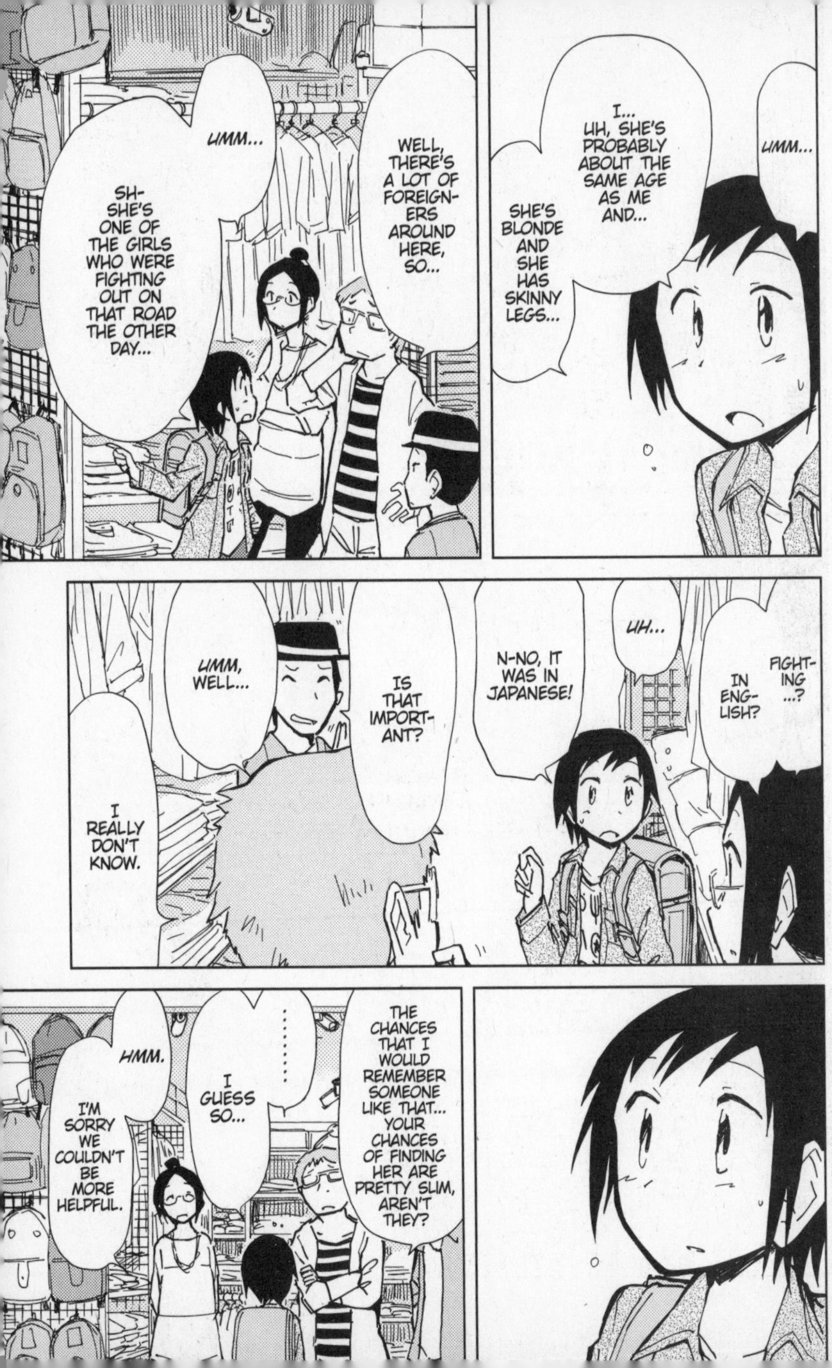
UMM...
I... UH, SHE'S PROBABLY ABOUT THE SAME AGE AS ME AND...
SHE'S BLONDE AND SHE HAS SKINNY LEGS...
WELL, THERE'S A LOT OF FOREIGN-ERS AROUND HERE, SO...
UMM...
SH-SHE'S ONE OF THE GIRLS WHO WERE FIGHTING OUT ON THAT ROAD THE OTHER DAY...
FIGHT-ING ...?
IN ENG-LISH?
UH...
N-NO, IT WAS IN JAPANESE!
IS THAT IMPORT-ANT?
UMM, WELL...
I REALLY DON'T KNOW.
THE CHANCES THAT I WOULD REMEMBER SOMEONE LIKE THAT... YOUR CHANCES OF FINDING HER ARE PRETTY SLIM, AREN'T THEY?
......
I GUESS SO...
HMM.
I'M SORRY WE COULDN'T BE MORE HELPFUL.

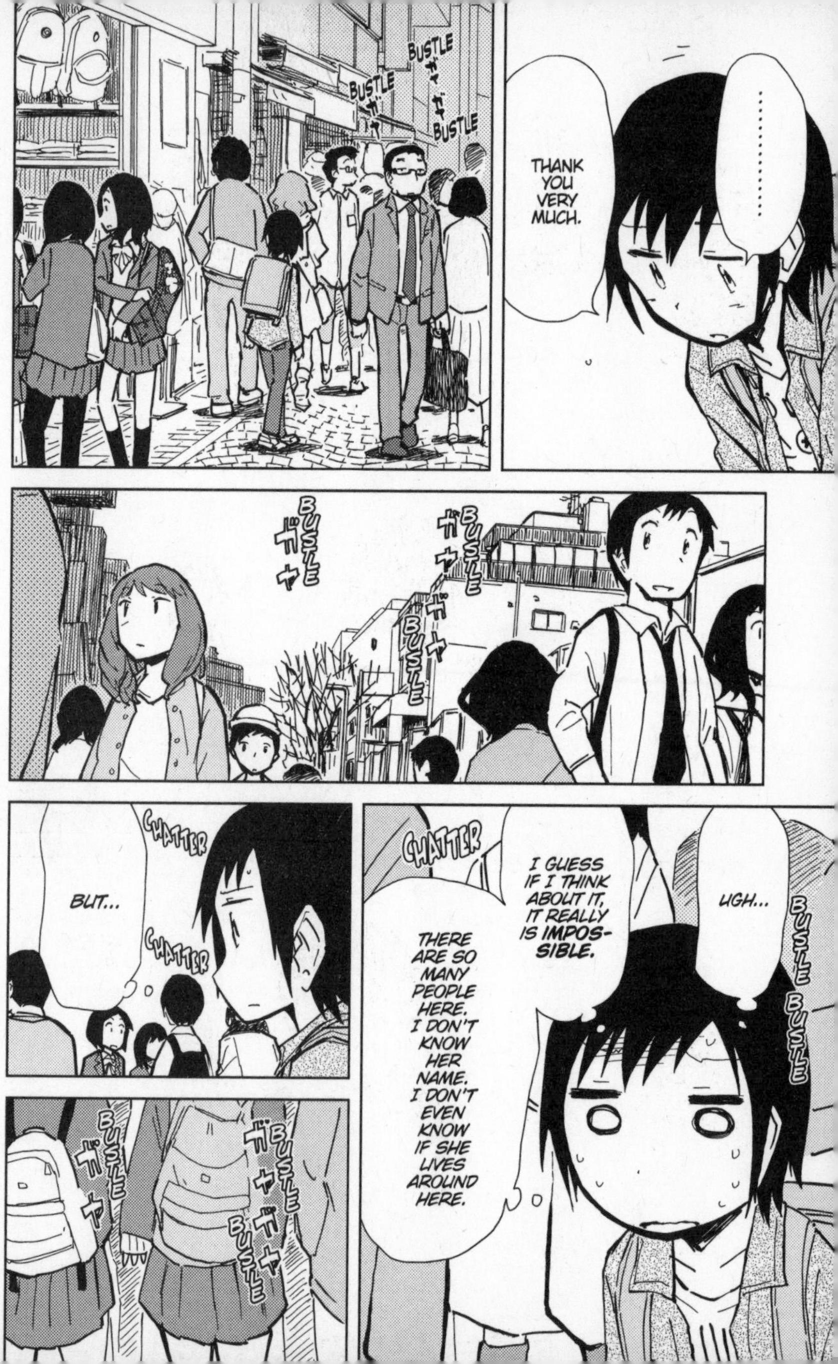
......
THANK YOU VERY MUCH.
BUSTLE
BUSTLE
BUSTLE
BUSTLE
BUSTLE
BUSTLE
UGH...
BUSTLE BUSTLE
I GUESS IF I THINK ABOUT IT, IT REALLY IS IMPOSSIBLE.
THERE ARE SO MANY PEOPLE HERE. I DON'T KNOW HER NAME. I DON'T EVEN KNOW IF SHE LIVES AROUND HERE.
CHATTER
CHATTER
BUT...
CHATTER
BUSTLE
BUSTLE
BUSTLE

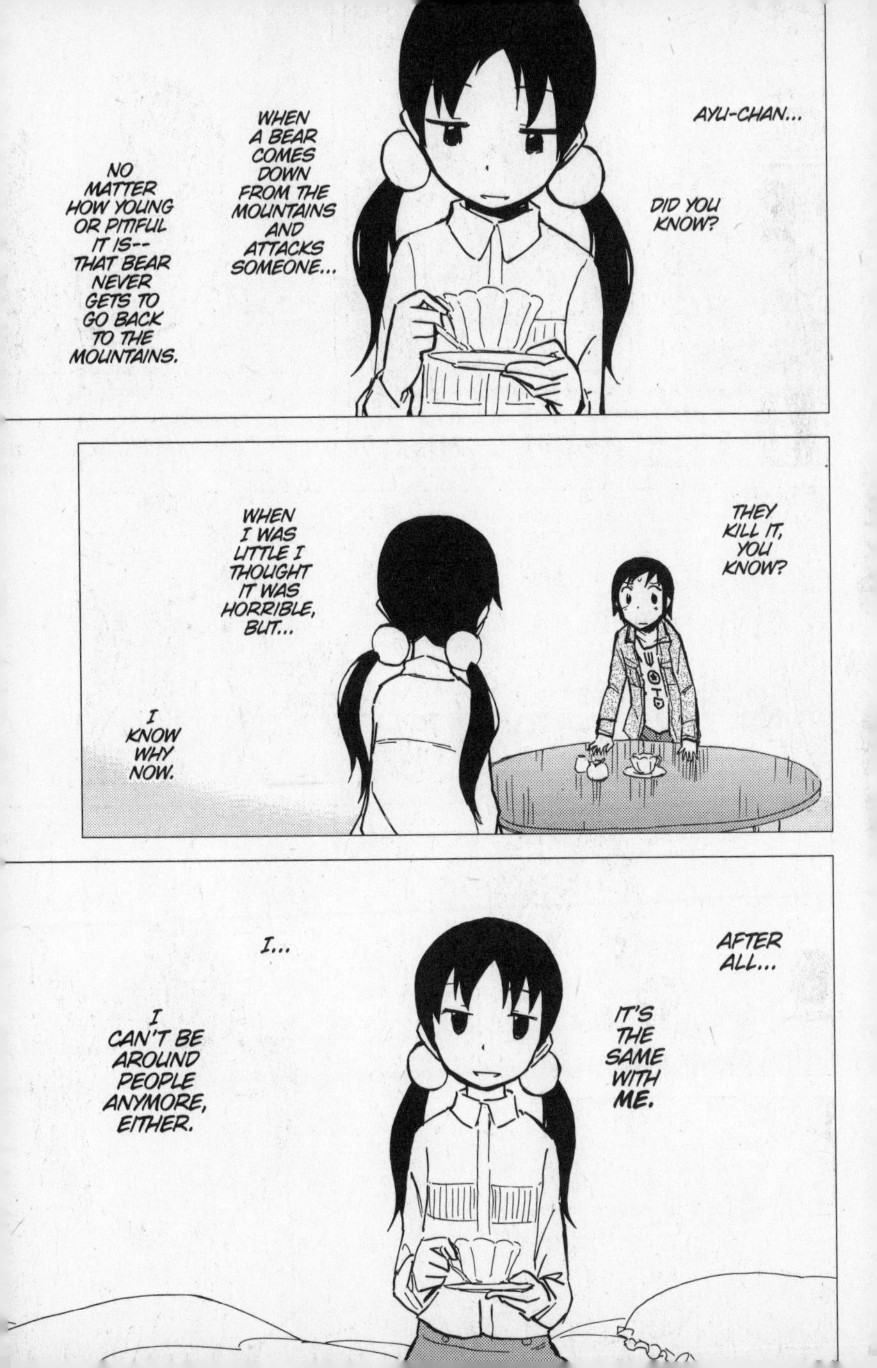
AYU-CHAN...
DID YOU KNOW?
WHEN A BEAR COMES DOWN FROM THE MOUNTAINS AND ATTACKS SOMEONE...
NO MATTER HOW YOUNG OR PITIFUL IT IS-- THAT BEAR NEVER GETS TO GO BACK TO THE MOUNTAINS.
THEY KILL IT, YOU KNOW?
WHEN I WAS LITTLE I THOUGHT IT WAS HORRIBLE, BUT...
I KNOW WHY NOW.
AFTER ALL...
IT'S THE SAME WITH ME.
I...
I CAN'T BE AROUND PEOPLE ANYMORE, EITHER.

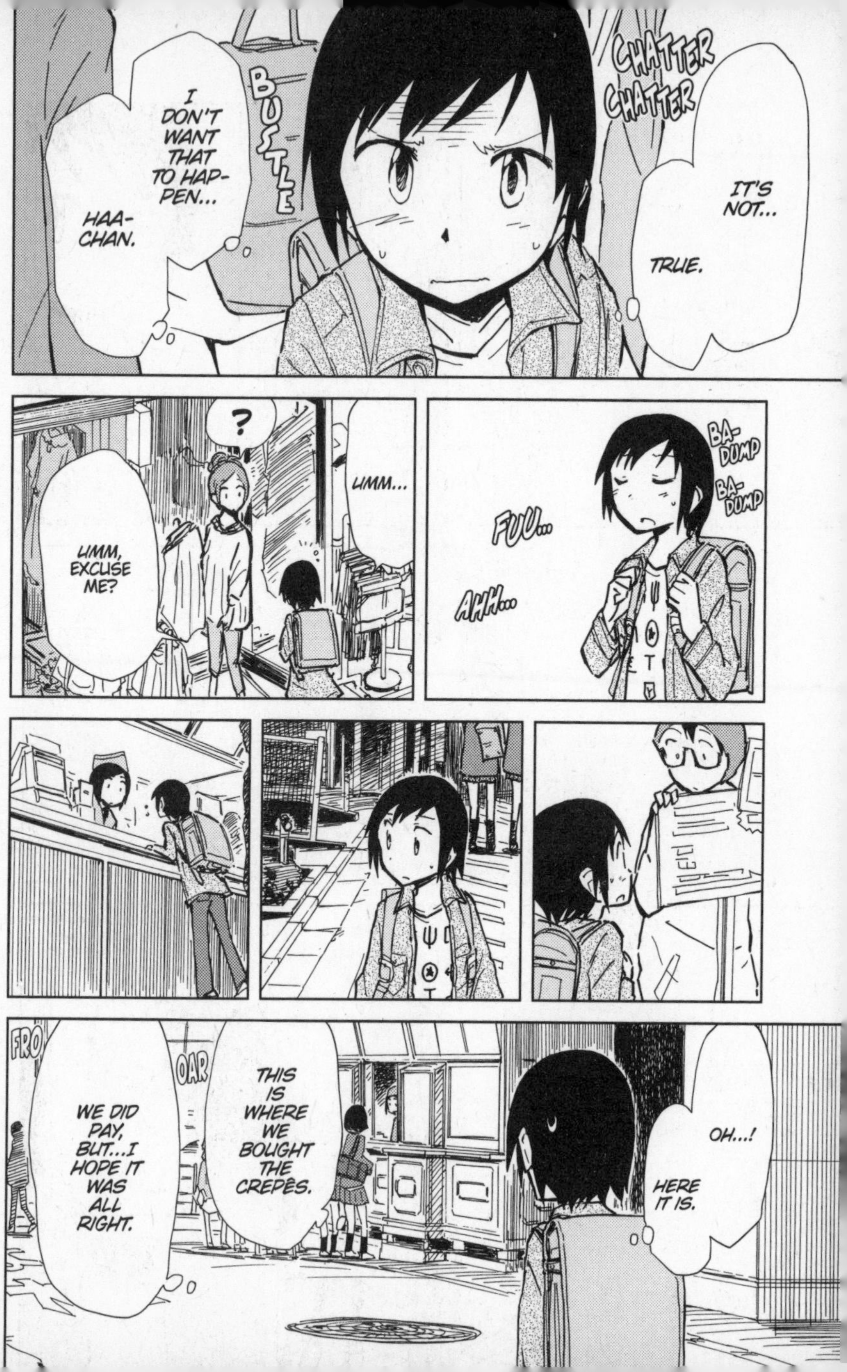
CHATTER CHATTER
IT'S NOT... TRUE.
BUSTLE
I DON'T WANT THAT TO HAP-PEN... HAA-CHAN.
BA-DUMP BA-DUMP
FUU... AHH...
?
UMM...
UMM, EXCUSE ME?
OH...! HERE IT IS.
THIS IS WHERE WE BOUGHT THE CREPES.
OAR
WE DID PAY, BUT...I HOPE IT WAS ALL RIGHT.
FRO

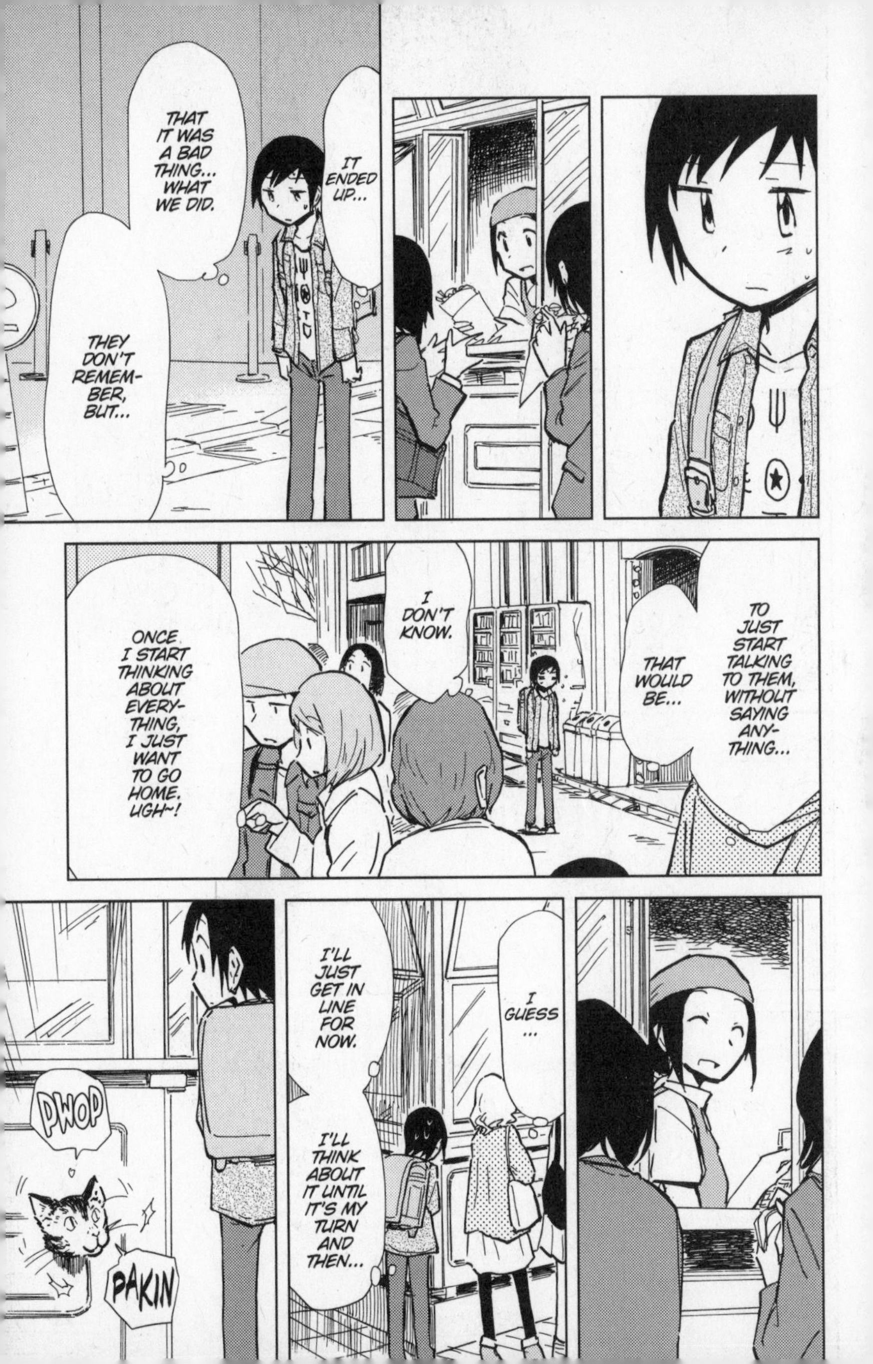
IT ENDED UP...
THAT IT WAS A BAD THING... WHAT WE DID.
THEY DON'T REMEMBER, BUT...
TO JUST START TALKING TO THEM, WITHOUT SAYING ANYTHING...
THAT WOULD BE...
I DON'T KNOW.
ONCE I START THINKING ABOUT EVERYTHING, I JUST WANT TO GO HOME. UGH~!
I GUESS ...
I'LL JUST GET IN LINE FOR NOW.
I'LL THINK ABOUT IT UNTIL IT'S MY TURN AND THEN...
PWOP
PAKIN

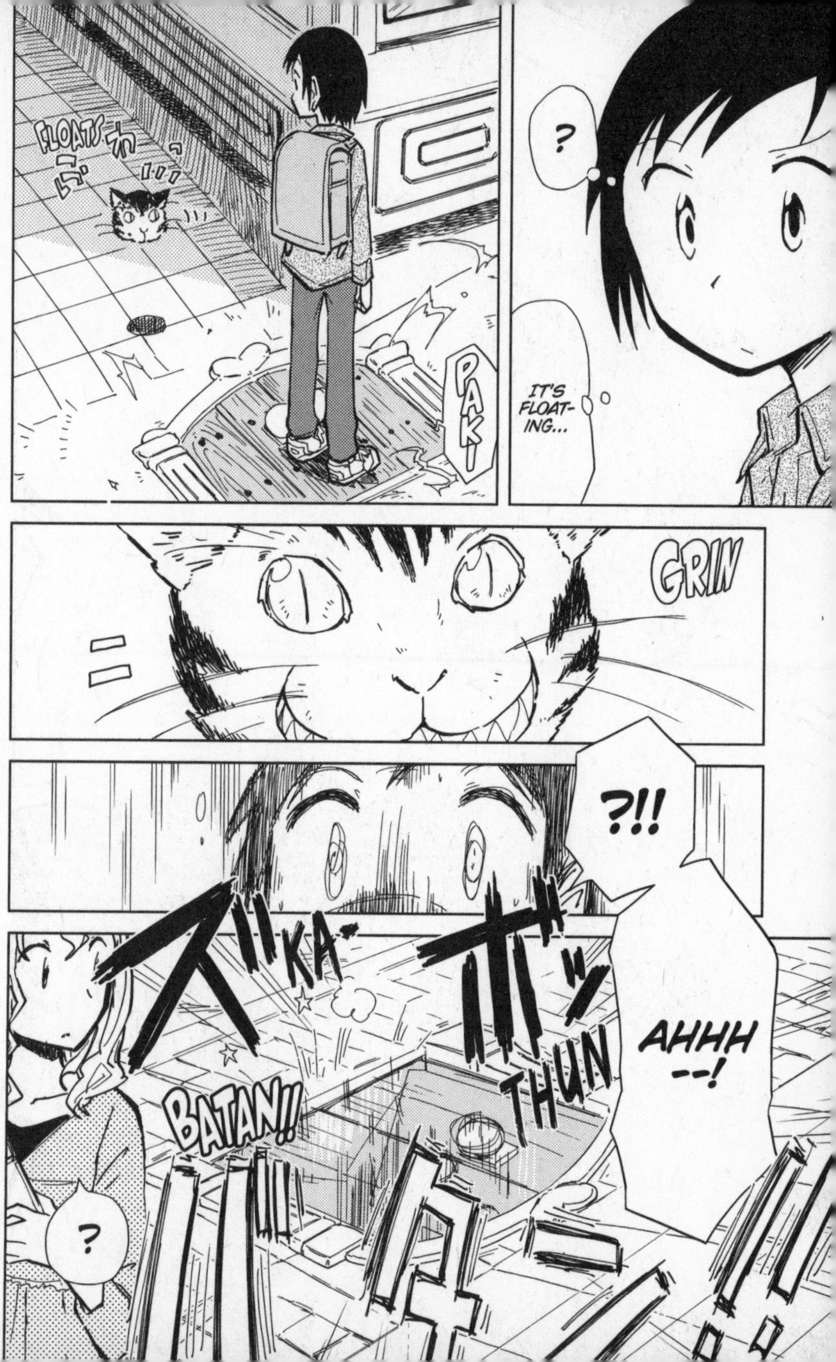
?
IT'S FLOATING...
PAKI
FLOATS
GRIN
?!!
AHHH --!
THUN
KA
BATAN!!
?

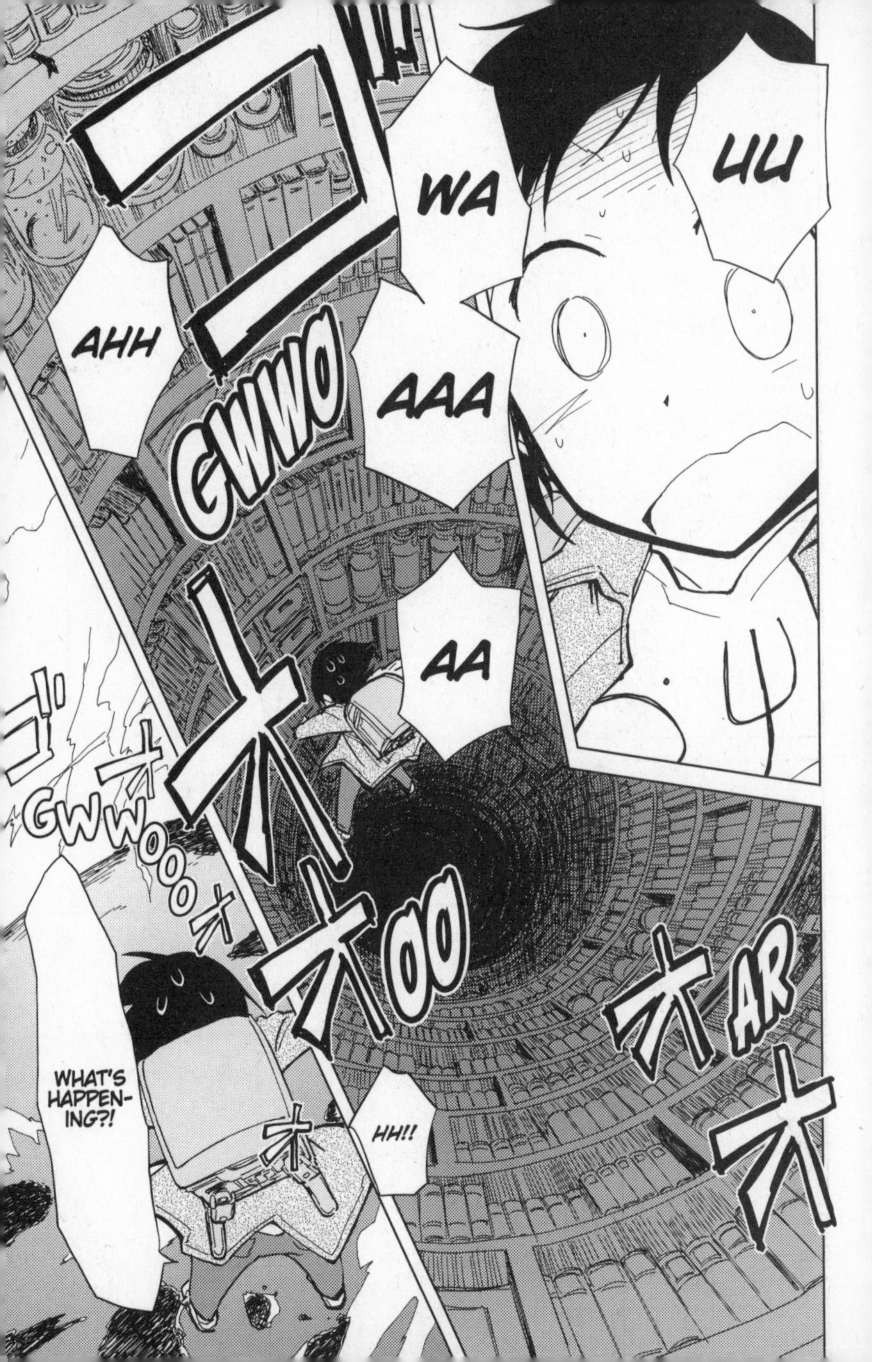
UU
WA
AAA
AA
AHH
GWWO
OO
AR
ゴオオオオ
GWWOOO
HH!!
WHAT'S HAPPEN-ING?!

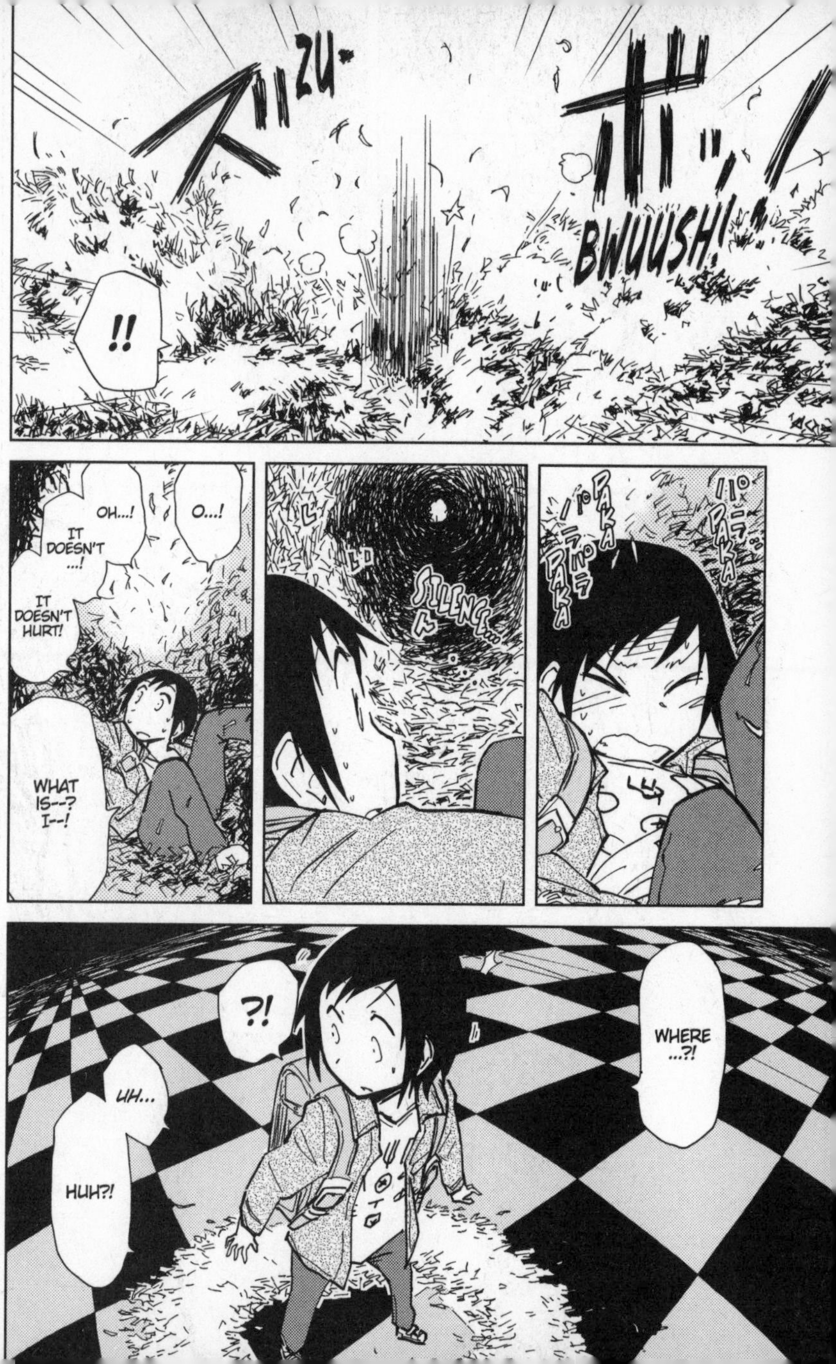

BWUUSH!!
ZU
!!
PAKA
PAKA
PAKA
PAKA
SILENCE...
O...!
OH...!
IT DOESN'T ...!
IT DOESN'T HURT!
WHAT IS--? I--!
WHERE ...?!
?!
UH...
HUH?!

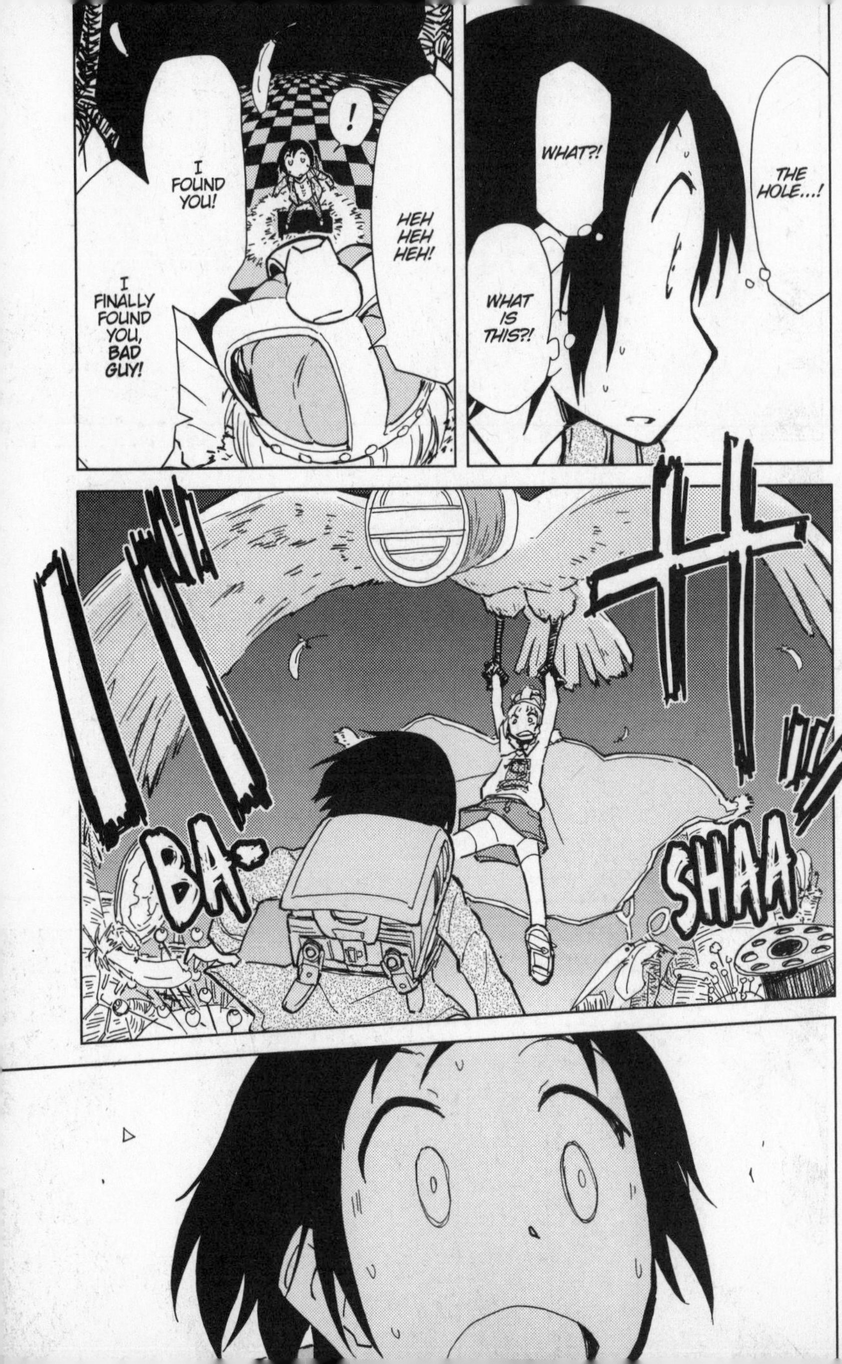
THE HOLE...!
WHAT?!
WHAT IS THIS?!
!
HEH HEH HEH!
I FOUND YOU!
I FINALLY FOUND YOU, BAD GUY!
BA-
SHAA

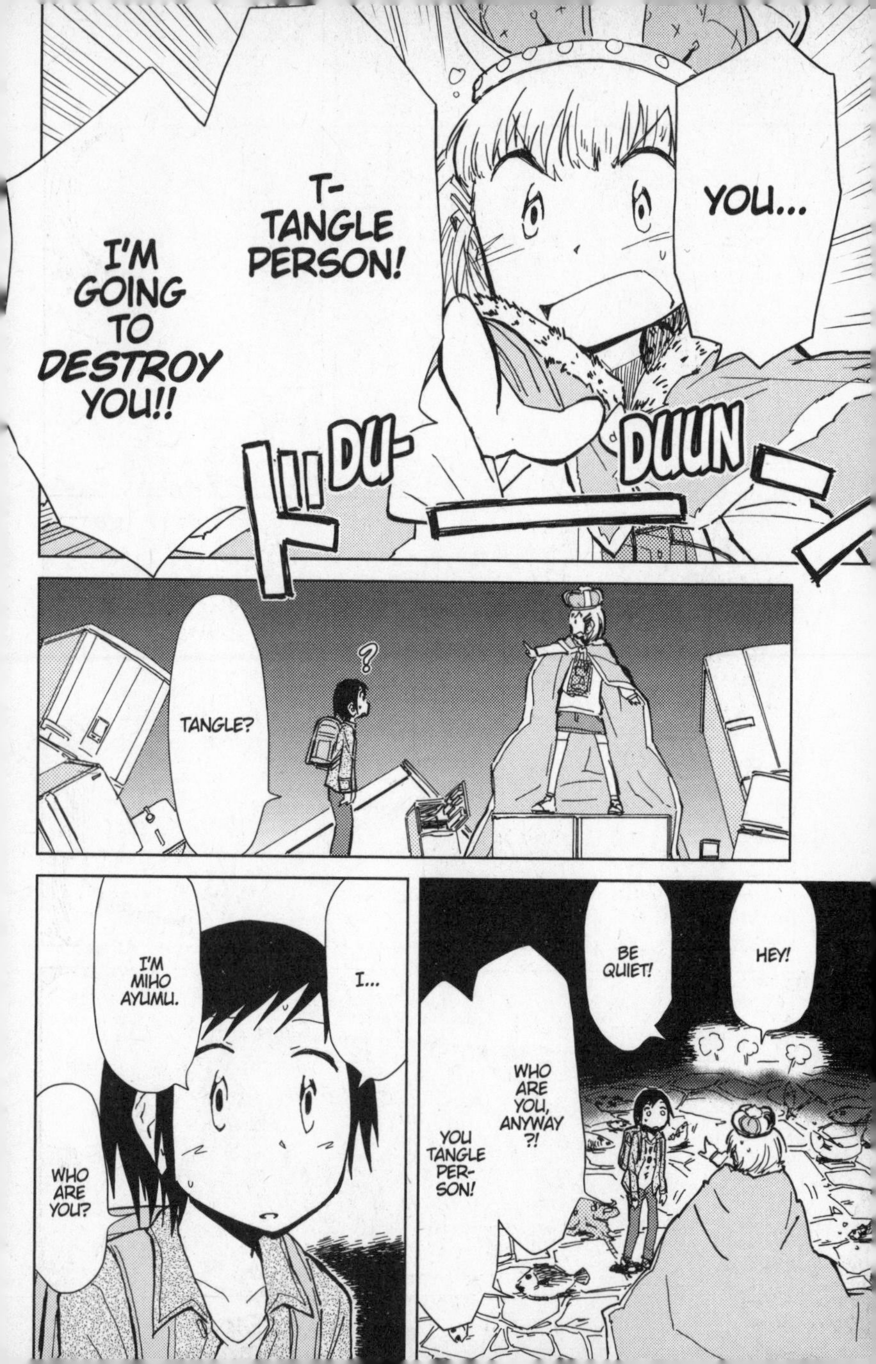
YOU...
T-TANGLE PERSON!
I'M GOING TO DESTROY YOU!!
DU-DUUN
TANGLE?
HEY!
BE QUIET!
WHO ARE YOU, ANYWAY?!
YOU TANGLE PERSON!
I...
I'M MIHO AYUMU.
WHO ARE YOU?

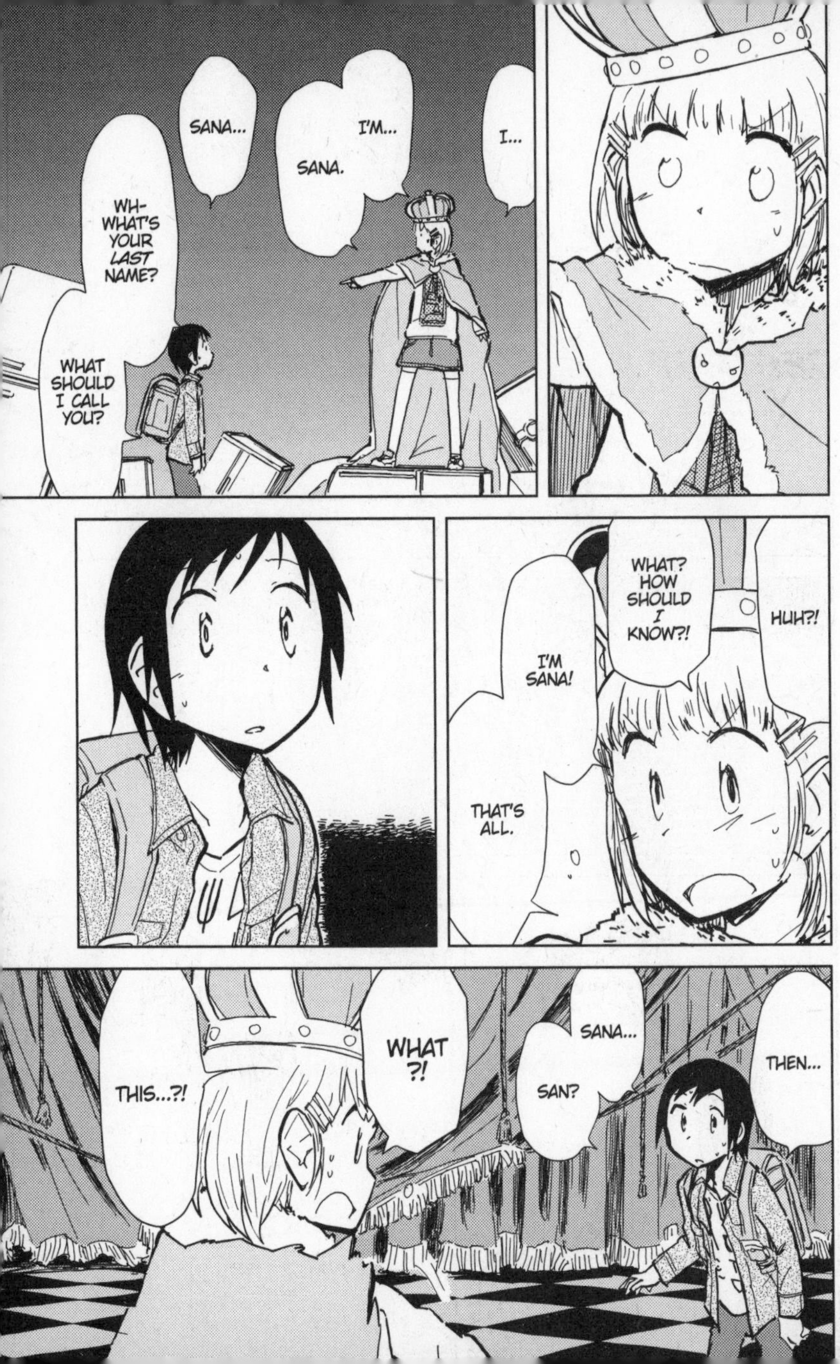
I...
I'M... SANA.
SANA...
WH-WHAT'S YOUR LAST NAME?
WHAT SHOULD I CALL YOU?
HUH?!
WHAT? HOW SHOULD I KNOW?!
I'M SANA! THAT'S ALL.
THEN...
SANA... SAN?
WHAT?!
THIS...?!

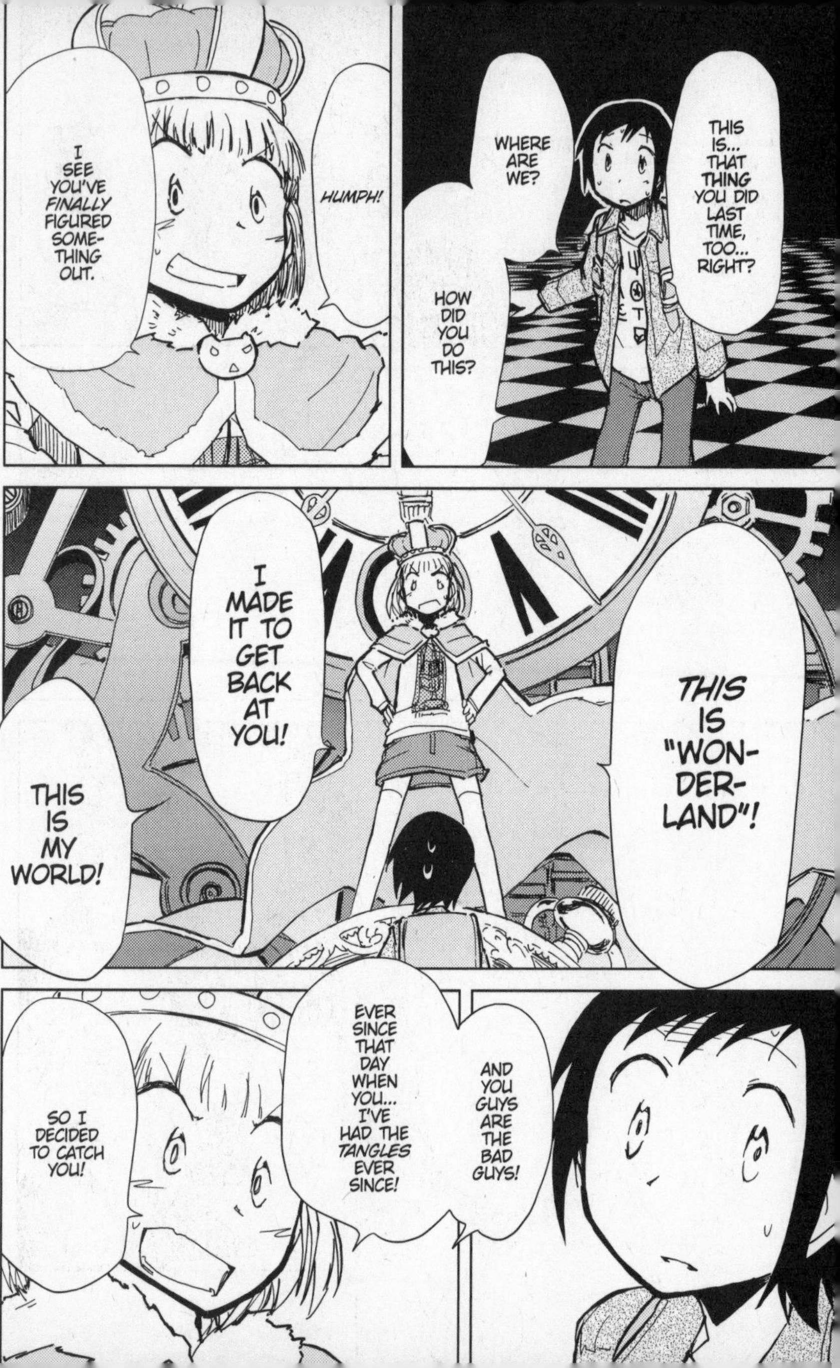
THIS IS... THAT THING YOU DID LAST TIME, TOO... RIGHT?
WHERE ARE WE?
HOW DID YOU DO THIS?
HUMPH!
I SEE YOU'VE *FINALLY* FIGURED SOME-THING OUT.
THIS IS "WON-DER-LAND"!
I MADE IT TO GET BACK AT YOU!
THIS IS MY WORLD!
AND YOU GUYS ARE THE BAD GUYS!
EVER SINCE THAT DAY WHEN YOU... I'VE HAD THE *TANGLES* EVER SINCE!
SO I DECIDED TO CATCH YOU!

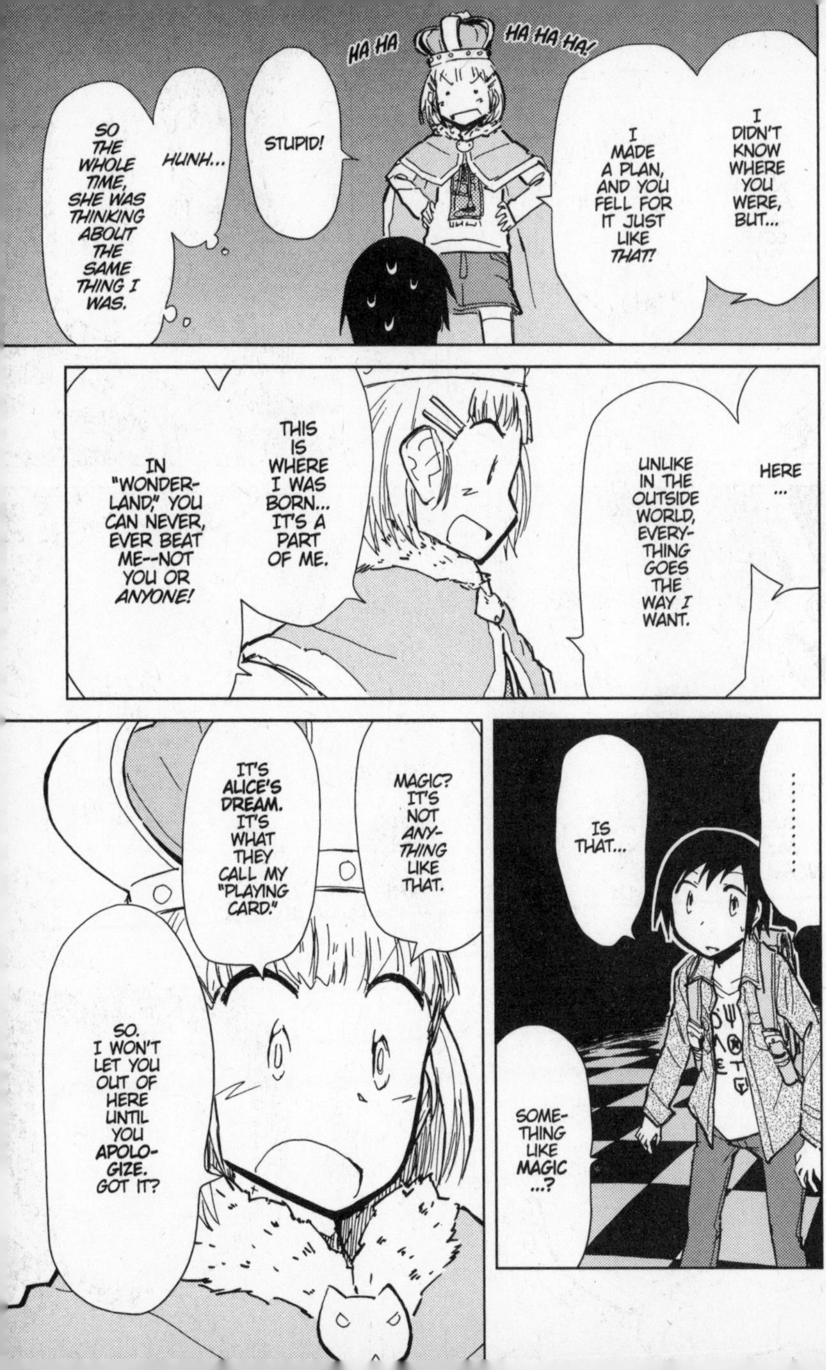
HA HA HA!
HA HA
I DIDN'T KNOW WHERE YOU WERE, BUT...
I MADE A PLAN, AND YOU FELL FOR IT JUST LIKE *THAT!*
STUPID!
HUNH...
SO THE WHOLE TIME, SHE WAS THINKING ABOUT THE SAME THING I WAS.
HERE...
UNLIKE IN THE OUTSIDE WORLD, EVERYTHING GOES THE WAY *I* WANT.
THIS IS WHERE I WAS BORN... IT'S A PART OF ME.
IN "WONDERLAND," YOU CAN NEVER, EVER BEAT ME--NOT YOU OR *ANYONE!*
......
IS THAT...
SOMETHING LIKE MAGIC...?
MAGIC? IT'S NOT *ANYTHING* LIKE THAT.
IT'S ALICE'S DREAM. IT'S WHAT THEY CALL MY "PLAYING CARD."
SO. I WON'T LET YOU OUT OF HERE UNTIL YOU APOLOGIZE. GOT IT?

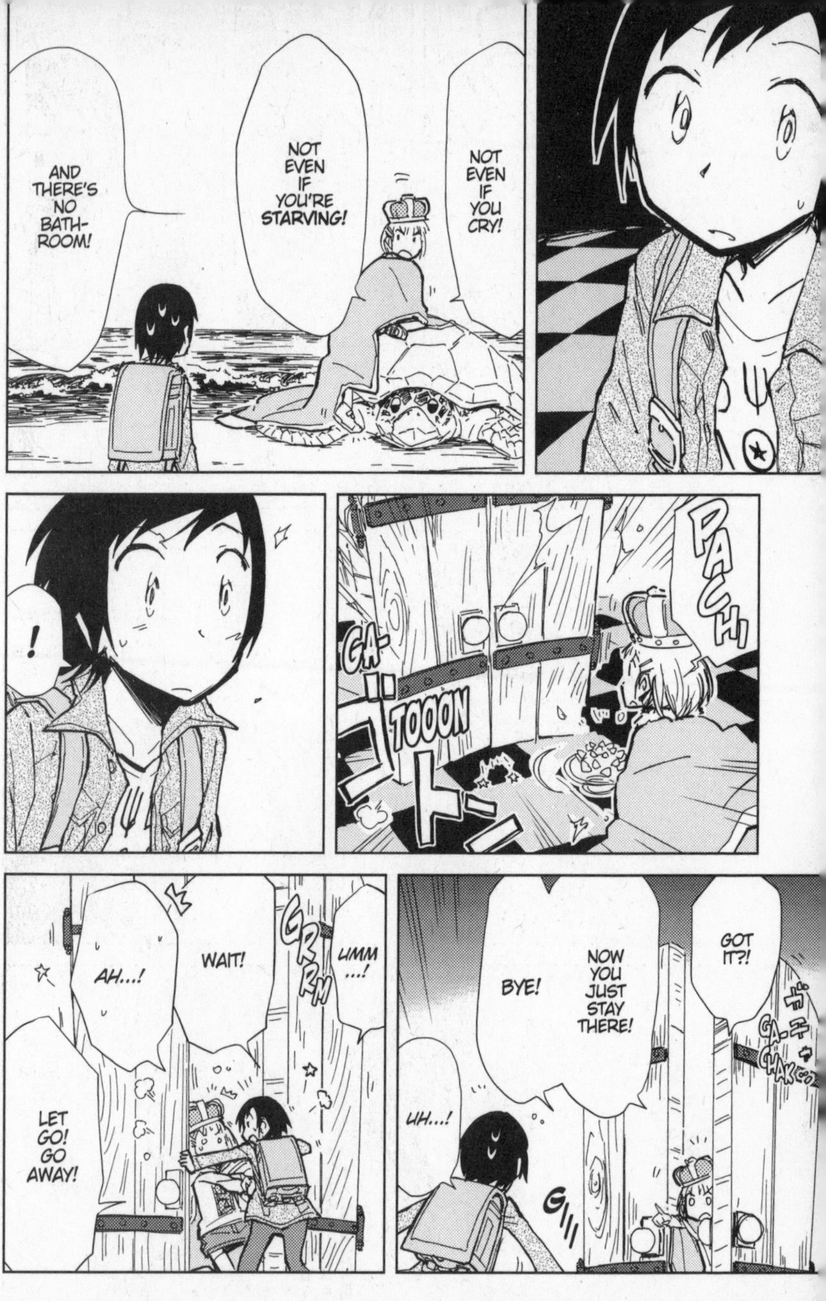
NOT EVEN IF YOU CRY!
NOT EVEN IF YOU'RE STARVING!
AND THERE'S NO BATH-ROOM!
PACHI
GA-
TOOON
!
GOT IT?!
GA-CHAK
NOW YOU JUST STAY THERE!
BYE!
UH...!
G
UMM...!
GRRM
WAIT!
AH...!
LET GO! GO AWAY!

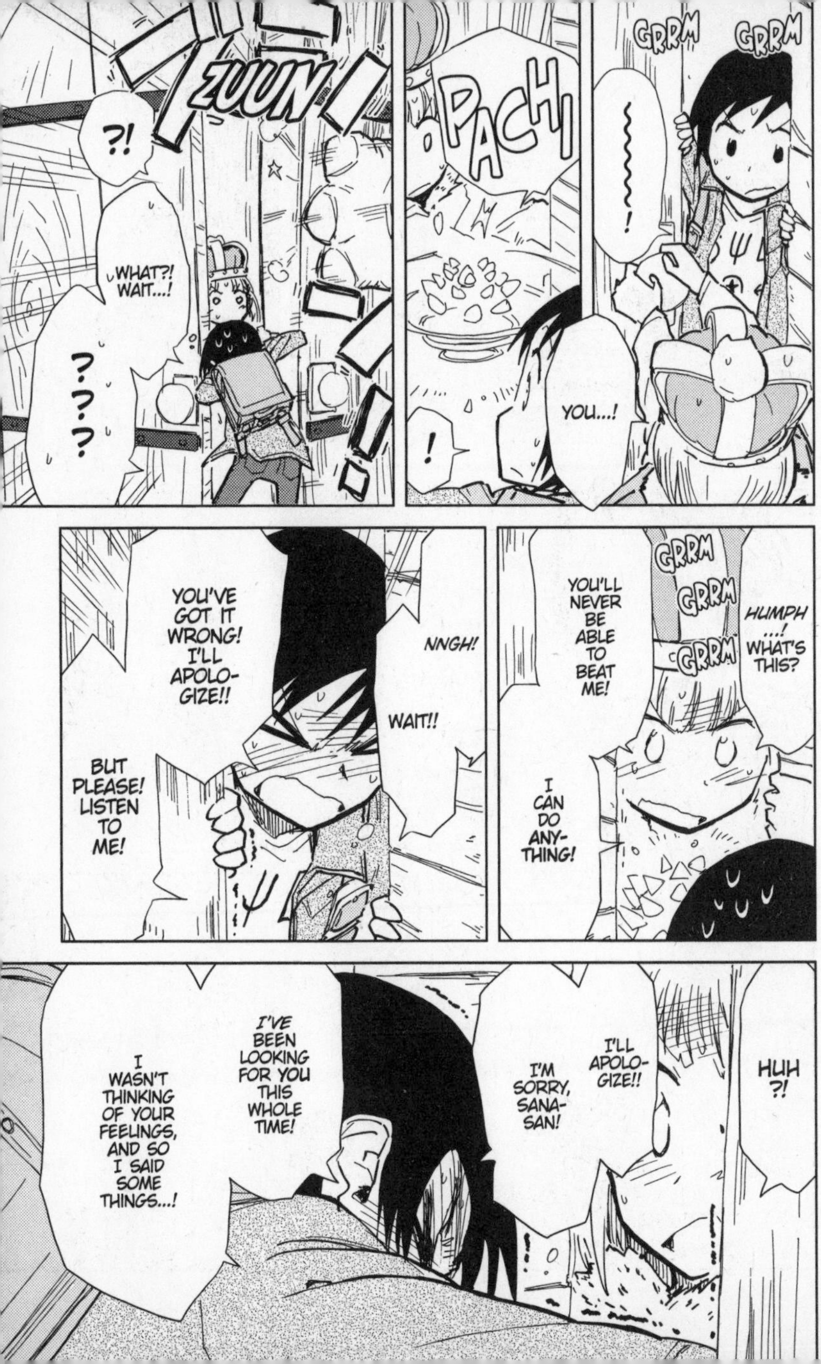
GRRM GRRM
~~~~!
YOU...!
PACHI
!
ZUUN
?!
WHAT?! WAIT...!
???
HUMPH...! WHAT'S THIS?
GRRM GRRM GRRM
YOU'LL NEVER BE ABLE TO BEAT ME!
I CAN DO ANYTHING!
NNGH!
WAIT!!
YOU'VE GOT IT WRONG! I'LL APOLOGIZE!!
BUT PLEASE! LISTEN TO ME!
HUH?!
I'LL APOLOGIZE!!
I'M SORRY, SANA-SAN!
I'VE BEEN LOOKING FOR YOU THIS WHOLE TIME!
I WASN'T THINKING OF YOUR FEELINGS, AND SO I SAID SOME THINGS...!
~~~~

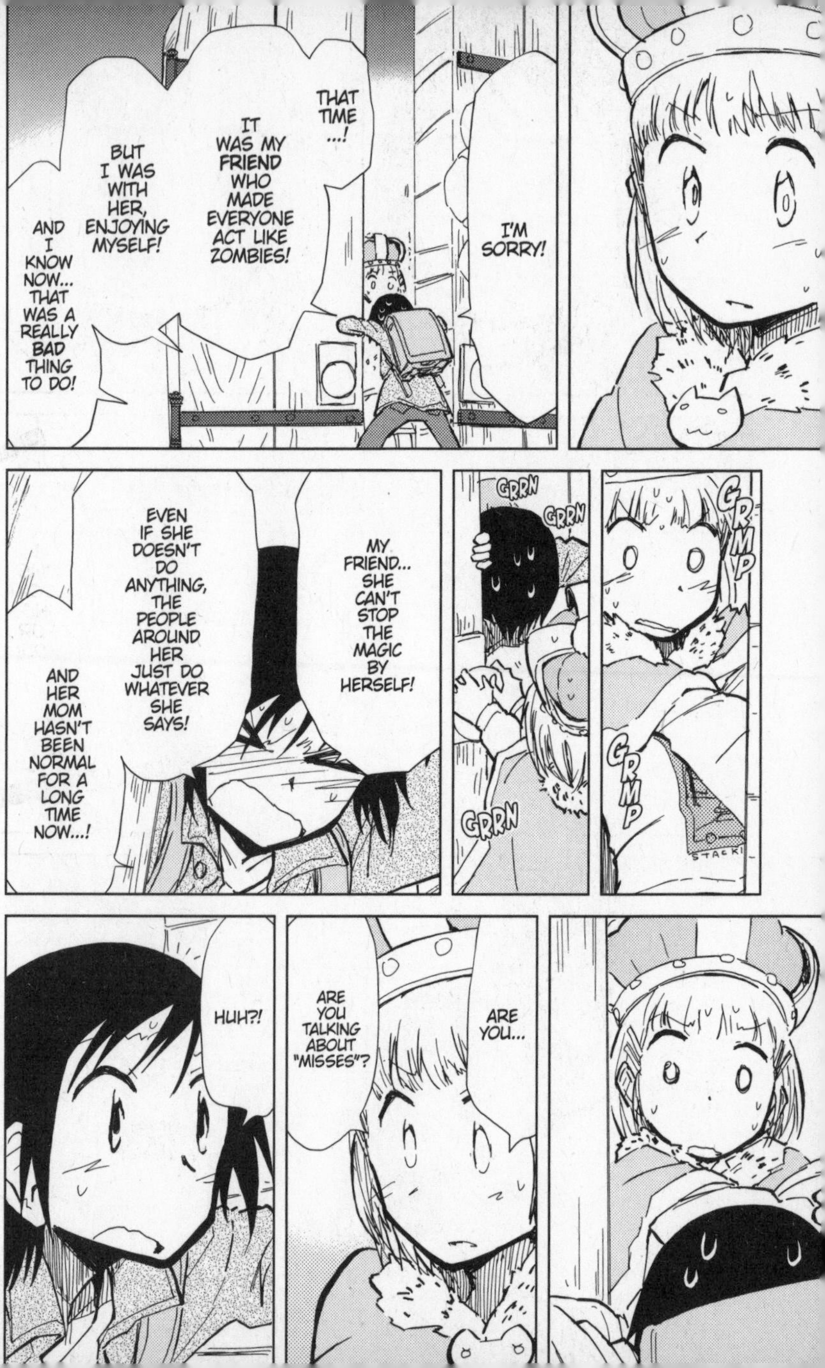
I'M SORRY!
THAT TIME ...!
IT WAS MY FRIEND WHO MADE EVERYONE ACT LIKE ZOMBIES!
BUT I WAS WITH HER, ENJOYING MYSELF!
AND I KNOW NOW... THAT WAS A REALLY BAD THING TO DO!
GRMP
GRMP
STACK!
GRRN
GRRN
GRRN
MY FRIEND... SHE CAN'T STOP THE MAGIC BY HERSELF!
EVEN IF SHE DOESN'T DO ANYTHING, THE PEOPLE AROUND HER JUST DO WHATEVER SHE SAYS!
AND HER MOM HASN'T BEEN NORMAL FOR A LONG TIME NOW...!
ARE YOU...
ARE YOU TALKING ABOUT "MISSES"?
HUH?!

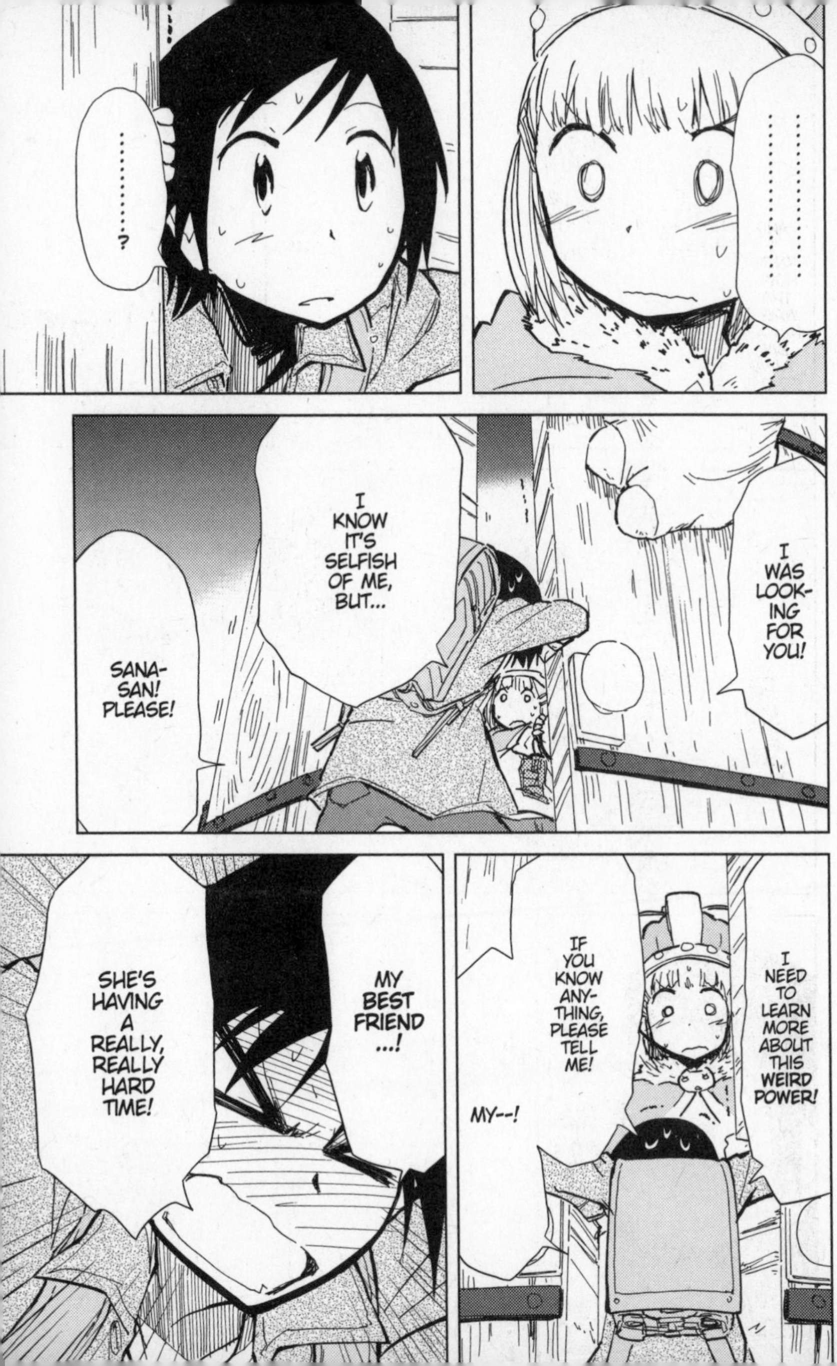
......
......?
I WAS LOOKING FOR YOU!
I KNOW IT'S SELFISH OF ME, BUT...
SANA-SAN! PLEASE!
I NEED TO LEARN MORE ABOUT THIS WEIRD POWER!
IF YOU KNOW ANYTHING, PLEASE TELL ME!
MY--!
MY BEST FRIEND ...!
SHE'S HAVING A REALLY, REALLY HARD TIME!

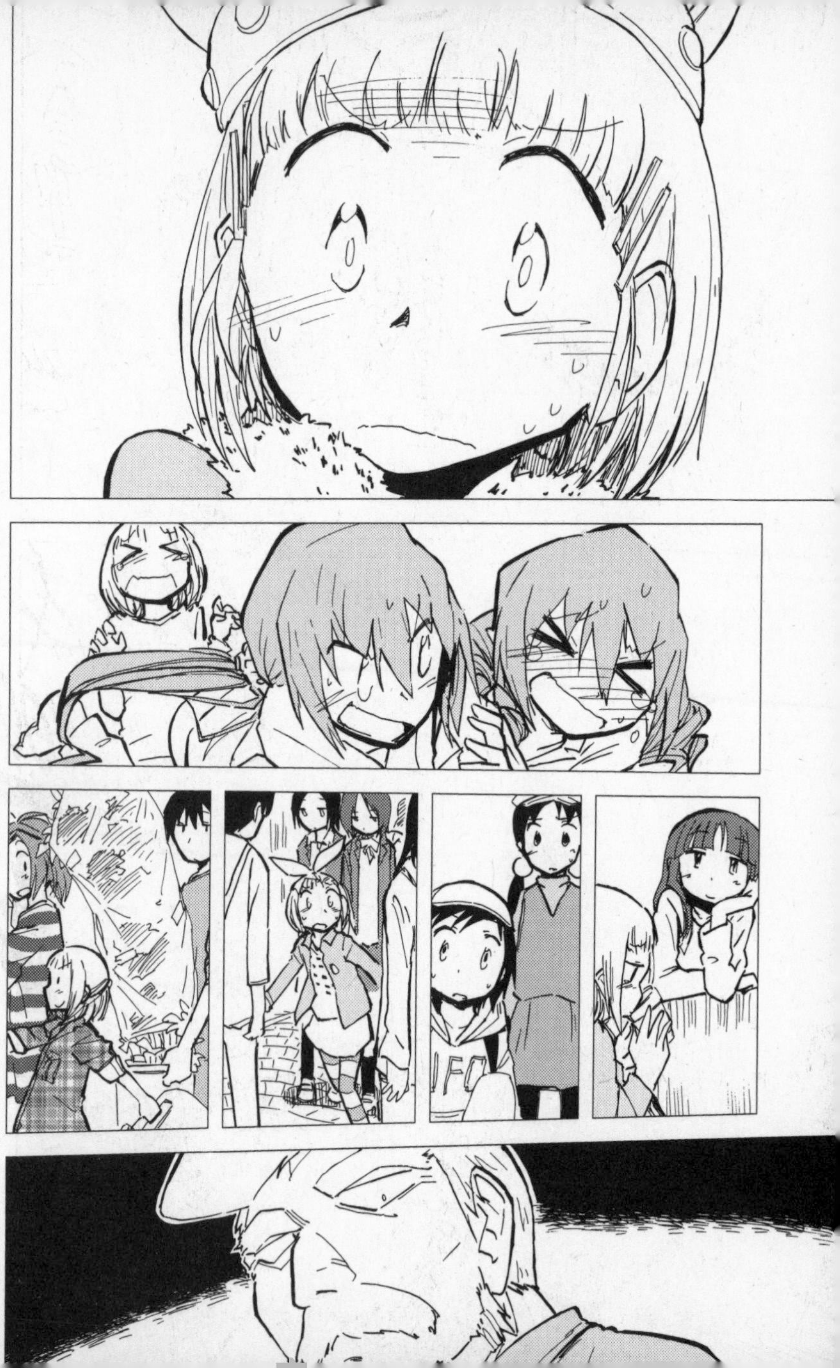

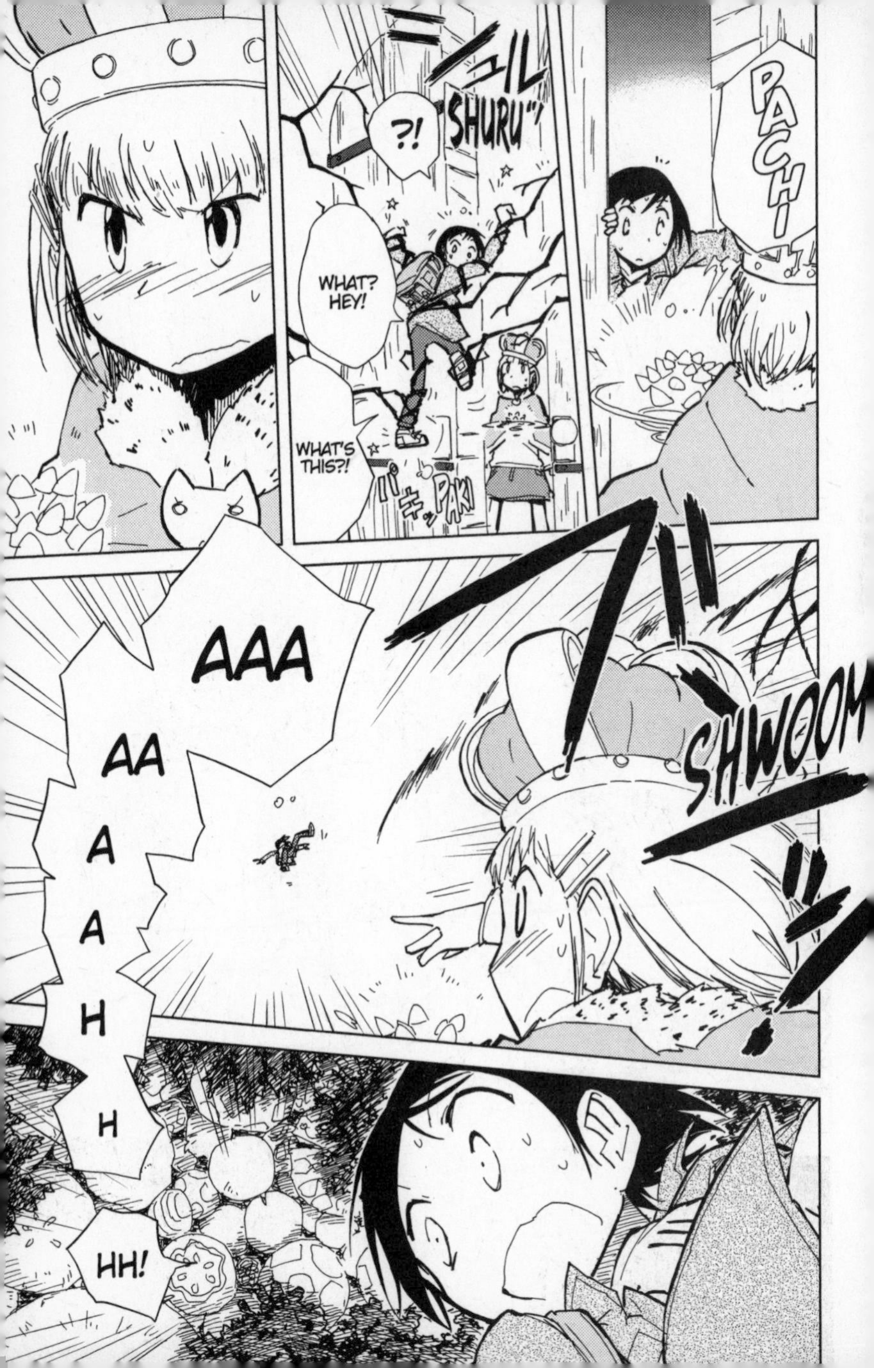
PACHI
シュル
SHURU
?!
WHAT? HEY!
パキッ
PAKI
WHAT'S THIS?!
SHWOOM
AAA AA A A H H HH!

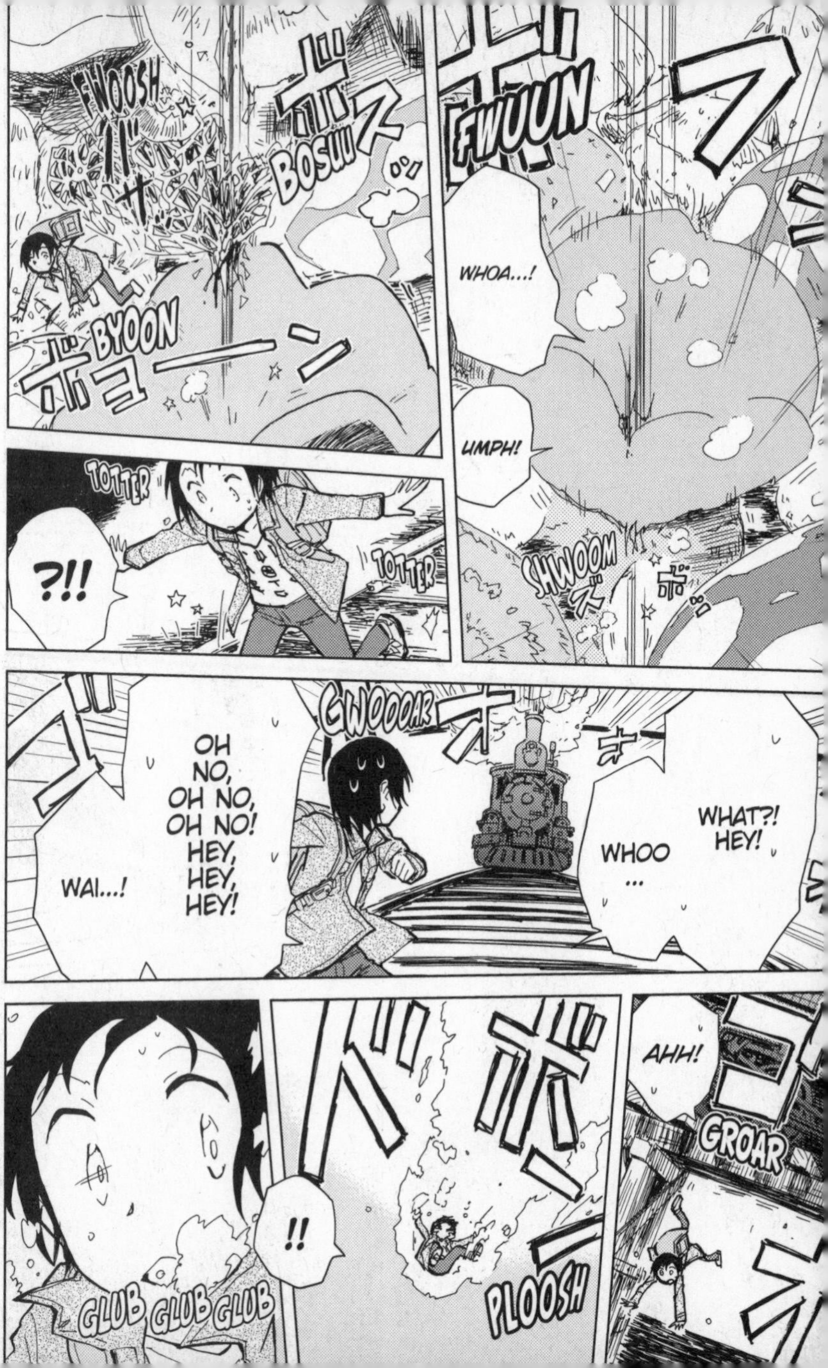
FWUUN
WHOA...!
UMPH!
SHWOOM
FWOOSH
BOSUU
BYOON
TOTTER
?!!
TOTTER
WHAT?! HEY!
WHOO ...
GWOOOAR
OH NO, OH NO, OH NO! HEY, HEY, HEY!
WAI...!
AHH!
GROAR
PLOOSH
!!
GLUB GLUB GLUB

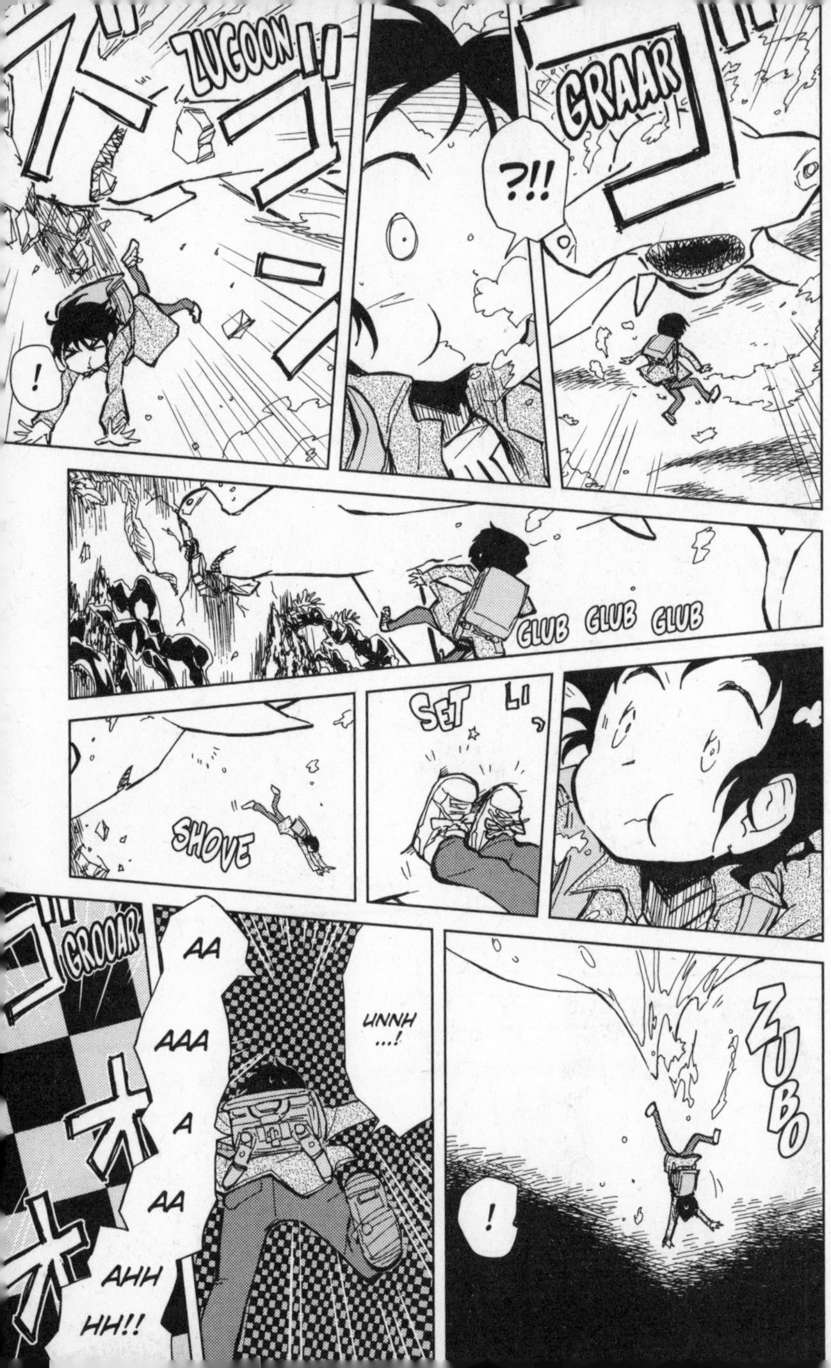
GRAAR
?!!
ZUGOON
!
GLUB GLUB GLUB
SET
LI
SHOVE
ZUBO
!
GROOAR
AA AAA A AA AHH HH!!
UNNH ...!

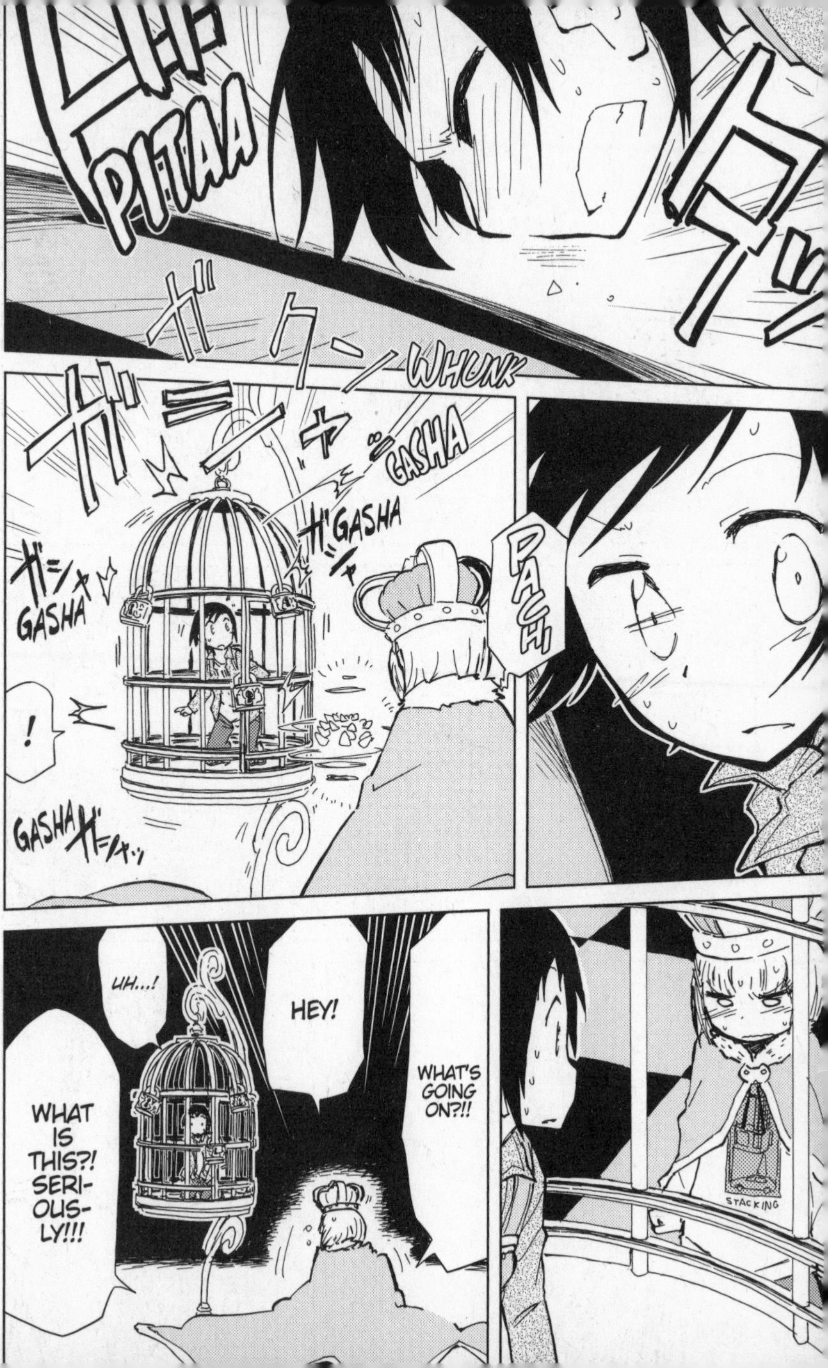
PITAA
WHUNK
PACHI
GASHA
GASHA
GASHA
!
GASHA
STACKING
HEY!
WHAT'S GOING ON?!!
UH...!
WHAT IS THIS?! SERIOUSLY!!!

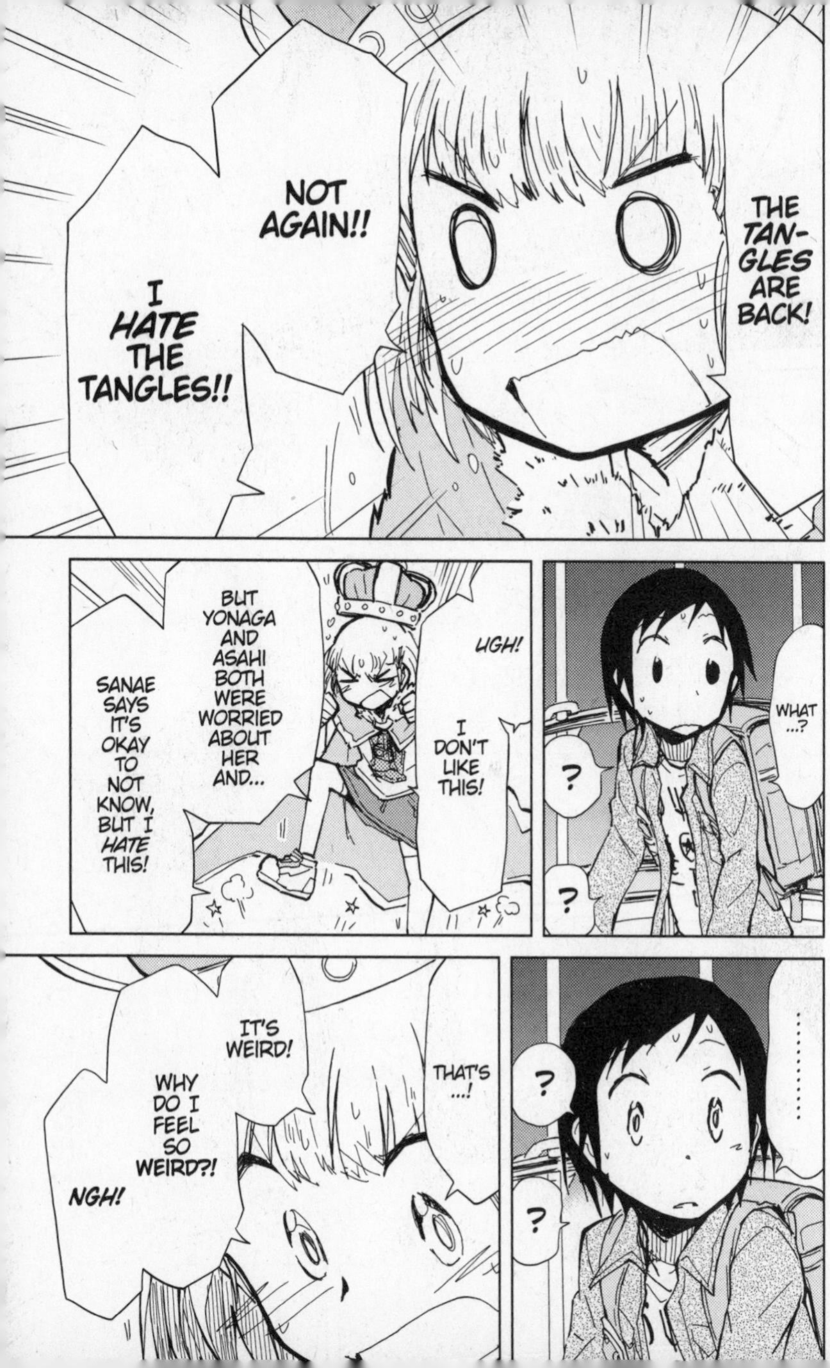
THE TANGLES ARE BACK!
NOT AGAIN!!
I HATE THE TANGLES!!
WHAT ...?
?
?
UGH!
I DON'T LIKE THIS!
BUT YONAGA AND ASAHI BOTH WERE WORRIED ABOUT HER AND...
SANAE SAYS IT'S OKAY TO NOT KNOW, BUT I HATE THIS!
......
?
?
THAT'S ...!
IT'S WEIRD!
WHY DO I FEEL SO WEIRD?!
NGH!

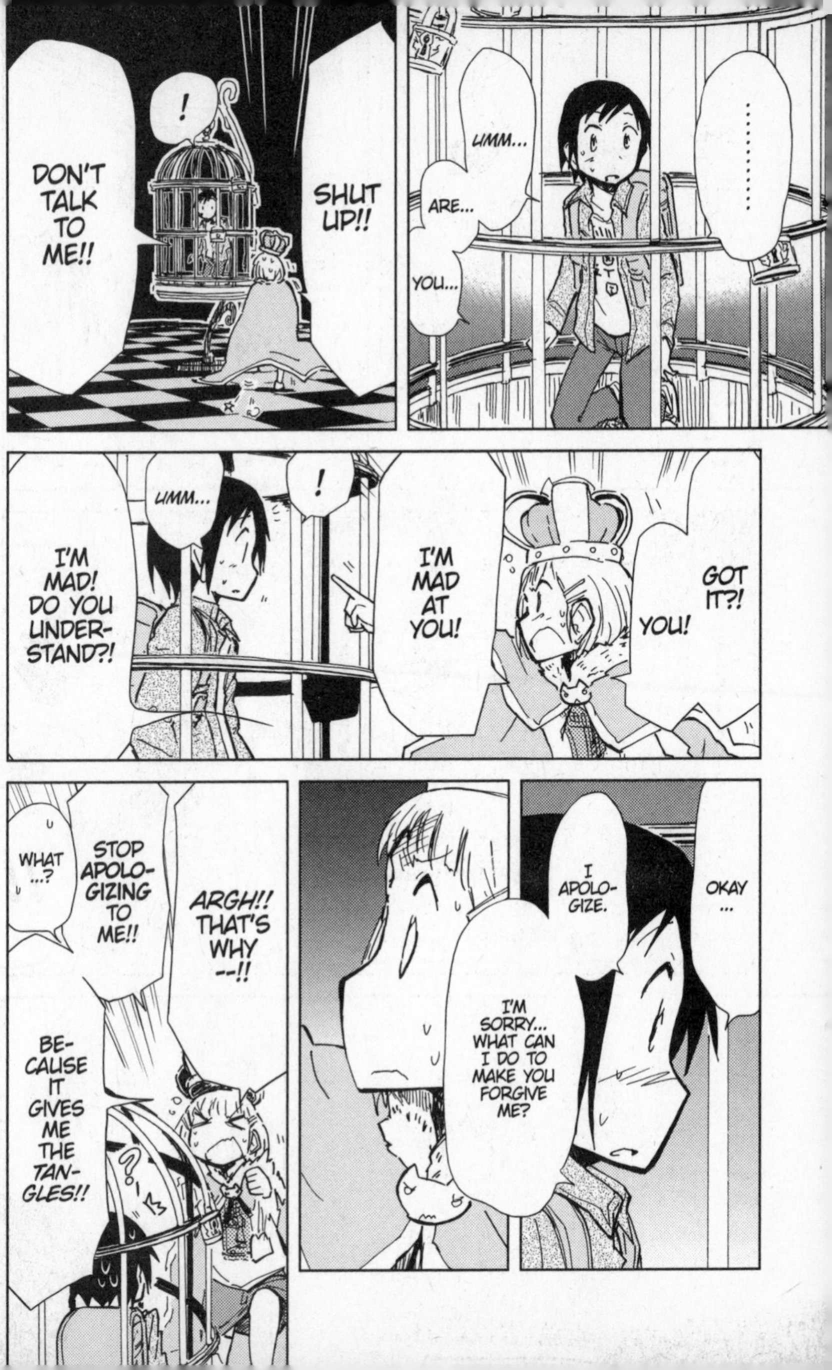
......
UMM...
ARE...
YOU...
SHUT UP!!
!
DON'T TALK TO ME!!
GOT IT?!
YOU!
I'M MAD AT YOU!
!
UMM...
I'M MAD! DO YOU UNDER-STAND?!
OKAY ...
I APOLO-GIZE.
I'M SORRY... WHAT CAN I DO TO MAKE YOU FORGIVE ME?
ARGH!! THAT'S WHY --!!
STOP APOLO-GIZING TO ME!!
WHAT ...?
BE-CAUSE IT GIVES ME THE TAN-GLES!!

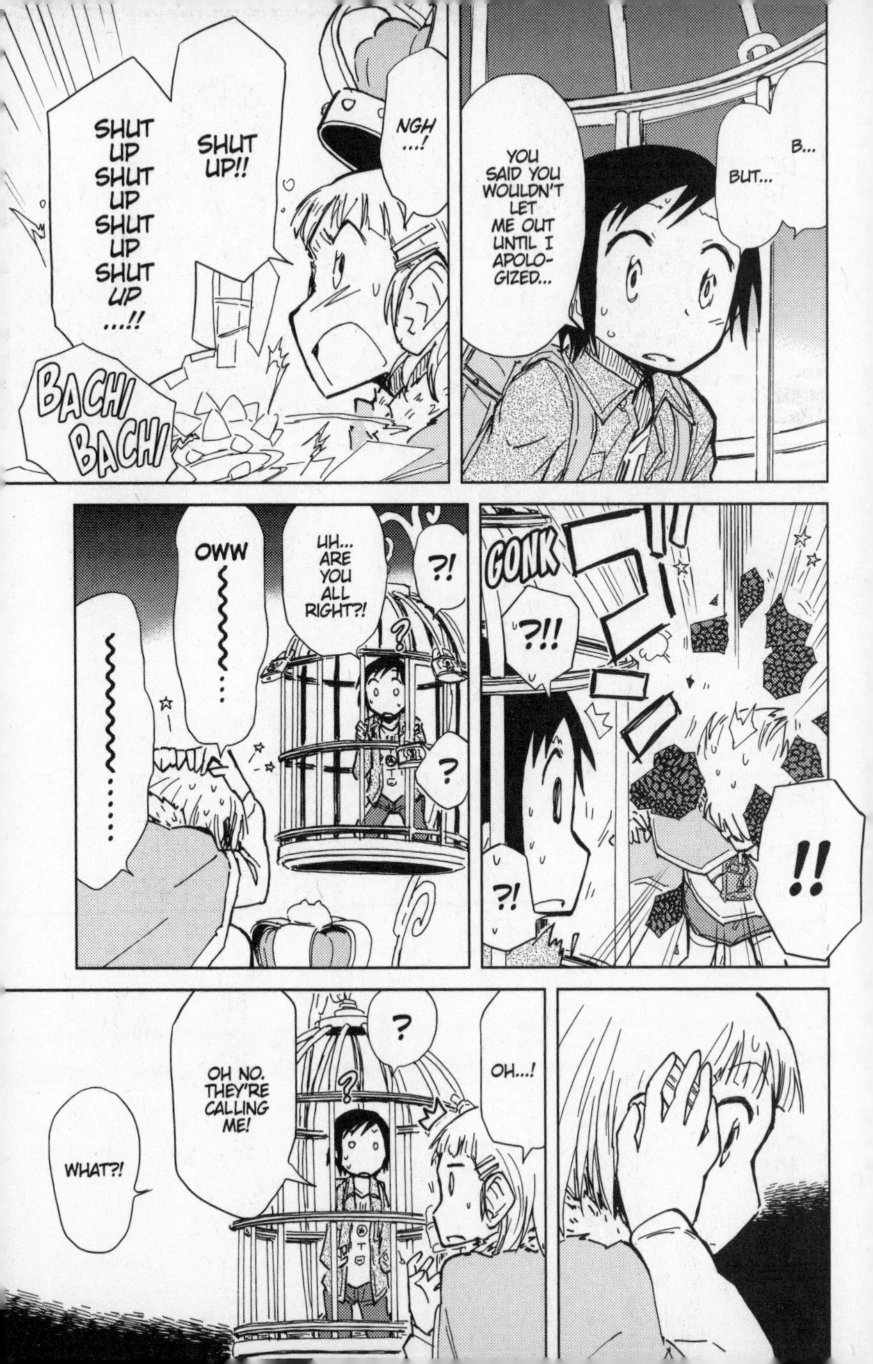
B... BUT...
YOU SAID YOU WOULDN'T LET ME OUT UNTIL I APOLOGIZED...
NGH ...!
SHUT UP!!
SHUT UP SHUT UP SHUT UP SHUT UP ...!!
BACHI BACHI
GONK
?!!
!!
?!
?!
UH... ARE YOU ALL RIGHT?!
OWW ......
?
......
OH...!
?
OH NO. THEY'RE CALLING ME!
WHAT?!

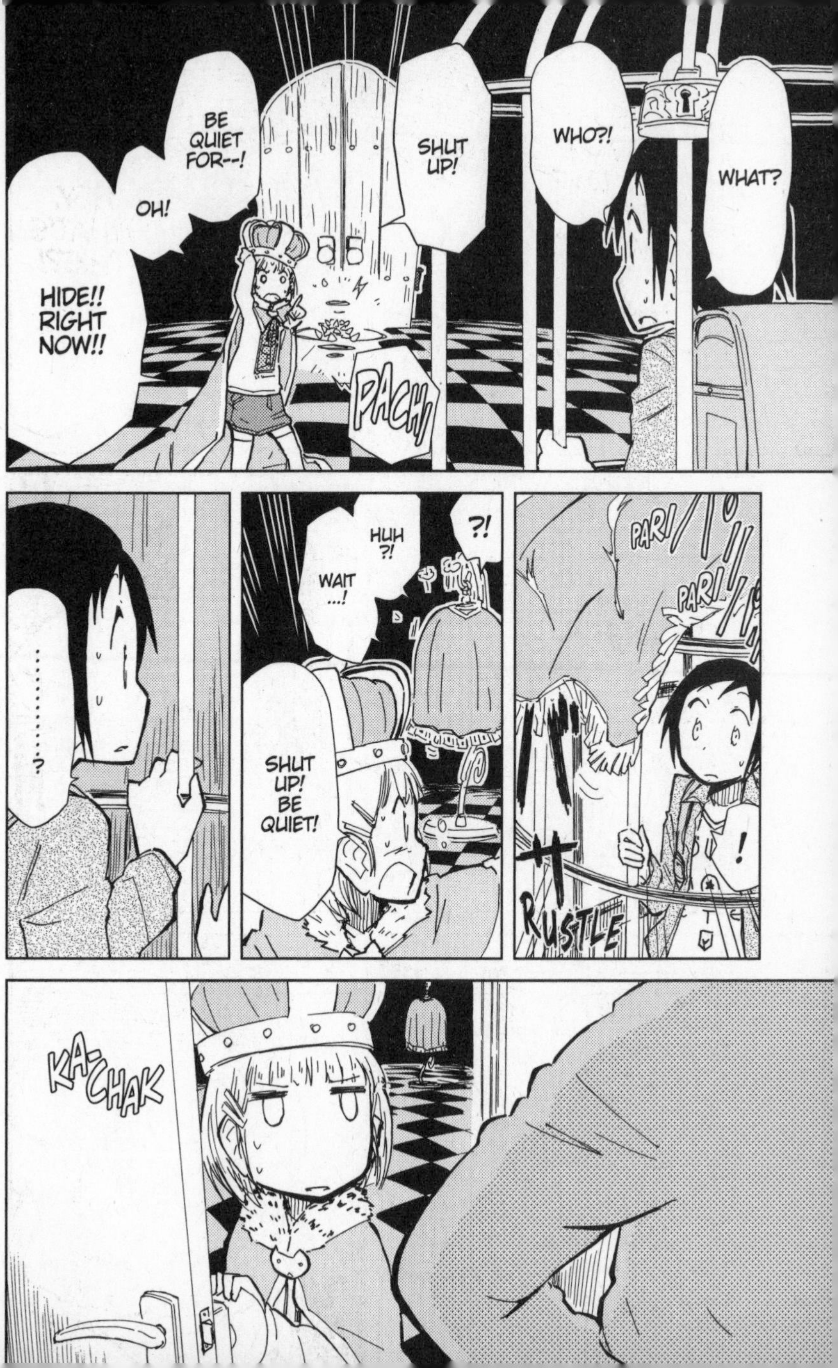
WHAT?
WHO?!
SHUT UP!
BE QUIET FOR--!
OH!
HIDE!! RIGHT NOW!!
PACH
PARI
PARI
!
RUSTLE
?!
HUH ?!
WAIT ...!
SHUT UP! BE QUIET!
......?
KA-CHAK

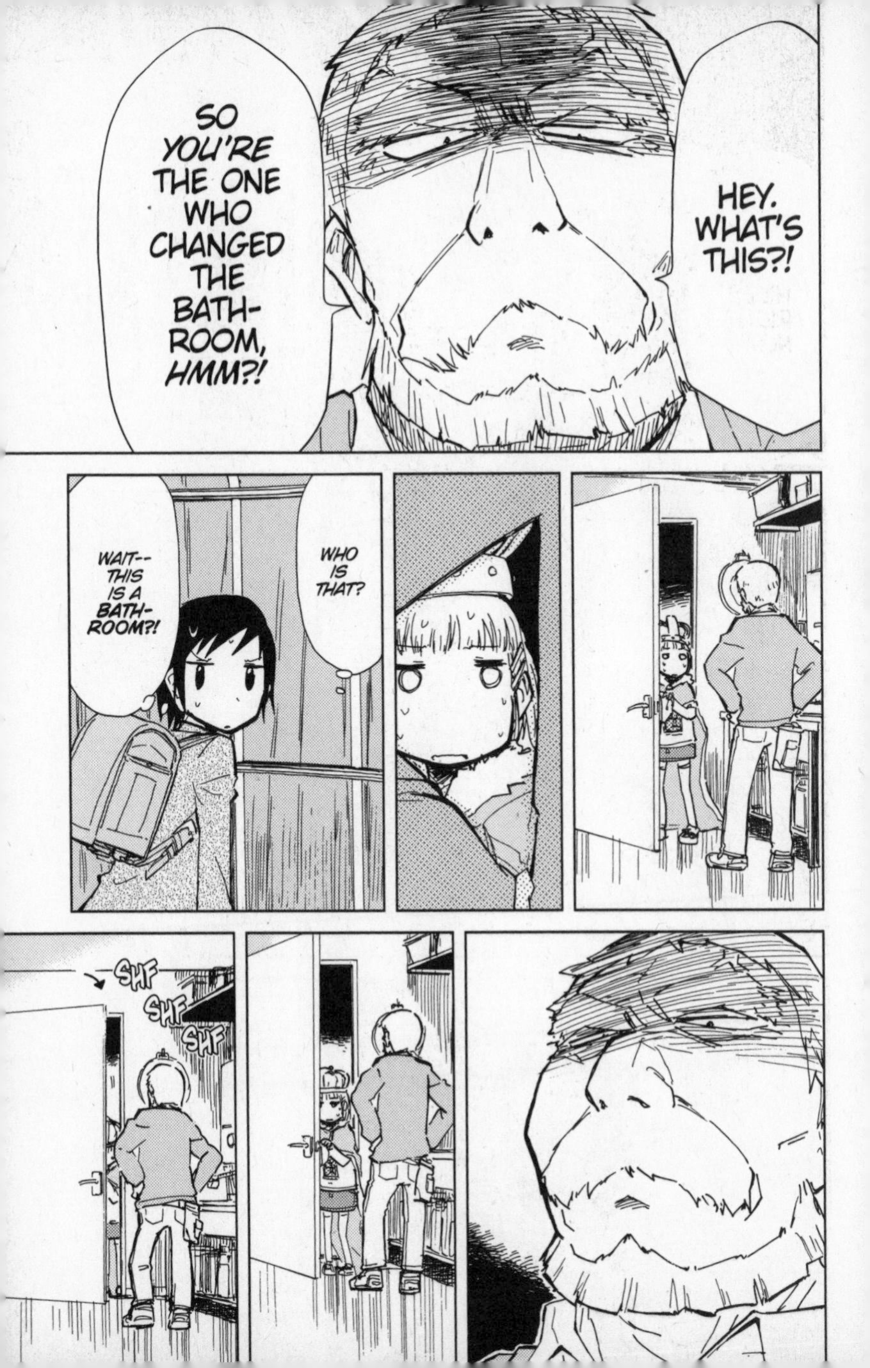
HEY. WHAT'S THIS?!
SO YOU'RE THE ONE WHO CHANGED THE BATH-ROOM, HMM?!
WHO IS THAT?
WAIT-- THIS IS A BATH-ROOM?!
SHF SHF SHF

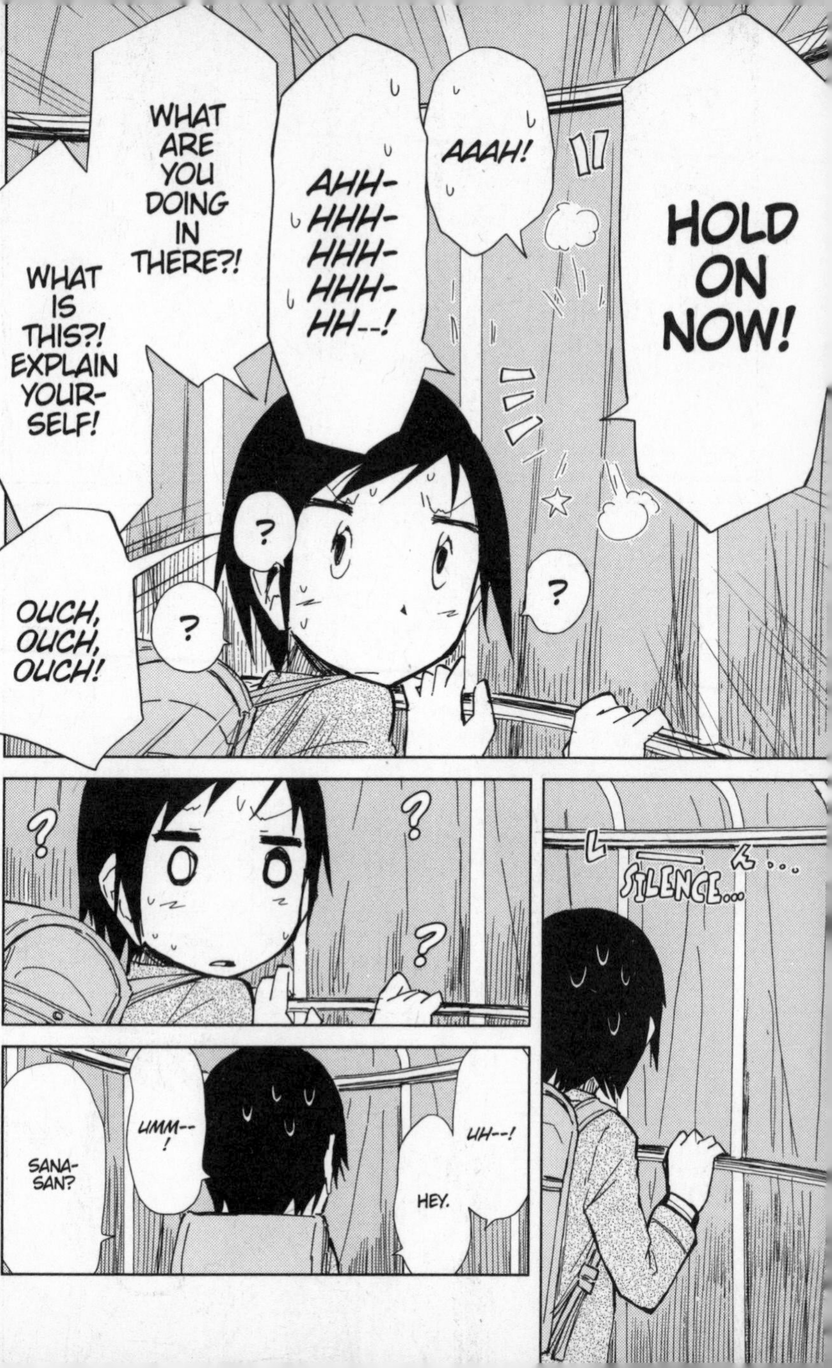
HOLD ON NOW!
AAAH!
AHH-HHH-HHH-HHH-HH--!
WHAT ARE YOU DOING IN THERE?!
WHAT IS THIS?! EXPLAIN YOURSELF!
?
?
?
OUCH, OUCH, OUCH!
しーん...
SILENCE...
?
?
?
UH--!
HEY.
UMM--!
SANA-SAN?

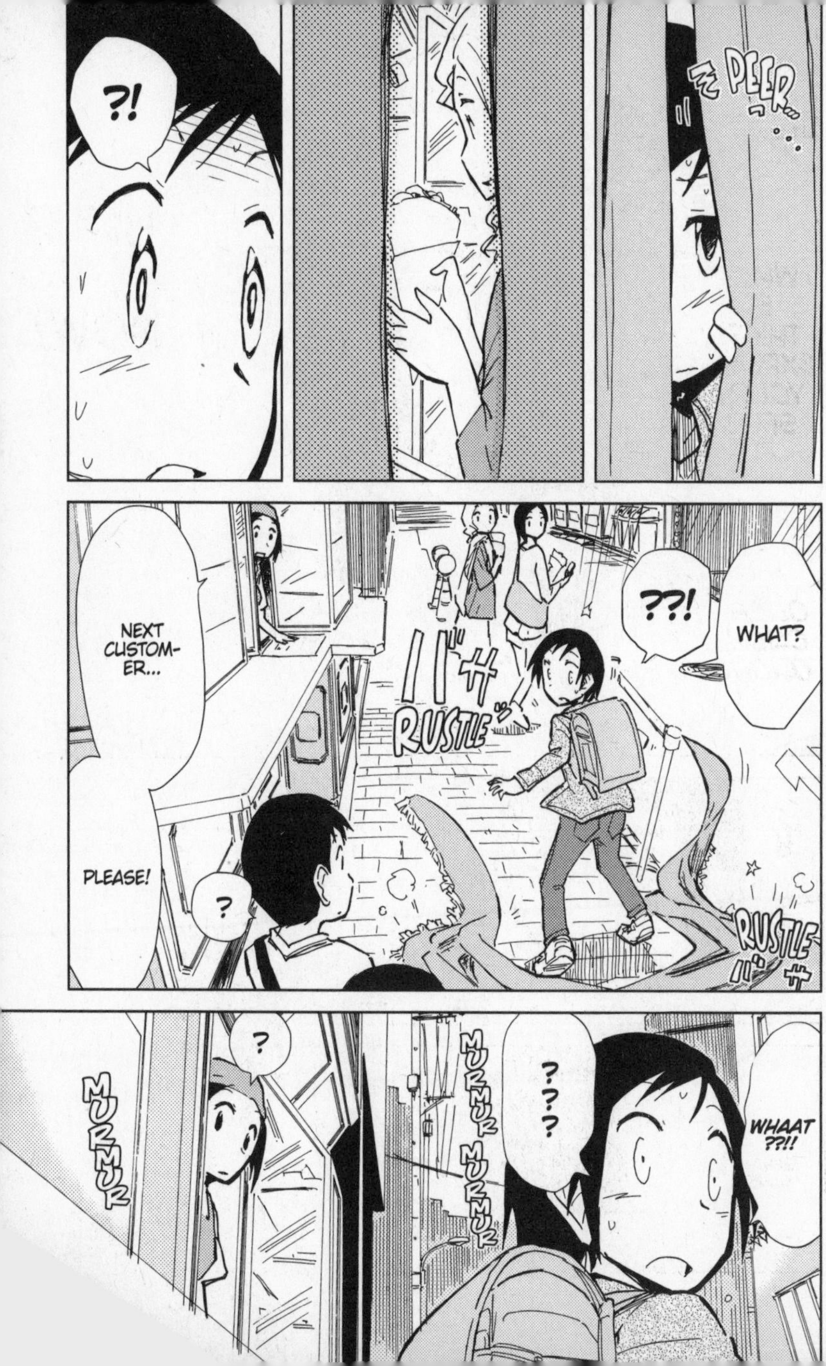
PEER...
?!
WHAT?
??!
バサ
RUSTLE
RUSTLE
バサ
?
NEXT CUSTOMER... PLEASE!
WHAAT ??!!
???
MURMUR MURMUR
?
MURMUR

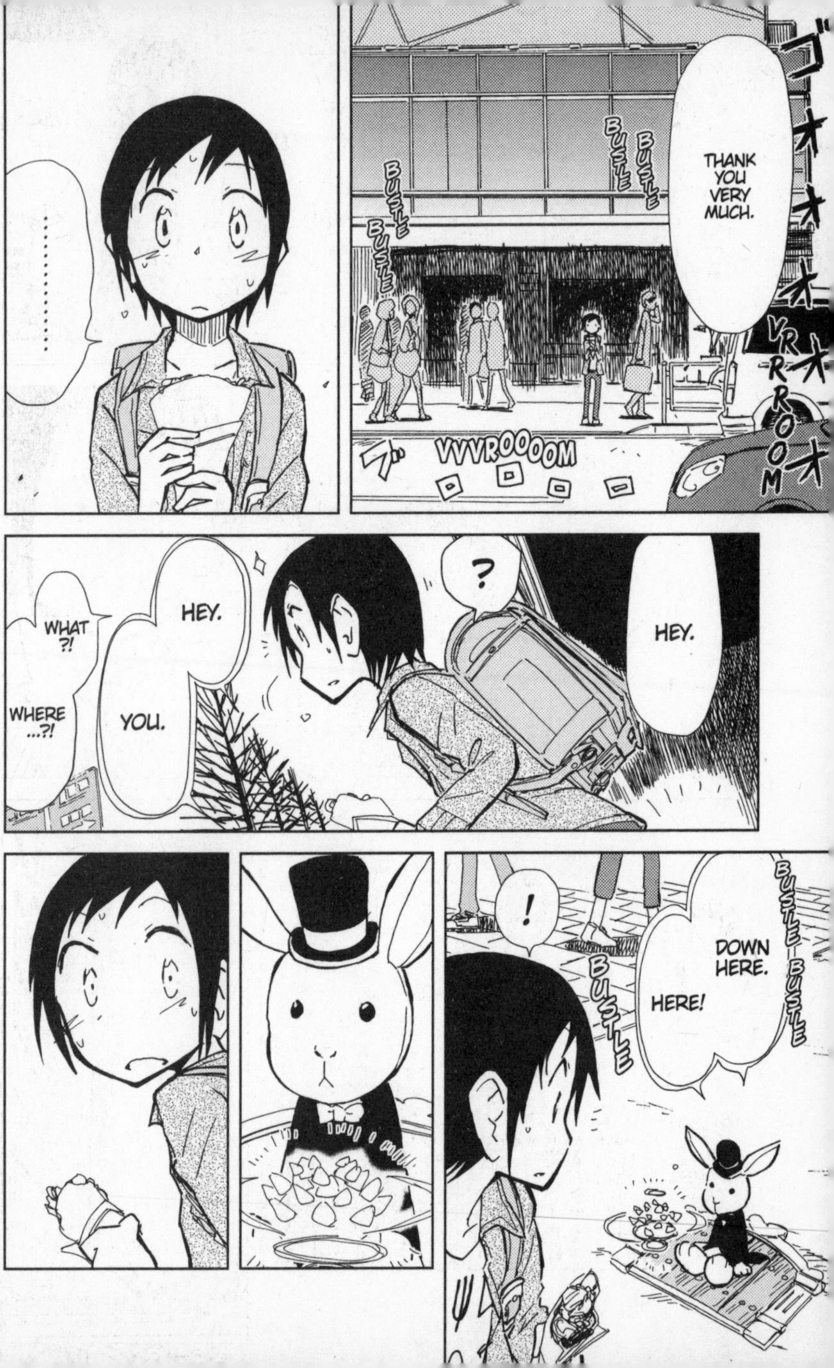
THANK YOU VERY MUCH.
BUSTLE BUSTLE
BUSTLE BUSTLE
VRRROOM
VVVROOOOM
HEY.
?
HEY.
YOU.
WHAT?!
WHERE...?!
BUSTLE BUSTLE
DOWN HERE.
HERE!
!
BUSTLE

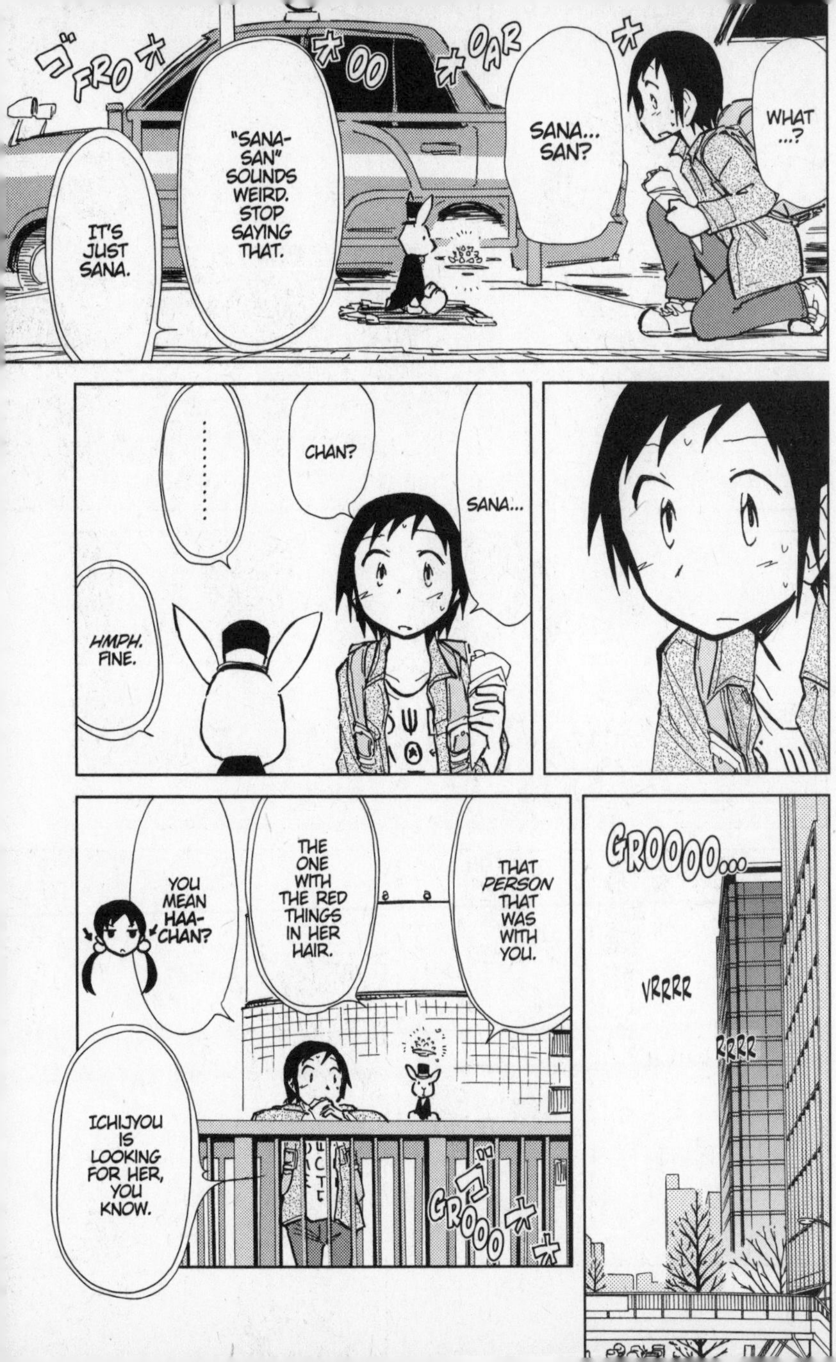
WHAT ...?
SANA... SAN?
ゴ FRO オ オ OO オ OAR オ
"SANA-SAN" SOUNDS WEIRD. STOP SAYING THAT.
IT'S JUST SANA.
SANA...
CHAN?
......
HMPH. FINE.
GROOOO...
VRRRR
RRRR
THAT PERSON THAT WAS WITH YOU.
THE ONE WITH THE RED THINGS IN HER HAIR.
YOU MEAN HAA-CHAN?
ICHIJYOU IS LOOKING FOR HER, YOU KNOW.
ゴ GROOO オ

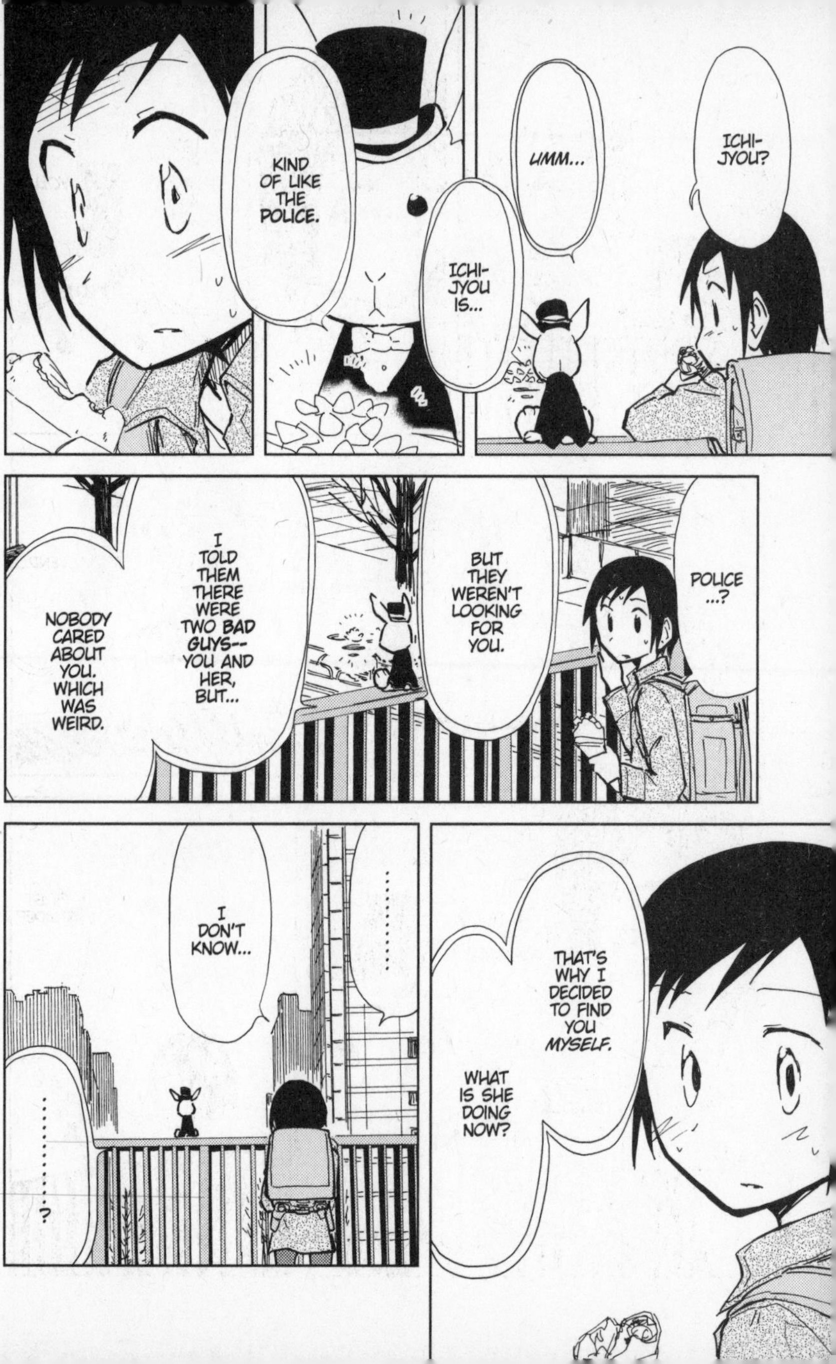
ICHI-JYOU?
UMM...
ICHI-JYOU IS...
KIND OF LIKE THE POLICE.
POLICE ...?
BUT THEY WEREN'T LOOKING FOR YOU.
I TOLD THEM THERE WERE TWO BAD GUYS-- YOU AND HER, BUT...
NOBODY CARED ABOUT YOU. WHICH WAS WEIRD.
THAT'S WHY I DECIDED TO FIND YOU *MYSELF*.
WHAT IS SHE DOING NOW?
......
I DON'T KNOW...
......?

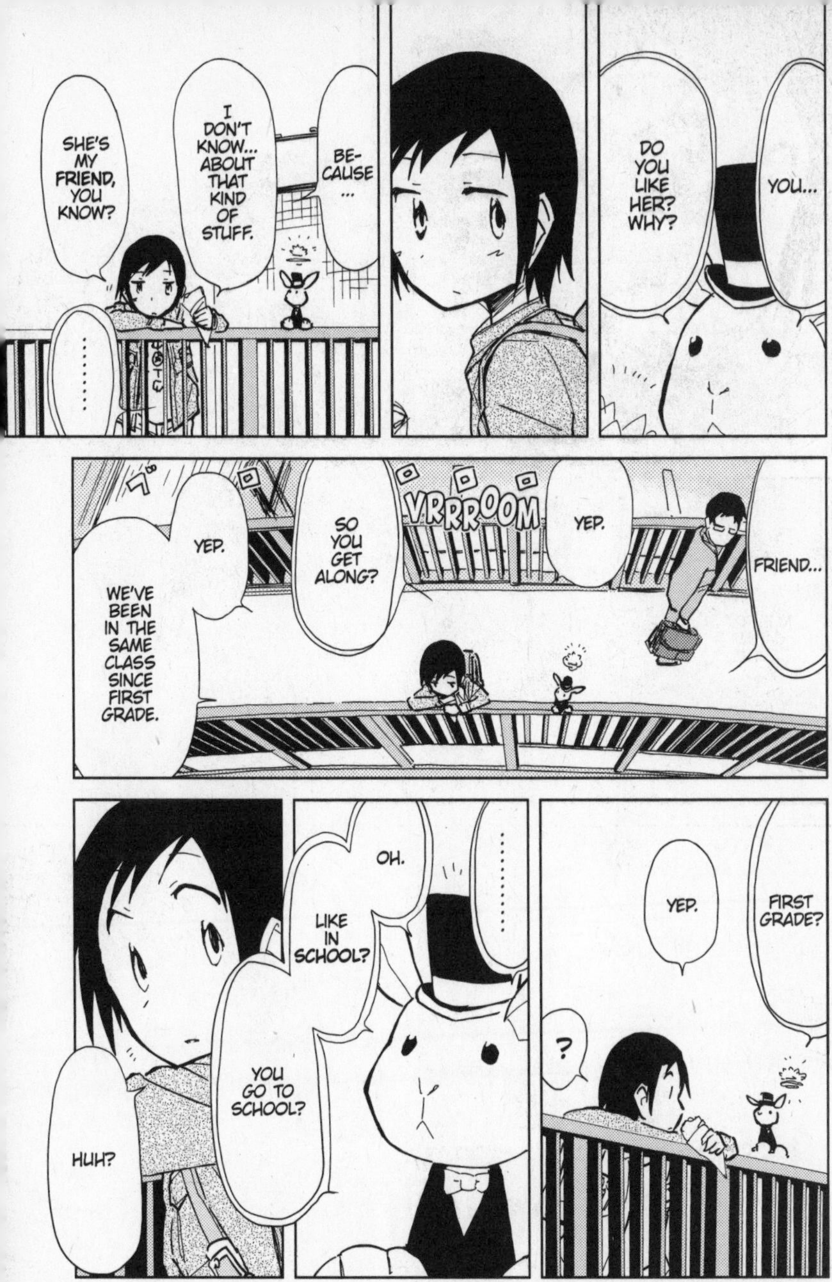
YOU...
DO YOU LIKE HER? WHY?
BE-CAUSE ...
I DON'T KNOW... ABOUT THAT KIND OF STUFF.
SHE'S MY FRIEND, YOU KNOW?
......
FRIEND...
YEP.
VRRROOM
SO YOU GET ALONG?
YEP.
WE'VE BEEN IN THE SAME CLASS SINCE FIRST GRADE.
FIRST GRADE?
YEP.
?
......
OH.
LIKE IN SCHOOL?
YOU GO TO SCHOOL?
HUH?

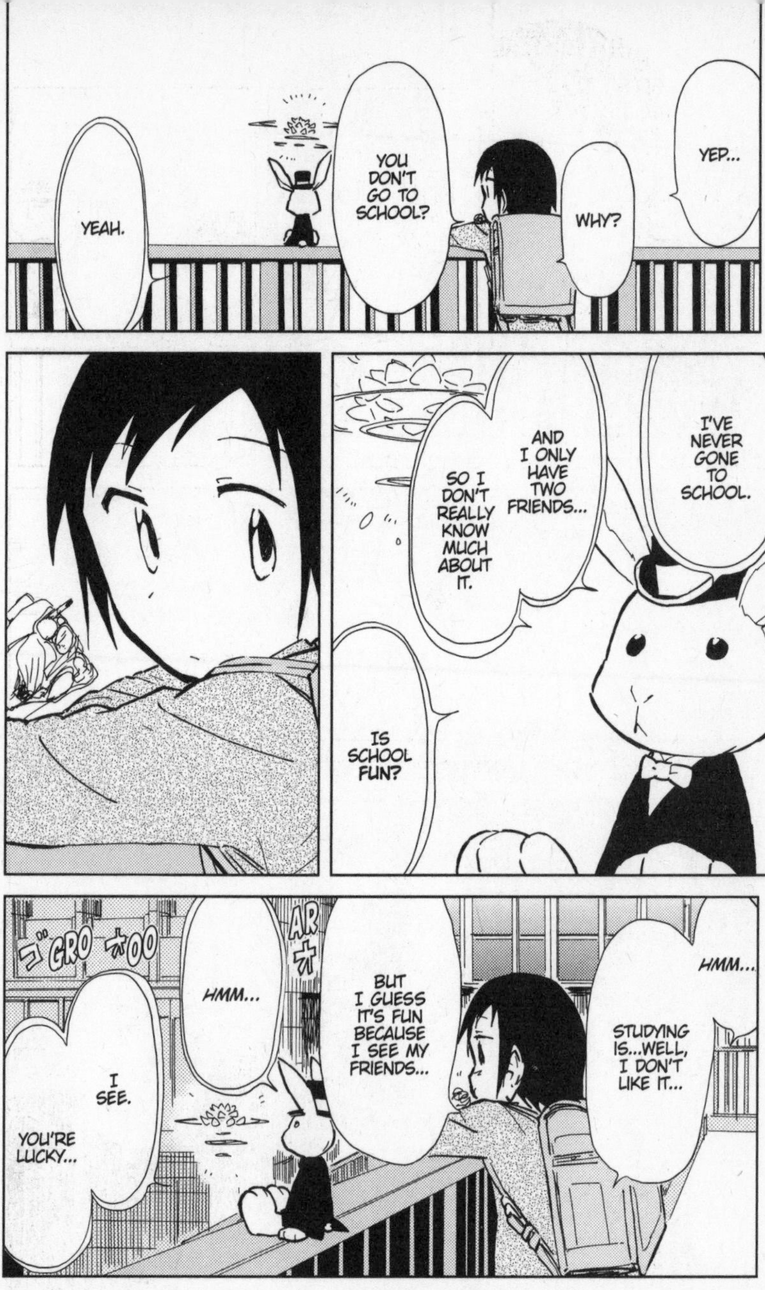
YEP...
WHY?
YOU DON'T GO TO SCHOOL?
YEAH.
I'VE NEVER GONE TO SCHOOL.
AND I ONLY HAVE TWO FRIENDS...
SO I DON'T REALLY KNOW MUCH ABOUT IT.
IS SCHOOL FUN?
HMM...
STUDYING IS...WELL, I DON'T LIKE IT...
BUT I GUESS IT'S FUN BECAUSE I SEE MY FRIENDS...
AR
HMM...
GRO
OO
I SEE.
YOU'RE LUCKY...

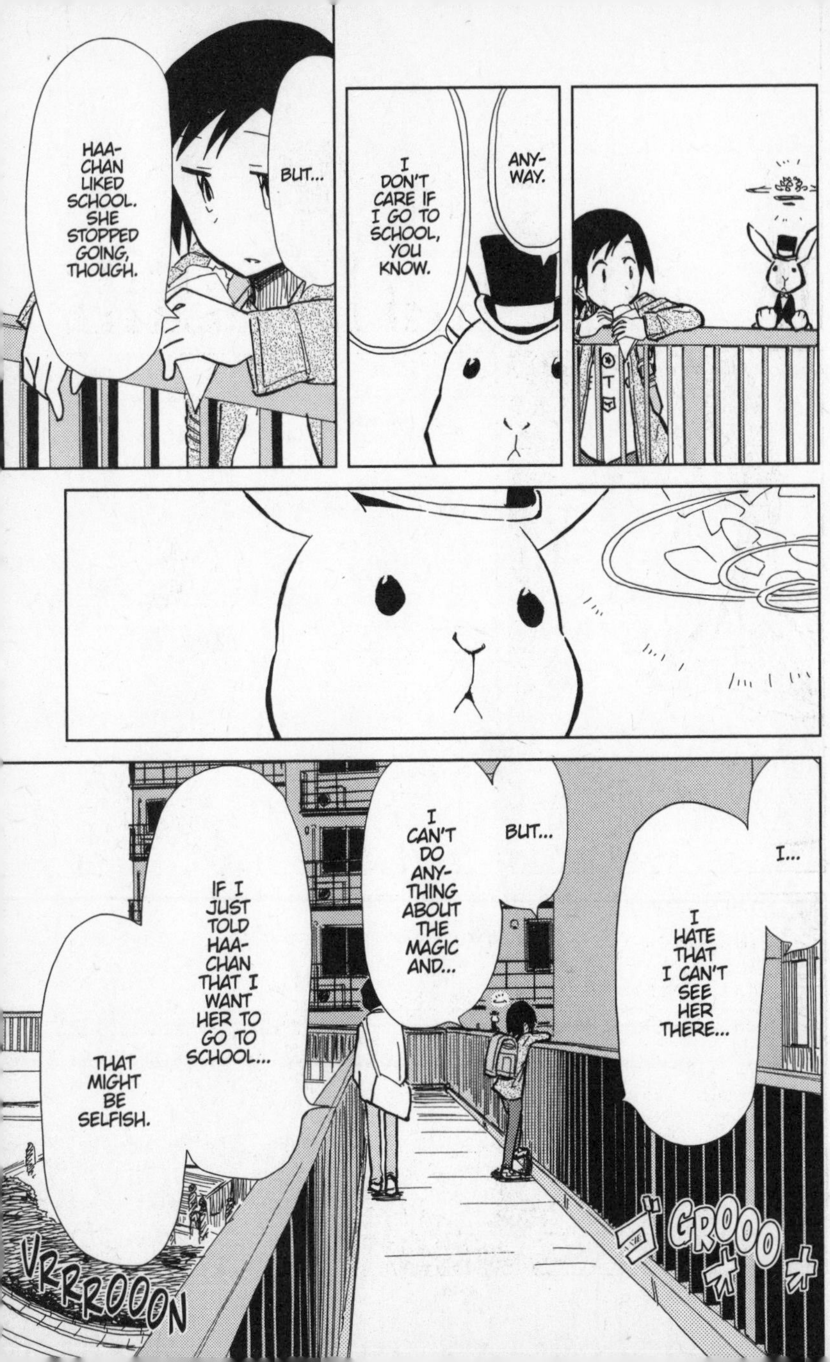
ANY-WAY.
I DON'T CARE IF I GO TO SCHOOL, YOU KNOW.
BUT...
HAA-CHAN LIKED SCHOOL. SHE STOPPED GOING, THOUGH.
I...
I HATE THAT I CAN'T SEE HER THERE...
BUT...
I CAN'T DO ANYTHING ABOUT THE MAGIC AND...
IF I JUST TOLD HAA-CHAN THAT I WANT HER TO GO TO SCHOOL...
THAT MIGHT BE SELFISH.
GROOO
VRRROOON

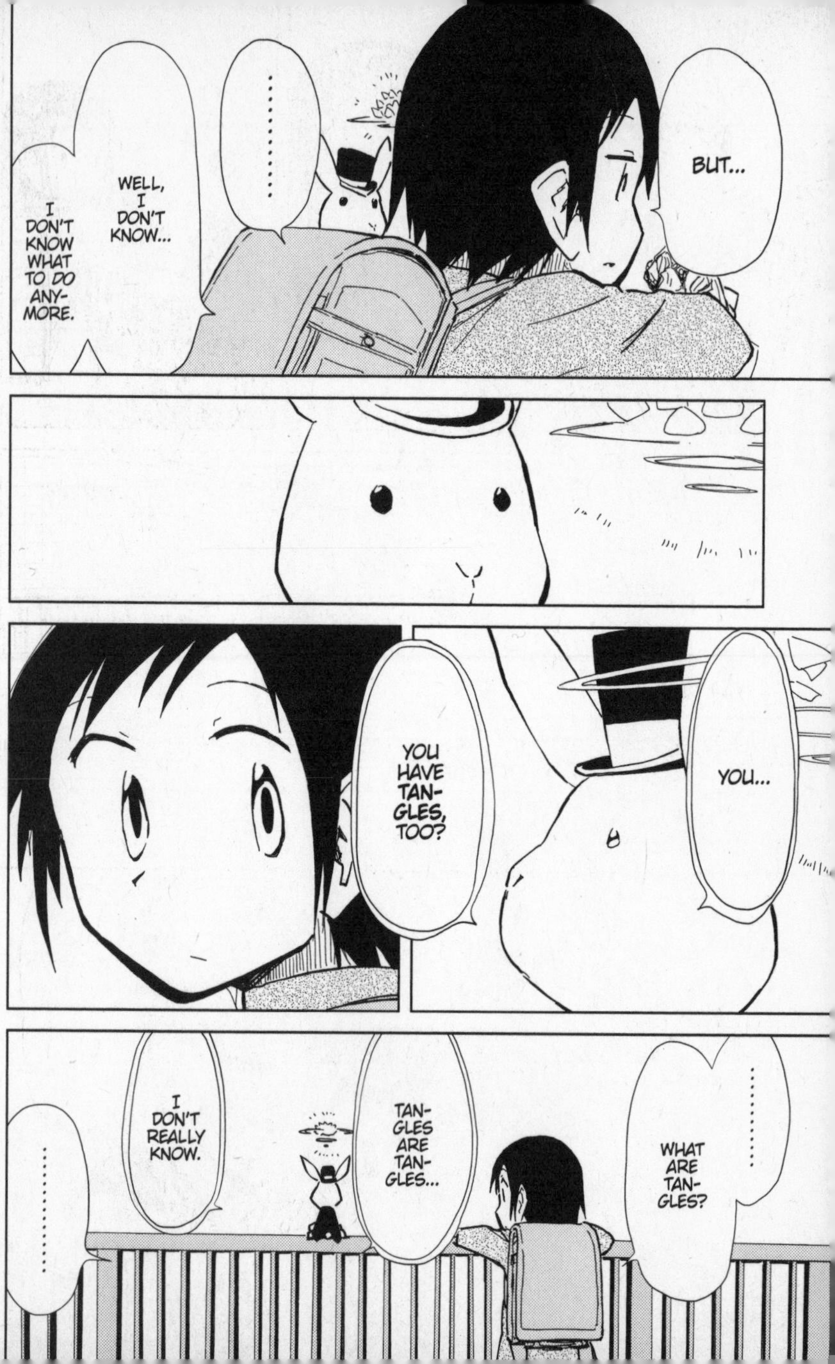
BUT...
......
WELL, I DON'T KNOW...
I DON'T KNOW WHAT TO DO ANYMORE.
YOU...
YOU HAVE TAN-GLES, TOO?
......
WHAT ARE TAN-GLES?
TAN-GLES ARE TAN-GLES...
I DON'T REALLY KNOW.
......

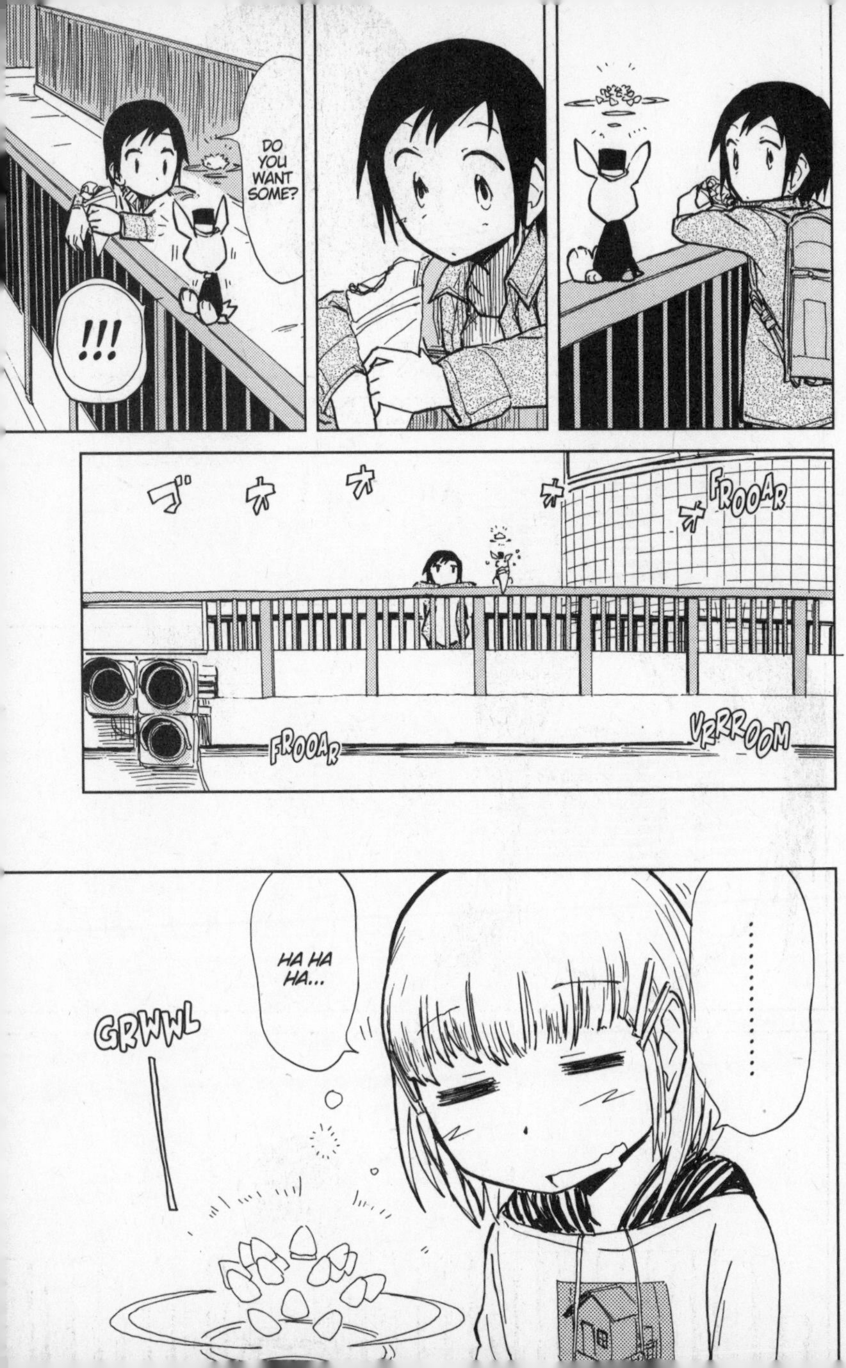
DO YOU WANT SOME?
!!!
FROOAR
ゴオオオオ
VRRROOM
FROOAR
......
HA HA HA...
GRWWL

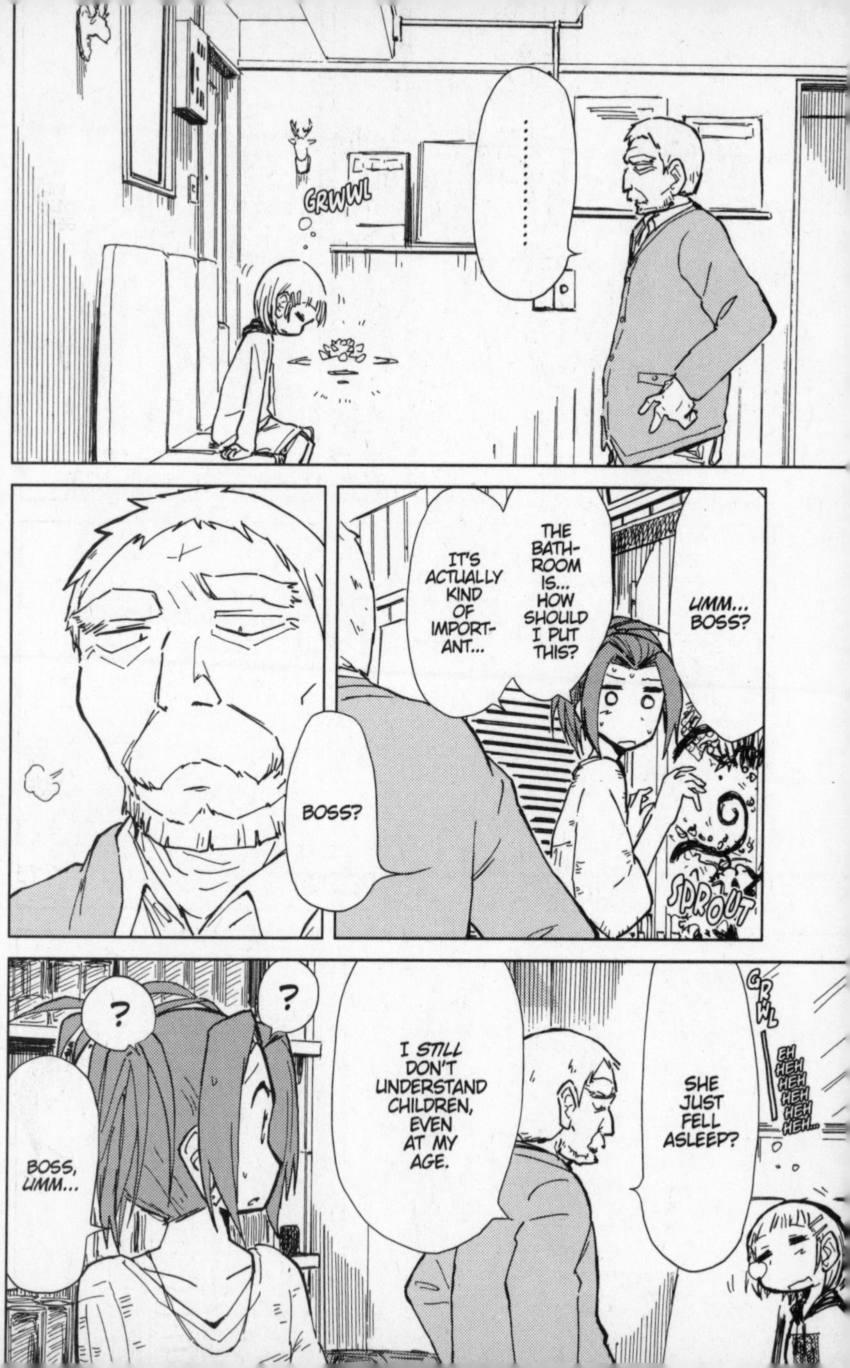
......
GRWWL
UMM... BOSS?
THE BATHROOM IS... HOW SHOULD I PUT THIS?
IT'S ACTUALLY KIND OF IMPORTANT...
BOSS?
SPROUT
GRWL
EH HEH HEH HEH HEH HEH...
SHE JUST FELL ASLEEP?
I *STILL* DON'T UNDERSTAND CHILDREN, EVEN AT MY AGE.
?
?
BOSS, UMM...

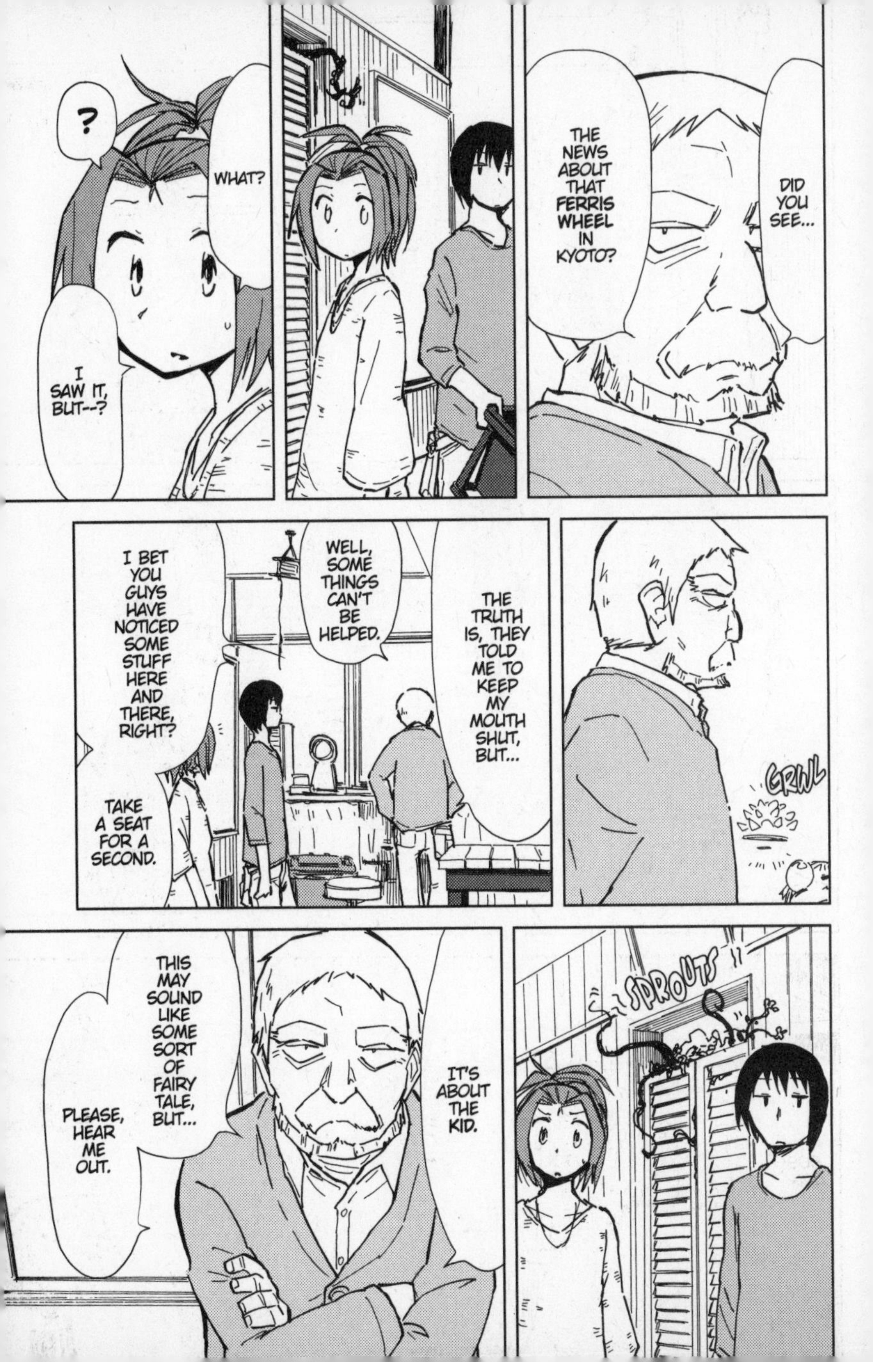
DID YOU SEE...
THE NEWS ABOUT THAT FERRIS WHEEL IN KYOTO?
WHAT?
?
I SAW IT, BUT--?
GRWL
THE TRUTH IS, THEY TOLD ME TO KEEP MY MOUTH SHUT, BUT...
WELL, SOME THINGS CAN'T BE HELPED.
I BET YOU GUYS HAVE NOTICED SOME STUFF HERE AND THERE, RIGHT?
TAKE A SEAT FOR A SECOND.
SPROUTS
IT'S ABOUT THE KID.
THIS MAY SOUND LIKE SOME SORT OF FAIRY TALE, BUT...
PLEASE, HEAR ME OUT.

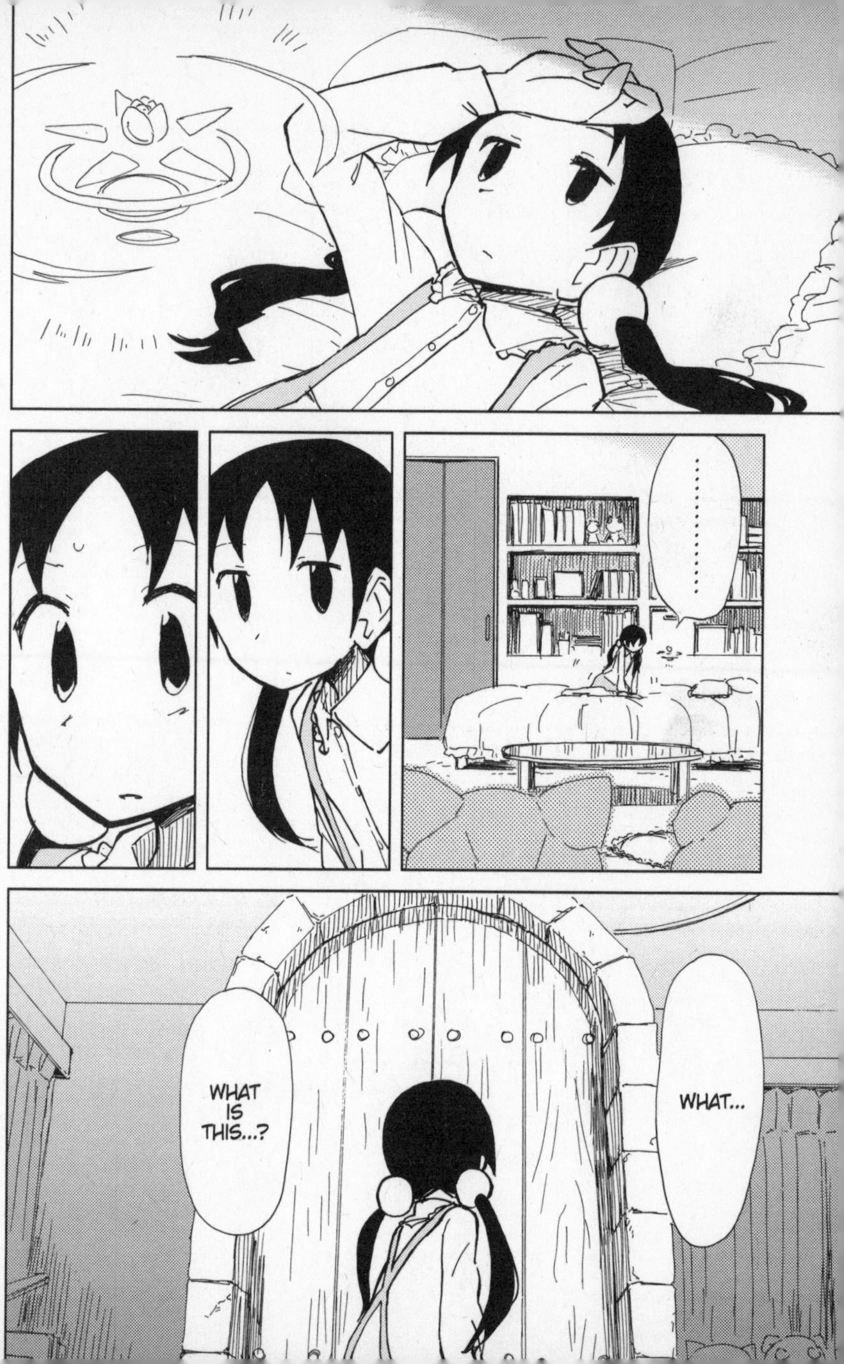
......
WHAT...
WHAT IS THIS...?

Alice & Zoroku

INTERLUDE

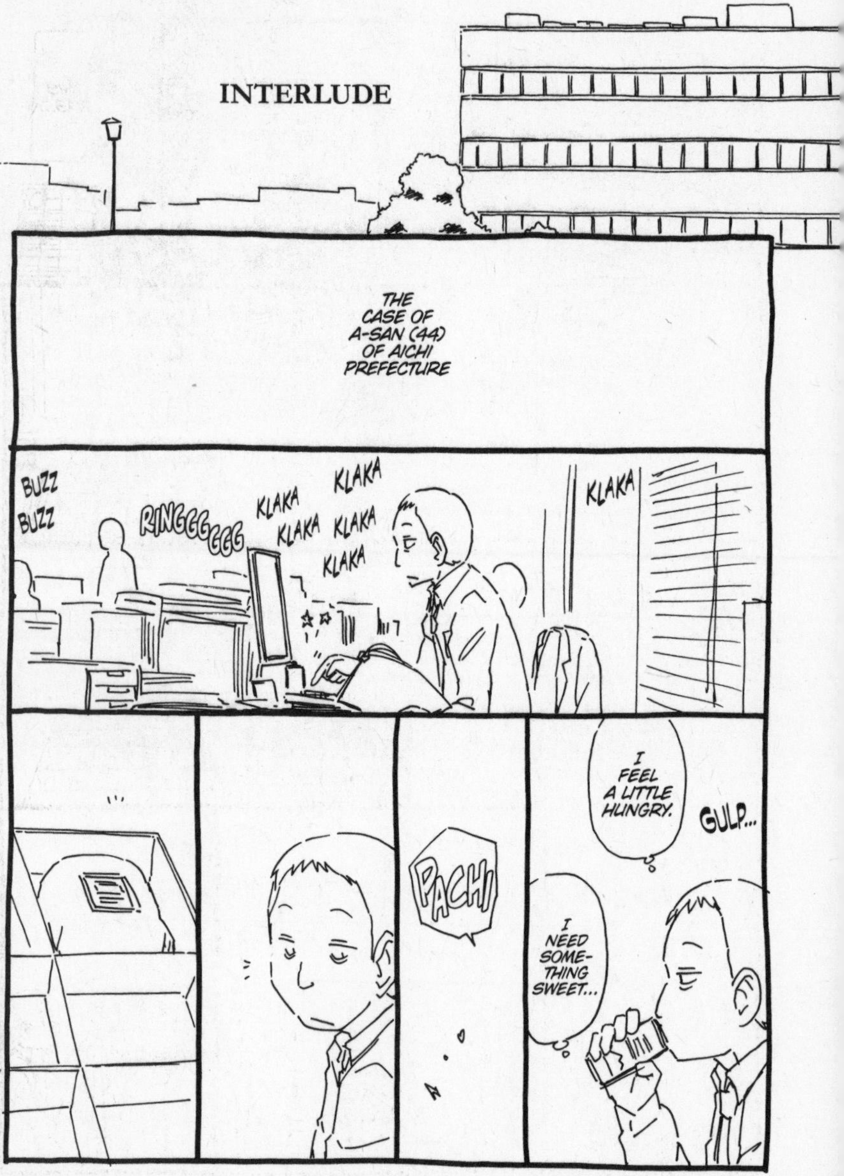
THE CASE OF A-SAN (44) OF AICHI PREFECTURE
KLAKA
KLAKA
KLAKA KLAKA
KLAKA
KLAKA
RINGGGGGG
BUZZ BUZZ
I FEEL A LITTLE HUNGRY.
GULP...
I NEED SOME-THING SWEET...
PACHI

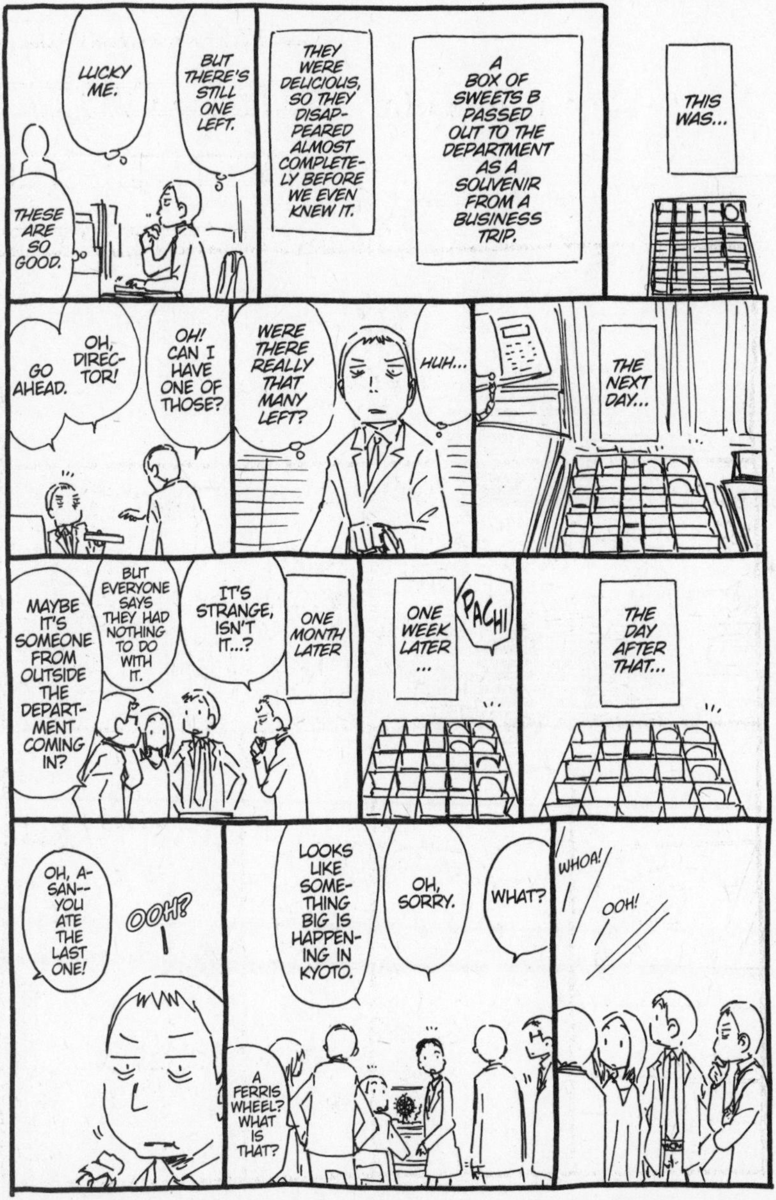
THIS WAS...
A BOX OF SWEETS B PASSED OUT TO THE DEPARTMENT AS A SOUVENIR FROM A BUSINESS TRIP.
THEY WERE DELICIOUS, SO THEY DISAPPEARED ALMOST COMPLETELY BEFORE WE EVEN KNEW IT.
BUT THERE'S STILL ONE LEFT.
LUCKY ME.
THESE ARE SO GOOD.
THE NEXT DAY...
HUH...
WERE THERE REALLY THAT MANY LEFT?
OH! CAN I HAVE ONE OF THOSE?
OH, DIRECTOR!
GO AHEAD.
THE DAY AFTER THAT...
PACHI
ONE WEEK LATER ...
ONE MONTH LATER
IT'S STRANGE, ISN'T IT...?
BUT EVERYONE SAYS THEY HAD NOTHING TO DO WITH IT.
MAYBE IT'S SOMEONE FROM OUTSIDE THE DEPARTMENT COMING IN?
WHOA!
OOH!
WHAT?
OH, SORRY.
LOOKS LIKE SOMETHING BIG IS HAPPENING IN KYOTO.
A FERRIS WHEEL? WHAT IS THAT?
OOH?
OH, A-SAN--YOU ATE THE LAST ONE!

THE END

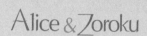

4

Editor
Inogai Kanta
(COMIC Ryu Editorial Department)

◆

Design and Formatting
AFTERGLOW

◆

Report Assistance
The People at Massa &Artists
Hanappa Nozaki Isao-san

◆

Illustration Assistants
Nagami Taro
Amanatsu Yuzuco
Watanabe Keisuke

SEVEN SEAS ENTERTAINMENT PRESENTS

Alice & Zoroku

story and art by **TETSUYA IMAI**

VOLUME 4

TRANSLATION
Beni Axia Conrad

ADAPTATION
Maggie Cooper

LETTERING
Ludwig Sacramento

COVER DESIGN
KC Fabellon

PROOFREADER
Janet Houck
Stephanie Cohen

EDITOR
Jenn Grunigen
Shannon Fay

PRODUCTION ASSISTANT
CK Russell

PRODUCTION MANAGER
Lissa Pattillo

EDITOR-IN-CHIEF
Adam Arnold

PUBLISHER
Jason DeAngelis

ALICE TO ZOROKU VOLUME 4
© TETSUYA IMAI 2014
Originally published in Japan in 2014 by TOKUMA SHOTEN PUBLISHING
CO., LTD., Tokyo. English translation rights arranged with TOKUMA SHOTEN
PUBLISHING CO., LTD., Tokyo, through TOHAN CORPORATION, Tokyo.

Seven Seas books may be purchased in bulk for promotional, educational, or
business use. Please contact your local bookseller or the Macmillan Corporate
and Premium Sales Department at 1-800-221-7945, extension 5442, or by
e-mail at MacmillanSpecialMarkets@macmillan.com.

Seven Seas and the Seven Seas logo are trademarks of
Seven Seas Entertainment, LLC. All rights reserved.

ISBN: 978-1-626927-33-9

Printed in Canada

First Printing: August 2018

10 9 8 7 6 5 4 3 2 1

FOLLOW US ONLINE: *www.sevenseasentertainment.com*

READING DIRECTIONS

This book reads from *right to left*, Japanese style.
If this is your first time reading manga, you start
reading from the top right panel on each page and
take it from there. If you get lost, just follow the
numbered diagram here. It may seem backwards at
first, but you'll get the hang of it! Have fun!!

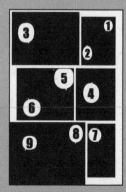